CELESTINA AND THE ENDS OF DESIRE

E. MICHAEL GERLI

Celestina and
the Ends of Desire

UNIVERSITY OF TORONTO PRESS
Toronto Buffalo London

©University of Toronto Press Incorporated 2011
 Toronto Buffalo London
 www.utppublishing.com
 Printed in Canada

ISBN 978-1-4426-4255-3

Library and Archives Canada Cataloguing in Publication

Gerli, E. Michael
Celestina and the ends of desire / E. Michael Gerli.

Includes bibliographical references and index.
ISBN 978-1-4426-4255-3

1. Rojas, Fernando de, d. 1541. Celestina. 2. Desire in literature. I. Title.

PQ6428.G47 2011   862'.2   C2011-900936-6

This book has been published with the help of a grant from the Program for
Cultural Cooperation between Spain's Ministry of Education and Culture and
United States Universities.

University of Toronto Press acknowledges the financial assistance to its publishing program of the Canada Council for the Arts and the Ontario Arts Council.

 Canada Council   Conseil des Arts   ONTARIO ARTS COUNCIL
for the Arts   du Canada   CONSEIL DES ARTS DE L'ONTARIO

University of Toronto Press acknowledges the financial support of the Government
of Canada through the Canada Book Fund for its publishing activities.

To the memory of C.B.J., who plumbed the depths and taught us to avoid the shallows.

Contents

Illustrations

A Note on Citations and Translations

Unless otherwise mentioned, all citations from *Celestina* in Castilian and their accompanying English translations are taken from Fernando de Rojas's *Celestina*, edited with an introduction and notes by Dorothy Sherman Severin (Warminster, UK: Aris and Phillips, 1987). The latter edition contains a facing-page English translation from 1631 by James Mabbe. From time to time, however, when Mabbe's translation fails to interpret certain words accurately (for example, when it renders the Spanish word *Dios* [God] as *Providence*), I have taken the liberty to substitute the word for its more accurate English form. All other translations are my own. Mabbe's 1631 translation was first edited and published by James Fitzmaurice-Kelly in 1894 (rpt. New York: AMS Press, 1967). Severin's edition includes interpolations taken from Mabbe's earlier 1598 manuscript not included in the 1631 printing and in Fitzmaurice-Kelly's edition.

Acknowledgments

This book is the product of several years of research, reflection, and teaching. During the course of its coming together, it was my privilege to share and discuss ideas about *Celestina* with my students at Georgetown University, the University of Virginia, and Emory and Duke universities, where I had the opportunity to offer seminars on Fernando de Rojas's work. The students' lively interest in the text, plus their spirited discussion, was what first convinced me that I should pursue the writing and completion of this study. I am grateful also to the colleagues who participated in my 2009 National Endowment for the Humanities Summer Seminar for College Teachers on *Celestina* and the Threshold of Modernity, and especially to my friends and colleagues in the Department of Spanish, Italian, and Portuguese at the University of Virginia for their observations, comments, good conversation, and fine fellowship. Among the latter, I am particularly indebted to Javier Herrero for his immense erudition, persistent good humour, unfailing goodwill, and wry irony. These are rare qualities indeed, which extend well beyond the scope of the present study and continue to play a part in our friendship and ongoing conversations. I am beholden as well to Alison Weber for her accommodating comments, her sharp insights into the representation of gender in early modern texts, and for restraining me from reading too much like a man. She reminded me pointedly that, although Melibea and the women in *Celestina* may be free to speak, 'freedom's just another word for nothing left to lose,' as Janis Joplin sang in a much later, equally double-edged age of change and liberation. My gratitude also extends to my old friends and colleagues Julian Weiss and Robert Archer, whose kind invitation to present some of my work-in-progress at King's College and the Cortauld Institute in 2006 played a crucial role in the evolution of this project. The lively comments and cultivated scepticism of my British colleagues during that visit allowed me, as ever, to refocus and refine some of the major tenets that have guided my work. David Nirenberg and Lillian von der Walde Moheno also deserve heartfelt thanks: the former for his keen observations on an early draft of chapter 9, and the latter for having appeared out of the ether like a cybernetic guardian angel at a crucial moment to resolve my doubts about Mirabella and Melibea, assuring me via a pdf file of one of her articles that I had not lost my mind somewhere in the library. Joe Snow also helped at critical junctures, allowing me to draw upon his prodigious knowledge of *Celestina* and over thirty years of friendship by responding to countless queries on all too many things.

Additionally, I wish to express gratitude to my colleagues, Eukene Lacarra Lanz and the late Louise Fothergill-Payne, for their enthusiastic response to some earlier drafts of some chapters. Sam Armistead, whose more than sizeable knowledge of proverbs, traditional poetry, folklore, and more than arcane arcana also pushed me along with some astonishing linguistic, textual, and cultural archaeology required to unpack some of the more recondite, and gamey (in all senses), passages of Roja's masterpiece. I am beholden also to my editors at the University of Toronto Press, Suzanne Rancourt, Barbara Porter, and Charles Stuart, for their unfailing assistance with the publication of this book; to those anonymous readers for the press who offered sensitive, detailed, and well-reasoned critiques of the original manuscript; and to the Dean of the College of Arts and Sciences and the Vice President for Research and Graduate Studies at the University of Virginia, who provided generous financial support for the completion of this project. Finally, the greater debt is to my friend and teacher, the late Carroll B. Johnson, to whose memory I dedicate this book. Although a mere five years older than I, from the moment he was fresh out of Harvard he became a guide and mentor. *Redde quod debes.*

Earlier versions of two chapters appeared as essays in books: chapter 4 under the title 'El placer de la mirada: Voyeurismo, fetichismo, y la configuración del deseo en *Celestina*' in *El mundo social y cultural de* La Celestina (Pamplona: Prensa Universitaria de la Universidad de Navarra, 2003); and chapter 7 as 'Dismembering the Body Politic: Vile Bodies and Sexual Underworlds in *Celestina*' in *Queer Iberia: Sexualities, Cultures and Crossings From the Middle Ages to the Renaissance*, edited by Josiah Blackmore and Gregory Hutcheson (Durham, NC: Duke University Press, 1999.) An earlier variant of chapter 5 was published as 'Complicitous Laughter:

Hilarity and Seduction in *Celestina*' in the *Hispanic Review*. One has been translated into English, and all three have been recast as well as accommodated to the larger design and context of the present study. I am grateful to the Universidad de Navarra, Duke University Press, and the University of Pennsylvania Press for permission to publish material from these previously published items in a more current, and hopefully more desirable, form.

CELESTINA AND THE ENDS OF DESIRE

Longing, we say, because desire is full of endless distances.
                                    Robert Hass, *Meditation at Lagunitas*

¡Qué esfuerzo!
¡Qué esfuerzo del caballo por ser perro!
¡Qué esfuerzo del perro por ser golondrina!
¡Qué esfuerzo de la golondrina por ser abeja!
¡Qué esfuerzo de la abeja por ser caballo!
                    Federico García Lorca, 'Muerte,' *Poeta en Nueva York*

'They told me to take a streetcar named Desire, and then transfer to one
called Cemeteries ...'
                            Tennessee Williams, *A Streetcar Named Desire*

Introduction

This is a book about one of the most popular books of early modern Europe, Fernando de Rojas's *Tragicomedia de Calisto y Melibea,* which has been commonly referred to as *Celestina,* the name of its chief female protagonist, since shortly after its initial publication at Burgos in 1499. *Celestina* the book, like the character whose name it ultimately adopted, traffics in desire, and when it was first published offered new, remarkable representations and expressions of it to an avid reading public more accustomed to witnessing desire's exaltation, interdiction, censure, or repression.

The present work argues that, while the control and policing of desire have been at the centre of human social formations since the beginning of civilization, but especially in early Christian and medieval times, its representation in *Celestina* took on new and unexpected immediacy and forms, and that the work's vivid portrayal of human desire is largely responsible for its fascination, popularity, and vast readership from the moment of its first appearance. To do this, this study examines the medieval theories and discourses of desire as epistemological categories, and their definition and representation in *Celestina* in relation to the latter's story of passionate love and prostitution played out against a background of class conflict and social transformation. It seeks to show how *Celestina,* situated at the bounds between the medieval and the early modern, has its own peculiar fascination, and clearly extended the notions of desire beyond their traditional medieval formulations directly into the social, economic, physiological, and psychological fields of human activity: to the transformation of *libido amandi* (lust for love) into *libido dominandi* (lust for power) and finally into *libido capiendi* (lust for knowledge). The final act of the work, which encompasses Pleberio's lament for Melibea,

I argue, exceeds even these new representations of desire, leading to the realization that desire itself is non-transcendental, and that it is always in excess of any thing or any capacity to contain or satisfy it. Desire in *Celestina* comes to its final, temporal, worldly end in Pleberio's soliloquy before the shattered body of his daughter, as Pleberio comes to grips with the futility of human ambition stripped of all illusion, provoking him to articulate a profound disenchantment with a fundamentally disenchanted universe. In this regard, Pleberio's lament, the subject of chapter 9, marks a crucial self-reflexive moment in the representation of the human subject in Spanish literature, a turn from consolation toward an understanding of ubiquitous desolation. It is in Pleberio's self-conscious awakening to the abyss at the ends of desire where I seek to the locate the striking novelty and early modernity of *Celestina,* which doubtless accounts for the work's continued readership and popularity into our own time. What follows, then, makes up a study that examines key moments and ways in which *Celestina* conjures the images, figures, and boundaries of desire as it explores the ends, and discovers the ultimate end, of human ambition and motivation.

For all the words that are uttered by the characters in *Celestina* to express desire, however, their true intentions, the desires that drive them, are rarely explicit or fully known to them. Indeed, they must be revealed through irony and close reading, processes that require understanding beyond the face value of a word or an utterance. To be sure, the best indications of concealed human motives can at times rather best be found in other, involuntary forms of human expression beyond language in *Celestina.* They may be discovered, as we shall see, in things like the laughter that cuts through Pármeno's and Celestina's circumlocutions when the latter attempts to enlist the former in despoiling Calisto. 'Symbolic language in *Celestina,*' as Roberto González Echevarría has remarked, generally 'is undone by both the appearance of an obstinate and excessive referentiality as well as by an appeal to the literal. To Calisto the girdle is Melibea's body; to Celestina the girdle is a girdle. The work invites either to allow desire to read through language to the object coveted or to read literally, putting aside the figurative meanings that a term may have acquired … In *Celestina* the symbolic or allegorical is still a shield, resistance to face the human, which is lodged in the literal' (15). Language in *Celestina* is moved in this way by a seemingly continuous falling away from its symbolic sense, gravitating always to its most immediate meaning, to the hyperliteral. It is thus the task of the reader to uncover the hidden resonances of the word, to see beyond it and expose its larger vibrancy.

In this regard, involuntary utterances and sounds made by a character in the work may often be better signifiers of intention than words themselves, which can be used by the characters both consciously and unconsciously to occlude purpose and meaning.

The representation of the astonishing mobilizing and destructive force of the desire for sex, money, status, recognition, and fulfilment in *Celestina* moves beyond the bounds of traditional forms of reading satisfied only with decoding a series of sexual or material signs and situating Rojas's work within the context of an emerging bourgeoisie in the late fifteenth century. Rather, *Celestina* propels us toward a rereading of it in relation to other texts in such a way as to compare it to the earlier texts' potential for portraying and mobilizing human want. The result of this comparison inevitably forces us to see *Celestina* as something quite different and entirely new – in short, as a modern text – because it constitutes an instance of the transformation of the relationship between conceptually distinct, historically locatable notions of human ambition and desire and newly emerging forms of them. Whereas desire and ambition in the Middle Ages remained discourses always allied with transcendental subjects (e.g., the redemptive desire or love of God in the context of theology, religion, and metaphysics, or the exalted, transfigurative power of courtly love in a secular, courtly setting), in *Celestina* they produce only conflict, violence, and ultimately death, leaving us with a radical, non-transcendent disillusionment with the world. Rojas's work takes as its object the fierce, self-sacrificing forms of human ambition that produce only abjection and, in the end, self-annihilation without the prospect of redemption. Want, desire, and ambition in *Celestina* cannot be contained by the framework of human social and religious relations as they were known to exist in the late medieval imaginary. The objects of human aspirations in the world portrayed in *Celestina* are not simply exalted; they form part of a way of life that ultimately demands the destruction of the desiring subject who pursues them. The result is a text that on the surface might be taken as a cautionary tale but at a deeper level is overwhelmed by the very grim finality and exorbitance of the deadly example it portrays. If, as Jacques Lacan asserts when imagining the origins of human language, language emerged from the expression of a desire to transcend and make an absence present, to recall something intuited but lost or out of reach, it was not until the last century, with Freud, that the larger importance of the link between desire and language was given significant attention. While many of Freud's ideas about sexuality have been called into question both by modern medicine and feminist theory, his overall perception of desire as the driving force of language and human existence remains intact. Freud also understood that not all desires could be expressed with the same facility; that the most difficult ones were frequently restricted or concealed, implicated in certain social taboos, like sex and death; and that the latter, especially, were often hidden or repressed in a region of the human imagination he called the unconscious. Hence, desires could be simultaneously present in individuals but absent from their immediate apprehension. Freud grasped that the hidden forces of repressed desire could often motivate significant events and changes in the lives of the subjects who possessed them. Yet in modern times Freud was responsible only for the systematic discovery, description, and theoretical formulation of the synergies of human desire and their effects on human conduct. The expression and representation of desire has, as Lacan rightly maintains, been part of the human condition since the very appearance of language, the most direct, audible manifestation of desire, and in the end comprises nothing more than the reflection of the human wish for something larger, namely, transcendence. Throughout *Celestina*, the problematic of desire arises in language, as we shall see, even when it seems invisible and its articulation remains incomplete, is blocked, or is incompatible with the notions that frame standards of social propriety and religious morality which seek to impede its articulation. In other words, although not often explicit, the stirrings of desire in *Celestina* can be discovered at every turn in the text, even in conflicts in which the enunciation of desire may at first seem difficult to discern, incomprehensible, illegible, or even inconceivable. The reading strategies employed in the pages that follow are, thus, fundamentally shaped by these convictions, recognizing that desire has always been with us as the driving force of language, and that *Celestina* serves as a testimonial to the materialization and transformation of certain forms of desire (sexual, social, political, even spatial, and, of course, metaphysical among them) at a critical juncture in the history of European culture, marking the subjective shift toward what we now refer to as early modernity.

Since Freud's first exploration of Shakespeare, medieval and early modern studies have increasingly turned to psychoanalysis as a heuristic tool, noting, in the words of Valeria Finucci and Regina M. Schwartz, how 'the writers of Renaissance literature were preoccupied with their versions of the inner life' and with the representation of 'the dynamics of sexual identity, gender definition, doubling, identification, voyeurism, memory, melancholy, the uncanny, even the unconscious,' and how these were 'concerns that arose, not in the context of nineteenth-century Vienna, but were already evident in the social, political, religious upheavals of the early modern period (as they were in the classical world)' (3). The power of psychoanalytical theory to illuminate the convoluted processes of language and identity in early modern texts is thus well recognized and established, confirmed by the work of contemporary early modern scholars, in addition to Schwartz and Finucci, like Margaret Ferguson (1983), Jonathan Dollimore (1991), Joel Fineman (1986), Marjorie Garber (1987), Stephen Greenblatt (1986), Valerie Traub (1992), Barbara Freedman (1991), Patricia Parker and David Quint (1986), Carroll B. Johnson (1983), and Ruth El Saffar and Diana de Armas Wilson (1993), to name but a few.

Likewise, the current challenges posed by post-structuralism to the traditional periodization of the medieval and the modern are equally consonant with the significance and utility of psychoanalysis to the understanding of medieval and early modern texts, especially in light of the now debunked but still lingering notion of Spain's cultural belatedness and the idea of its presumed lack of a Renaissance, propagated across the humanities mainly by German, French, and English scholars from the nineteenth century forward. As Jennifer Summit and David Wallace argue in the 2007 issue of the *Journal of Medieval and Early Modern Studies* they edited entitled *Rethinking Periodization*, these temporal taxonomies and geographical demarcations forced upon cultural history have become increasingly vexed, and are often arbitrarily used, in the words of Margreta de Grazia, one of their contributors, simply to determine 'what matters and what does not' (3). The editors and the contributors to *Rethinking Periodization* all persuasively maintain that the idea of the modern itself, according to de Grazia, 'misrepresents the historical consciousness of the very "early modern" period that is drafted to inaugurate it, a period that characterized itself not through its novelty – then used as a term of suspicion – but through its backward-looking identification with the antique past' (3). Similarly, in addition to the contributors to the issue of JMEMS edited by Summit and Wallace, the work of colleagues like Moshe Sluhovsky (2006), Kathleen Davis (2006), and Judith M. Bennett (1992) has examined and challenged these categories, calling into question the existence of what Bennett calls 'the great divide' that supposedly separates the medieval from the early modern.

While no single theory or methodology guides the present study, one persistent belief shapes the interpretive and critical strategies employed here. In tune with the general principles of psychoanalysis as laid down by Freud and Lacan, it defies the conviction that all of the characters' behaviour portrayed in *Celestina* comes from conscious intentions, suggesting that the aims and values uttered by them do not direct their behaviour as much as we might wish to believe. For this reason, language is the principal focus of this book, as I seek to gain insight into the linguistic and mental operations that lead the characters' behaviour astray of their professed goals, exploring these processes as preconditions for predicting and understanding their implicit values. As Freud and Lacan have taught us, much of human behaviour is governed by mental synergies that exist outside of conscious awareness and conscious control, and these synergies are best approached through an understanding of their mediation through language, physical gesture, and other signs.

In connection with this, then, the present study examines the way desire is enunciated and mediated in *Celestina*, or the manner in which the work represents, mobilizes, translates, and communicates desire in and through language (chapters 1, 2, 3, and 6), as well as by other means: via the body (chapter 7); in the representation of physical space (chapter 8); through sight, hearing, and other significant material vehicles for the conveyance and discovery of human want (chapters 4 and 5). All of this culminates in the total breakdown of desire, the collapse of meaning in the face of a yearning for something metaphysical; in the failure of language and of interpretation, in the end of a desire for an object beyond desire itself, which at its conclusion produces an understanding of life as being something only of the material world (chapter 9).

The historical and cultural backdrop for this questioning of metaphysical presence at the conclusion of *Celestina* reflects a period in Iberian, but especially Castilian, life of acute crisis and vertiginous human change. The events of the social and political panorama of the second half of the fifteenth century leading to 1499, the date of the work's first publication, produced nothing short of a series of tectonic shifts in the civic and psychic landscape of Castile. With the accession of Enrique IV, known to history as El Impotente, to the throne of Castile in 1454, there erupted a series of controversies regarding the king's fitness to govern centring on his character and personality that culminated in a carnassial struggle over monarchical succession lasting more than a decade. The struggle was profoundly implicated in issues of gender, sexual potency, and paternity, terminating in a civil war that pitted the king and his supporters against his half-sister, Isabel, and her consort, Fernando de Aragon, that would eventually result in Isabel's accession to the throne and produce no few cultural and political anxieties concerning female monarchy, religious zeal, and the consolidation of all power in the newly centralized state. At the same time, daily life resounded with rumours and recriminations regarding apostasy and the sincerity of the staggering number of *conversos*, or *nuevos cristianos* (Jews who had converted from Christianity and their descendants), in the kingdom (estimated by some scholars to be upwards of 350,000); statutes on blood purity promulgated by their 'Old Christian' co-religionists designed to contain the converts' social advancement; and the establishment of the Holy Office of the Inquisition for the Purity of the Faith (1477), to examine and deal with the religious, cultural, and social disorder produced by mass conversion, doctrinal and spiritual confusion, and ethnic and political discord.

The very decade in which Fernando de Rojas published *Celestina* saw striking events that shook the kingdom of Castile to its foundations and held profound consequences for the rest of Europe and, indeed, the world. These encompassed no less than the Christian conquest of Granada (the last Muslim kingdom in Europe), the expulsion of the Jews, renewed mass conversions now in the form of converts both from Judaism and Islam to Christianity, the discovery of America, the Castilian-Aragonese intervention in Italy, and, finally, the promulgation of a divinely ordained Catholic state whose security, purity, and orthodoxy were ensured by the vigilance of the firmly establish Santa Hermandad (rural militias) and the Inquisition. As Fernando and Isabel, who are known to history as the Catholic Monarchs, sought to forge an empire through the extirpation or suppression of all signs of difference in their realms, the entire cultural spectrum of Castilian life during the last decade of the fifteenth century was distinguished by persistent strain and focused on questions of order and orthodoxy, status and identity, power and legitimacy, truancy and transformation – circumstances that racked every boundary of belief, all notions of possibility, and every category of human existence.

Celestina, which inscribes these tensions, is a book that provides dramatic proof not only of the presence and the power of the desire for transcendence and fulfilment in all human utterances and actions, but a crucial recognition of it at the threshold of early modernity as an all-embracing force of the human subject. Crossing all boundaries of class and gender, desire in *Celestina* is ubiquitous, uttered openly in dialogue and in asides by prostitutes and lackeys as well by the high born, embedded in discourses both lofty and low minded, in gestures, in signs of and on the body, and inscribed in the very spaces that those bodies transit and inhabit. By the work's end, however, in Pleberio's final soliloquy, desire points only to its radically non-transcendent, physical constitution, and hence ultimately to death. The progression of desire released from the opening words of *Celestina* follows a desacralization of it, of love and passion and yearning, and gives emphasis to the materiality of existence that points to a human subjectivity rooted exclusively in the body, defined by its demands and haunted by its limitations. In *Celestina*, Fernando de Rojas and his fellow authors (it was begun by an anonymous author and completed by Rojas in 1499, just to be amplified and rewritten later by Rojas himself at the request of his first readers), found and inculcated intransitive yearning in all the characters of their literary universe. Quite simply, none of them ever ceases to express their desire. At every step, the characters' yearnings are shown as inconvenient, often difficult to recognize and voice, or completely hidden even though menacingly deadly, but ever necessary and as the main cause and consequence of their ongoing existence. It is the representation of the lives of the characters in *Celestina* as continuing performances of ceaseless want acted out in dramatic dialogue before the reader that makes these characters memorable and stand out, projecting the illusion that, more than abstractions, they resonate with living forms of need and serve as mirrors that reflect the reader's own desire in the process of the plot's unfolding. However notable all the characters are, among them the old whore Celestina stands apart; not because her desires are more shocking, disgraceful, or diabolical than those of the others who share her world, but because Celestina dares to incarnate and speak her own desires unabashedly, as well as to reveal and actualize desire in everyone she encounters, including, as we shall see, the very authors and readers of the work.

The *Tragicomedia de Calisto y Melibea*'s early change in name to *Celestina* is important in this regard. It serves as an indicator of how the work was perceived, received, and interpreted by its early modern reading public since this appellation gave primacy to the old bawd and registered a shift in interest away from Calisto and Melibea, the two aristocratic protagonist lovers of the original title, *Comedia* (later *Tragicomedia*) *de Calisto y Melibea*. It was clearly the go-between and the industry she practises – the manipulation and increase of desire – that fascinated, held the attention, and marked the memory not only of the work's first readers but all its subsequent readers as well, to the point where the very book singularly held on to the old bawd's name and continued to incite readers through the ages to speak about it and ask for it simply by invoking Celestina.

The personage whom all in the work refer to as *la puta vieja* (the old whore) embodies desire, she is the subject who seemingly has mastered it and seeks to bring it to fruition both in herself and in all others. The revelation and realization of desire are at once the reasons for *Celestina's* vibrant popularity across the centuries (it remains the only widely read work of the sixteenth century in Spain that is still popular today; see Whinnom 1980), but at the same time desire serves as the springboard for the action and conflict of the *Tragicomedia*. In the latter desire circulates and motivates, yet few without the assistance of Celestina can recognize, understand, or seek to make it transitive.

On the one hand, Celestina helps unfold the range of meanings and propositions of desire in the world in which she moves; and on the other, she uncovers and makes comprehensible a whole chain of interconnected, partial meanings – a synthesis – in any single act where she encounters human yearning. The process that mediates Celestina's interaction with all the characters in the work is thus essentially a hermeneutical one; it is a process in which her chief role is to reveal and then interpret the meanings of their desire, as she creates a network of interconnected meanings necessary for their comprehension through the threads she weaves between all their lives.

Celestina as book and Celestina as character stage agons of desire in everyone they encounter – characters and readers alike. At the time the work was initially circulated in its sixteen-act version, Fernando de Rojas tells us that he was moved to amplify it at the behest of his readers, all of whom yearned for more. Although the ancient cultural prohibitions that shape the laws and rules by which society lived were acutely felt, considered inviolate by the Roman Catholic Church and the public standards of morality and rules of propriety, there was doubtless titillation in reading this work, a sense of excitement at encountering human passion and ambition expressed in such a conspicuously earthbound fashion. At every turn, readers sought to discover more of the world in which the characters moved as they transgressed every standard of propriety and showed resistance to the repression of desire through their every action. It is for this reason that works like *Celestina* probably still matter and continue to hold the interest of the contemporary reading public, as readers discover a material understanding of the world, an unembellished encounter with the effects of ambition on the human spirit, and their own interest in learning about the private lives of other people (both high and low). *Celestina* is a work that continues to appeal to a reading public's desire for bold, racy narratives that test the limits of propriety, often under the very guise of claims to moral exemplarity.

What follows, then, is an exploration of the way desire manifests itself, materializes, and is ultimately blocked in *Celestina*. It does not, however, constitute a description of how desire simply makes itself evident in the work, but rather an examination of the way desire shapes *Celestina*'s fundamental epistemology: how desire becomes knowledge, action, moral life, experience, and above all, political, social, and urban experience in the world it portrays. The following chapters seek to provide not just a textual but also a theoretical exploration of the radical transformation and new understanding of the ends of desire at the threshold of early modernity. Additionally, they constitute an attempt to locate just what in *Celestina* is responsible for its continued appeal, and for the disturbing sense of amazement and revelation readers still feel after their first encounter with it.

1 The Chain of Desire: Linking Language and Longing in *Celestina*

> 'Does not Desire, performing many miracles, to use antiphrasis, change the shapes of all mankind? Though monk and adulterer are opposite terms, he forces both of them to exist together in the same subject.'
>
> Alain de Lille, *De planctu Naturae*, Metre 5, 47

Celestina, the name commonly given to the *Comedia* (subsequently *Tragicomedia*) *de Calisto y Melibea*, is one of the most remarkable works produced at the close of the fifteenth century in Iberia. A text composed initially of sixteen 'acts' written entirely in dialogue, its earliest known edition (Burgos, 1499) was published anonymously. By the publication of the 1502 edition, however, five more acts were added, along with a prefatory 'letter from the writer to a friend' and an acrostic verse identifying an author. Although uncertainty still clouds the identity of the individual who composed the original act 1, the remaining acts (2–21), the acrostic tells us, were written by one Fernando de Rojas (ca 1465–1541). Rojas was a lawyer educated at the University of Salamanca and the son of recently converted Jews (*conversos*). Late in his life Rojas served as chief magistrate of Talavera de la Reina, an important commercial centre in the province of Toledo during the late Middle Ages.

Translated into all the major European languages and reprinted in some eighty-four separate Castilian editions before 1650, Rojas's *Celestina* was by all accounts one of the most popular, best read, and influential books of early modernity.[1] Celebrated by Cervantes in the prefatory pages of *Don Quixote* as a 'divine if human book,' and imitated, among many others, by Lope de Vega, the verbal profanity and sexual licence it portrays seems to have caused little distress to its readership. The plot revolves around the young patrician, Calisto, and his passion for Melibea, daughter of the wealthy Pleberio. When Melibea rejects Calisto's advances, he enlists the aid of old Celestina, an unscrupulous former prostitute who now makes her living as a witch and go-between. With the help of Calisto's manservants, Sempronio and Pármeno, and some apprenticed whores named Elicia and Areúsa (who consort with the latter), Celestina persuades Melibea to relent. Just when the liaison is progressing, however, Calisto dies from a fall suffered as he scales the wall of Melibea's garden after a heated night of love. In despair, Melibea kills herself by leaping from a tower into the garden as her father watches from below. Shortly before Calisto's plunge, Celestina is stabbed to death by Pármeno and Sempronio in a dispute over the spoils, a gold chain; the two are publicly executed by the civil authorities for the murder. Although Calisto and Melibea move in a world of ardent, idealized passion and aristocratic breeding reminiscent of medieval courtly romances (especially sentimental romances), most of the interest in the work centres on the demonic Celestina and her low-life confederates, who paint a vivid picture of a sexual underworld driven by competing desires and economic and social imperatives.

For all its achievements *Celestina* scholarship has in the main – with the exception of the work of scholars like Américo Castro (1970), Stephen Gilman (1956, 1972), and Francisco Márquez Villanueva (1994) on *converso* mentalité, Alan Deyermond (1993) on female societies, and José Antonio Maravall (1968) on social transformations – focused on textual technicalities, questions of authorship, characterization, and other formal, bibliographical, or artistic considerations. Conspicuous principally for its ahistoricity and its aversion to broad interpretation as it invokes the text's ambiguity (Russell 1991, 157), *Celestina* criticism, while it has served to resolve thorny textual issues and to illuminate the prodigious artistic achievements of the work, has declined (with the exception of the individuals mentioned) to confront the larger problematical connection between literature and life, text and context, at the threshold of early modernity.

Yet a close reading of *Celestina* reveals that the Church, private morals, sex, and public order were in fact in profound conflict, challenged by a rapidly changing social and historical horizon and the existence of an increasingly visible underworld inhabited by human subjects whose currency was the pleasures of the human body, lucre, personal ambition, and the proclamation of the sovereign self. It is a work which shows incontrovertibly that self-awareness, desire, and the ideals of private freedom and their restraint were not self-sufficient, uncontested abstractions but ideas that could be construed as contradictory expressions of a single principle in late fifteenth-century Spain – the good – whose pursuit by one and the many was capable of producing a distinctly unstable moral and cultural arrangement. *Celestina* registers and advocates definite ways of being and thinking about the world while it thwarts others; and it constitutes itself as a site of struggle and a catalyst for change whose implications are ineluctably political, ideological, and cultural. The law, love, money, morality, ambition, the body, nutrition, and sexuality in particular are all intertwined and become the loci where dramatic early modern battles of caste, rank, class, and ethics are played out and where desire is revealed to be the thriving, driving force behind all human action, the unstoppable motor of the human spirit.

Indeed, *Celestina*, as José Antonio Maravall notes, 'nos presenta el drama de la crisis y transmutación de los valores sociales y morales que se desarrolla en la fase de crecimiento de la economía, de la cultura y de la vida entera, en la sociedad del siglo XV' (1968, 20) [offers up the drama of the crisis and transformation of the social and moral values developing during the phase of economic growth, the growth of culture – of all life – in fifteenth-century society]. It is a work that portrays not only the blurring but also the deliberate encroachment of socially consecrated boundaries of power, authority, sexuality, and notions of the self in order to test them and to portray new styles and mores that were daily transforming the collective imagination of late fifteenth-century Castile.

As *Celestina* gives ascendancy to new and unexpected voices and portrays novel ways of being human in the world, it centres its interest on desire, which pulls, entices, and entraps, and finally threatens to unravel the very foundations of culture, order, polity, language, and belief. Desire, manifested in *Celestina* chiefly as eros and *cupiditas*, is inherently totalizing, encompassing an overarching ambition for more, contending always to possess and to be more. Its relentless forward progress in the text creates and maintains interest, making the characters' inner selves act upon the world through imagined scenarios of fulfilment. At the same time, desire in *Celestina* circulates and motivates in ways that cannot be directly grasped by language. It is always in excess and manifests itself through the gaze, in laughter, by means of the body and fetishized objects, and through the very space the characters move in and inhabit. Ultimately, however, the powers of desire induce alienation and deny the constraints of community and the potentiality of control.

From its outset, the plot of *Celestina* consists of an exploration of the structure and nature of human desire, where desire is manifested as an impulse that pursues a series of counterfeit objects or substitutes for what cannot be fully known or consciously recovered. Calisto mistakes Melibea for the grandeur of God, Pleberio sees his daughter as the guarantor of his honour, and Celestina and her minions see the key to wealth and happiness in the despoilment of all three. Figured as a chain of yearning pursued by those who are not capable of fully understanding their desideradum, desire in *Celestina* both enslaves and binds all the characters together as it impels them to transgress the limits of caste, class, and conscience, enacting all manner of civic boundary crossings and disruptions of moral prescriptions, linking their mutual destinies just as it destroys their individual lives. We see actions in which desire in each person rises up and fails to locate and obtain its object. That unachievable object is in turn substituted by another, which then crumbles and is replaced by yet other forms of yearning that multiply until ultimately they collapse and find their end in either death, despair, or alienation. In remarkably Lacanian terms, as the plot unfolds the characters in *Celestina* all misrecognize the objects of their desire in an endless chain of believable but self-deluding falsehoods, performing a *méconnaissance* of the object of their longing as they project their yearning toward its counterfeit.[2]

All of the characters in *Celestina* are constituted as desiring subjects that pursue an impossible and perpetually obscure object under the impression of knowing what it is. Their desire is materialized metonymically, as a constant forward impulse in a chain of language and signification that asserts itself toward an object whose essence is thought to be known but cannot be fully ascertained. Desire is in this way central to the forces that move the world in *Celestina*, and it is portrayed in the work as a type of unavoidable condition, the engine of all human cause and consequence, attached always to a sense of absence, and a deep longing for something more that incites the trespass of social as well as physical boundaries and animates individual passion in perpetuity.

Fernando de Rojas understood well that the onset of desire always portends its end. When he read and then took up his pen to advance the fragmentary plot he found circulating at Salamanca, he foresaw in it a dark denouement inexorably linked to its beginning. When he tells us that, upon reading and rereading the anonymous manuscript that fell into his hands, he felt compelled to compose the end that its beginning heralded ('compuse tal fin que el principio desata' [10] [I composed such an ending as the beginning suggests]), he reveals that, as a reader of texts and as an observer of human life, he could already perceive the dark shadow cast over the characters whose lives he would complete. He saw that, from the outset of the work, mortality lurked in the pleasures pursued by all of them. As Rojas saw it, the death that stalked the folios of the *antiguo autor* announced no mystical union, no redemption, no transfiguration of the lovers. The piece was cast in a more frightening light. Its ironic language failed to signal a poignantly transfigurative *Liebestod*, and its peculiar characters were tied neither to heartfelt sacrifice nor grave transcendence. It was, rather, plotted by a sinister, coarse fate tied to black irony, linked both tragically and absurdly to human instincts and the hazards and blindness of a fundamentally earthbound passion. Rojas perceived in the *antiguo autor*'s portrayal of Eros a deadly force connecting its beginnings to an end, to Thanatos, across a tragic human comedy of self-deception and misrecognition. For Rojas, desire's realization materialized in menacing forms, always destructive of the self. Its fable was sustained by a movement toward death, or a perceived instinctual, compulsive drive to achieve a condition beyond his characters' own lacklustre lives. If the motor of existence for the characters in act 1 was desire, the ultimate determinant of desire's meaning for them would lay at the deadly end Rojas would confer upon the *antiguo autor*'s initial story. The story Rojas envisioned implied an ominous consummation. Desire, he understood, ignites the fires of existence just to immolate the subjects whose spirits it enkindles.

In the end, then, *Celestina* unleashes the demons of human yearning, acknowledging that their fury constitutes not only the mark of a beginning but also the likeness of a violent, capricious, and material end. In this way, *Celestina* denies both the spiritual and tragic values of desire embraced by the medieval intellectual tradition, situating human ambition at the centre of a bleak and abysmal material universe that lacks a presence and a *telos*. The work thus problematizes and reconceptualizes the two dominant discourses of metaphysical transcendence at the centre of medieval civilization up through the late fifteenth century – Christianity and the exalted secular vision of passion called courtly love – in their relation to desire, demythifying their transfigurative powers while dislocating them from their stable medieval cultural and existential matrices. In *Celestina* love and desire can no longer be defined in terms of the soul's infinite quest for meaningful fulfilment, its recognition of a movement toward a defining, rapturous centre. Through the work's ironical denial that either of these expressions of love and lack may constitute a purifying, heroic, or transcendent experience, and by locating an essentially material vision of death at the heart of all human want, *Celestina* exceeds the very premises on which it rests, abjuring the god of love and the love of God to cross the threshold of early modernity. To be sure, its modernity lies precisely in its insistence on the pedestrian, material, unstable, protean, and dangerous nature of desire as something immanent that inhabits every human heart and informs and drives all human commerce in the world.

Celestina thus compels us to move beyond the bounds of a reading that is content simply with subsuming and decoding a series of thematic and ideological tensions that situate it at the end of a textual tradition. Rather, it forces us to see it as a radical rethinking of these texts and the cultural logic that informs them as it defines the world's broad potential for mobilizing the pervasive presence of human yearning. That is, we are obliged to take *Celestina* as an expression of a terminal transformation of two conceptually distinct but related, historically identifiable master narratives of the Middle Ages – religion and courtly love – that eclipses all possibility of the nobility of their values and pious ideals to represent an undifferentiated universe where all distinctions of caste, class, and sensibility are erased by an indistinct, incontinent want that inhabits every human heart. The result is the emergence of a culturally ambiguous space populated by equally ambiguous desiring subjects whose identities and relationships can no longer be defined by well-defined categories of the social order but by the circulation of sexual and economic capital advanced and structured by unrestrained material yearning.

A theological anthropology of the Middle Ages shows that, in contrast to what is found in *Celestina*, desire had been understood as a state of being that could be directed in essentially two distinct but always transcendent directions, toward God or toward damnation. The Church steadfastly taught that humankind was created with a capacity for union with God and with an inherent tendency toward that union. Even after the Fall, humans, who had been made in His image (Gen. 1:26), possessed a vestige of prelapsarian goodness that moved the soul toward desiring its pre-existing state. Because humans had been made in God's image, they could not be wholly satisfied by the realities of their own existence. Driven thus by a natural propensity to transcend their own order and seek their origins in the divine, Christian theology taught that union with God was the ultimate goal and the reality of every human life. As a consequence of the very act of being, such a disposition existed above and beyond the free will of every individual. It was a faculty that God had endowed to Adam and his descendants at the very moment of Creation.

Support for this metaphysical, essentially Platonic, theory of desire drew authority from patristic doctrine, and although there was some early discrepancy of opinion among theologians regarding the interpretation of Genesis 1:26, by the twelfth century it had become orthodox since it was generally agreed that God's creation of humankind in His likeness denoted a basic spiritual capacity that raised human beings above the other animals. Although it could be subjected and sullied by sin and egoism, which led to eternal damnation in hell, this natural affinity to find God was universal and vouchsafed the *ordo* constituted by Him at the Creation. Desire, as it was understood by the medieval Church, was a conscious reflection of this fundamental state of being. The movement toward God became a component in conscious life to the extent that humans were in contact with the truth of their own existence and were responsive to the demands that confronted them. For the medieval Christian, human desire consisted of a desire for God that, if rightly directed toward the metaphysical, coincided with finding oneself and the perception of oneself to be in motion beyond what can be seen and known. Endowed by the Creator, the human soul was animated by a yearning for the Absolute that led to redemption and resurrection. The object that stirs every spirit is a longing for transcendence and repose in the love of God.[3]

The power of love to transport human perception to a spiritual plane beyond the ordinary also took form in a secularized version of human desire currently known among scholars as courtly love (the Provençal term *fin amours* was mostly applied to it in the Middle Ages). In its ideal manifestation, the latter represented a worldly alternative to the role of love and want in human aspirations but offered an equally deep level of experience and an awareness of desire as a mobilizing and purifying force of the human spirit. Love was conceived of as an ennobling power that merged the ideal of spiritual attainment with erotic yearning. It was, according to Francis X. Newman (1973), 'a love at once illicit and morally elevating, passionate and self-disciplined, humiliating and exalting, human and transcendent' (vii). Although its inspiration came from earthly desire, like its theological congener – which it exploits both structurally and linguistically – courtly love was configured as a quest for a state of existence above and beyond the material experience from which it took flight. The courtly ideal pursued the infinite in human garb through the refinement and idealization of worldly passion.

Although the exact nature of courtly love continues to be a matter of critical debate among medievalists, several things remain clear: courtly love was a masculine discourse that claimed to conceive of women as ennobling moral and spiritual forces, an assertion that, of course, put it in opposition to the ethos espoused by the Church. Rather than characterize passionate exaltation and physical love as sinful, courtly lovers valued it as the highest form of good and as a means of spiritual purification and refinement. The sacrament of marriage did not appear on courtly love's horizon, and if the institution of marriage did, it usually did so as an obstacle to achieving the most elegant, exquisite height of romantic passion. By the beginning of the thirteenth century the courtly version of human desire was condemned by the Church as anathema and heresy; it was entirely the wrong choice for channelling the pursuit of spiritual transcendence.

Despite its polemical nature both then and now, beginning in the eleventh century courtly love doubtless had a civilizing effect on aristocratic ideals and behaviour. Georges Duby (1994) has suggested that, through its conjunction of erotic love and the desire for personal transcendence, it filled the psychological and emotional needs of newly emerging subjectivies in late medieval Europe. Salvation, previously found in the love of God, could now be found in the delicate, carnal hands of a lady. That said, however, in its darker incarnation passionate secular love in the Middle Ages was often linked with both physical and spiritual death (eternal damnation), depending on the way it was presented, and it could be viewed either as a tragic but ennobling force – as a part of love's inevitable fulfilment, as in the case of Tristan and Iseult's sacrificial *Liebestodt*, or Leriano's hieratic, ritualistic death in Diego de San Pedro's *Cárcel de Amor* – or as a sinful and degrading, if stylized, form of concupiscence leading to perdition – as in Alfonso Martínez de Toledo's *Corbacho*, a widely disseminated mid-fifteenth-century Castilian reprobation of worldly love. To be sure, the convergence of death and desire after the thirteenth century was pervasive in literature and art and involved, according to Denis de Rougemont's influential study titled *Love in the Western World* (1956), a displacement of the religious quest for transcendence by a defiantly secular form of alternative religion that seeks spiritual fulfilment in human desire and emotional intensity. Passionate love in the late Middle Ages entailed the dislocation of the mystical thirst for transcendence with worldly desire and emotional suffering, through which lovers, although they may find death in it, reach self-awareness, understanding, nobility, and fame through sacrifice and pain (De Rougemont 1956, 53–4). What is important to note, however, is that in both its medieval theological and courtly formulations, the discourses of love and desire in general were implicated in metaphysical and transcendental consequences; they were thought to be driven toward ends beyond any immediate material reality. Mystical love was directed at union with, and repose in, God; courtly love at achieving spiritual nobility, eternal fame, and privileged understanding, even at the expense of death.

Although the juxtaposition of love and death is a central concern and even a commonplace of medieval and early modern art, in *Celestina* it takes on an unmitigatedly sombre and starkly material perspective that modern theories regarding the nature and origins of human desire help to clarify. Viewing *Celestina*'s staging of the plots of desire aided by means of contemporary social and psychoanalytical theory centring on the expression of desire through and beyond language leads to a deeper understanding of the work's liminal location at the entrance to modernity. The theories of Jacques Lacan especially help us to elucidate how the aims and imaginings of desire in *Celestina* – its performance in response to dream-like scenarios of fulfilment – move from the realm of basic drives to highly elaborate sublimations of social and sexual ambition whose goals always conceal the drive for power and an impulse toward material death.

Lacan, Language, and Desire

In his ground-breaking *The Order of Things*, Michel Foucault compared the early modern understanding of the relationship of words to things (*signum* to *signatum*) with the same affiliation as it was envisioned by means of rational scrutiny in the late seventeenth and early eighteenth centuries. Foucault noted that during the early modern period language was thought to exist as an independent entity in its own right. Words and language were vague, multivalent, copious things that pointed toward a proliferation of other things or ideas in the universe. The best proof of the copiousness of words and language could be found in their ability to evoke an ancillary language of interpretation aimed at explaining the nature and functioning of these word-objects and their organization. Later, after the rise of Cartesianism in the seventeenth and eighteenth centuries, as language was subsequently subjected to rational examination, Foucault contends that words and language lost their ability to exist as polysemous, multivalent things that shared in the mystery of creation. As a result, language lost its supplementarity and ceased to endure as an independent object in the human imagination, having been transformed into a mere vehicle of representation that lacked the need of exposition.

It was in the late nineteenth century, however, through the questioning of rationalism, that a new awareness of how language could exist independently and signify in multiple ways reappeared to challenge the prevailing rationalist assumptions about its transparency.

The rediscovery of the supplemental nature of language in the nineteenth century can be traced to Freud and his development of the theory of psychoanalysis. For Freud, understanding could not be achieved through rational equivalencies or the direct translation of words into the things they represented. To the contrary, meaning could only be achieved through the understanding of language as a symbolic system capable of signifying in multiple, extravagant ways, by intuiting and grasping its rich symbolic repertoire that was deeply rooted in human drives and desires. In this fashion, Freud's interest in the symbolic aspects of language inaugurated a preoccupation with the question of metonymic and metaphorical association that pointed to, but did not specify, suppressed human thoughts and needs. Language and images for Freud became nothing less than the vehicles for conveying and disclosing the presence of concealed desire. Freud conceived of desire in terms of what he called *Treiben* (translated as 'drives' in English) and even compulsions that found their origin deep in instincts buried in the human psyche. Freud's differentiation between the primary and secondary processes of the psyche, and between what Lacan would later define as the split between the Imaginary and the Symbolic realms of human consciousness, in this way hold the key to understanding the obscure, often occluded, nature of desire in a philosophical and psychoanalytical context.

In Freud's psychoanalytical model, the primary processes are the most directly involved in conveying the need for the immediate satisfaction of desire. Infants, for example, represent the forces of these primary processes at work when they are observed sucking in the absence of their mother, doubtless envisioning an image of their mother's breast, or whatever object that may have provided them with prior satisfaction. The infants' enacted fantasy repeats the perception linked to the fulfilment of a need, giving rise to the phenomenon that Freud in *The Interpretation of Dreams* called 'perceptual identity' (1965, 79), or the perceived relationship between something actually experienced and something actually imagined. Perceptual identity in this way constitutes an imaginary avenue toward satisfaction that in the end, because of its purely illusory nature, fails to appease real needs and desires. As a consequence, the secondary processes, guided by what Freud called the Reality Principle, disabuse the infant and teach it not to be misguided by the intensity of

its perceptual images and identities. The outcome of the intervention of
the secondary processes thus results in the modification, deferral, or inhibition of the urge for immediate satisfaction.

Where Freud spoke of the differences between the representation of
verbal language and dream images in the psychic economies of desire,
Jacques Lacan posited the psyche's duality by likening it to language itself, comparing its make-up in terms of concepts taken from structural
linguistics. Lacan, rethinking Freud in terms of contemporary linguistics, underscored the figural nature of desire and its indicators, positing
that the signifiers of desire are protean and conventional in relation to
the thing they signify, which remains unavailable to the conscious mind.
For Lacan, the discourse of the unconscious and the conscious may be
compared to the Saussurian relationship of *langue* to *parole*, in which every utterance implies the pre-existence of a system that renders its enunciation possible. Thus, just as in language the network that endows a
word with sense, although implicit, cannot be present when the word is
uttered, the double discourse of the psyche cannot be simultaneously
actualized or apprehended. The linguistic sign is thus defined by what it
is not and exists in a chain of signification in which the absence of the
sign's opposite is always implicated. A conscious utterance to another person therefore invokes a chain of signification that is not under the speaking subject's control, which thus opens up the unconscious or the realm
of desire. Lacan thus stresses the figural nature of desire and its symptom
as the different positions of a sign in relation to the thing it signifies,
which always remains out of reach of the signifier and of the conscious
mind. For Lacan, the nature of desire can thus never be known to the
desiring subject. It is always elusive and always obscured from consciousness. As we will see in the chapters on *Celestina* that follow, the characters
in the work operate in a strikingly similar universe, constantly seeking to
articulate, yet perpetually misidentifying, the object of their sublimated
desires. The language of desire in both Lacanian theory and in *Celestina*
is always contingent, always metonymical; it can describe only indirectly
and is indicative always of something other.

The uncertain, constantly changing, figural nature of desire served as
an important principle that subtended the depiction of the dynamics of
love in late medieval Castilian courtly literature, especially poetry. Tapia,
perhaps the most widely copied and read *cancionero* poet of the first part
of the sixteenth century, for example, records his conception of the protean nature of love and the object of one's desire in the *Cancionero
General,* published in 1511. There, in a poem in which he responds to a

lady's query to the question of what love is, he stresses its shifting, metonymical, and ultimately abstract nature and says:

Es amor una visión
que cuan presto se figura
tan presto desapareçe;
afición y no raçón,
un bulto de hermosura
que los ojos entristeçe.
Es un doblado dolor,
es un senzillo plazer,
nascido del desear.
Éste, señora, es amor,
tan liviano de perder
cuan pensoso de ganar.   (Gerli 1994, 326)

[Love is a vision
that disappears
as soon as it appears,
ardour and not reason,
a gathering of beauty
that saddens the eyes.
It is pain redoubled,
it is a simple pleasure
born of desire.
This, lady, is love,
so easy to lose,
so difficult to gain.]

The notion of the ineffable and uncertain nature of ever-changing desire was thus firmly ensconced in the discourse of love and desire at the time Fernando de Rojas completed *Celestina* and in large part determined the conventions of its representation in courtly culture.

Structured by the opposition between presence and absence, need and demand, language and the expression of desire in *Celestina,* as in Tapia's poem and in the theories of Lacan, erase their original objects and become its substitute.[4] This is so because the sign of presence in language is always linked with the sign of absence, and the desire for gratification can only be expressed but never achieved. Desire emerges from the split between lack and necessity and manifests itself as a perpetual human want that remains inherently unsatisfied. Satisfaction remains endlessly out of reach, to be infinitely substituted by new forms of desire articulated through language but destined to end in equal disappointment. Desire is thus set in motion by means of signifiers that are constituted as Other and points always to the presence of lack or incomplete satisfaction that becomes the motor of actions whose significance is blocked from consciousness. The object of desire constitutes an object of gratification that remains unobtainable – forever out of reach – representing itself in a chain of objects with which it is not consubstantial, destined always to be misrecognized.

Human discourse in this way constitutes the linking of signifiers in a signifying chain where access to the meaning of the unconscious object of desire does not reside in any single link but continually asserts its suppressed presence. Language thus arises from the obstructed expression of desire and its inability to come to terms with its objects and its meaning. It is condemned always to defer meaning, signify other than what it would mean, moving centrifugally away from a meaning that is the end of its objective. The use of the signifier, which marks the separation of the word from the thing, therefore, denotes the onset of linguistic alienation and, for Lacan, parallels the distinction between Freud's Primary and Secondary Processes. However, these are not separate mechanisms but parts of a complex psychic whole that is the function of three different but related orders: the Imaginary, the Symbolic, and the Real. Of fundamental interest for us, and for the reading of *Celestina* outlined here, is the linking of the latter two; the way the one leads to, or is subsumed in, the other.

Lacan's Symbolic Order is the domain of language, of linguistic representation, and of the separation of words and things. It comes as an intrusion and rupture of the unitary feeling infants experience with their mothers before they become aware of themselves as individuals. In the Symbolic realm, language mediates the relation to reality, forever distancing subjects from a direct grasp of their own psychic reality, marking a disjunction between lived experience and the sign that replaces it. This is the case with all the characters in *Celestina*, who seek to articulate their desires in a torrent of dialogue that only leads to a deepening sense of estrangement, distance, and despair in the work. In both Fernando de Rojas and Lacan, the definitive thing signified is thus lost in the process of symbolization and the human subject remains divided from itself, alienated by the effect of language, desire, and the signifier. All desire is in this way a desire for what is lost in the subject itself.

Lacan's Real Order, structured around constitutional and emotionally powerful experiences like desire, sexual consummation, and death, is the most profound and most inaccessible of the three realms of the psyche. The Real becomes apparent only in the fleeting, final instants of ecstasy or terror, at the shattering points of the Symbolic that Lacan labels *jouissance*. It is there, beyond the Imaginary and the Symbolic, that, as we shall see in Pleberio's final summation of the events in *Celestina*, the kernel or truth at the heart of all subjectivity resides, a condition Lacan identifies with the perception of 'lost immortality' (1977, 166). Immortality, he notes, is what is sought at the deepest level of all human yearning: it is the essence of all human lack. Immortality is, in fact, the real thing that is lacked by all human subjects, and the realization of its impossibility is where the tragic dimension of the *Tragicomedia de Calisto y Melibea* comes into play.

The Symbolic Order – the order of the perception of Otherness and of difference, and therefore of the need for communication with the abstract signifiers of language – encompasses both a feeling of conquest and a profound sense of loss and deficiency. It is at this moment that a quest for subjective wholeness manifested through desire begins, accompanied by deep feelings of lack sensed by an identity that sets itself apart as an individual. As such, a sensation of constitutional want prevails in the realm of the Symbolic, which is always characterized by an unquenchable desire to gain an ineffable object, whose reality is death itself, and the realization of the impossibility of immortality.

The conquest of the power of language to signify what is lacking, according to Lacan, is, like meaning itself, always deferred and forever out of reach. Speech, in this way, is animated by a form of insatiable desire whose object remains always beyond reach. It is both presence and absence. In recognizing the insatiable drive of desire for the impossible in language, the human subject must come to terms with the nontranscendental nature of mortality as the only legitimate reality. It is only at this point, when the subject recognizes the true object of its desire, that he or she ceases to search for another fuller reality beyond the empirical self, producing mourning and the death of language. The sense of mourning that is produced is distinct from the rite that Hegel describes, designed to preserve the dead from the ravages of mortality. It is in fact a mourning that rises from a deep well of alienation for which there is no philosophical or religious cure. It constitutes the inability to affirm in any way the value of ongoing life. This is the condition beyond desire, beyond language, beyond the final residue of the hopeless pursuit of the ever obscure object of desire. This is the condition reached by Pleberio, the lone voice that is finally extinguished at the end of the *Tragicomedia de Calisto y Melibea* as it recedes into the depths of a valley of tears.

In this way, the conjunction of want and death acts as a metaphor for the workings of an unquenchable desire beyond the Symbolic, leading Lacan to conclude that desire, especially in the form of love, is always 'a form of suicide' (1988, 149). Desire, both for Lacan and in *Celestina*, ultimately transports the desiring subject beyond the illusory identifications and ephemeral assurances of language to a confrontation with the Real, the terrifying, permanent, unfulfillable abyss, the lack that resides at the centre of all desiring subjects.

Slavoj Zizek, a pre-eminent applicant of Lacan to cultural theory, maintains that the instinctive sense of lack is itself the constitutional sight of human subjective identity and that it coincides with the Hegelian notion of the transformation of nothing into something (1989, 195–6, 214–15). In the end, neither Lacan's Symbolic or Imaginary Order can offer what the human subject always lacks. Nothing, including the Other, can fully appease the subject's desire. The missing object will always remain missing as desire itself always demands something else. Only the Real – death – can fill the gap and remedy the sense of lack by killing it.

Celestina: The Links and Bonds of Desire

Celestina is a work inscribed in a remarkably similar teleology of desire. Like the theory of desire just outlined, the characters portrayed in it never cease to express and pursue the objects of their desire, only to fail to understand and attain them as they are led to the edge of the mortal abyss. To be sure, the work from its outset is inscribed in the discourse of desire since it is presented as an act of civic responsibility written to counter the spiritual disorder in the world arising from misdirected passion and the confusion of love with religion. This purpose is made plain in the *incipit* of the work, which claims that it was 'conpuesta en reprehension de los locos enamorados que vencidos en su desordenado apetito, a sus amigas llaman y dizen ser su dios' (20) [composed in reprehension of those foolish and brain-sick lovers, who overcome by their disordinate appetites, cleep their loves their gods]. In the prefatory letter to an anonymous friend, Fernando de Rojas inscribes *Celestina* firmly within a dialectic of secular truancy and metaphysical orthodoxy, spiritual order and disorder, that appeared to be shaping the closing years of the fifteenth century in Castilian life. In the letter, he underscores sexual, class, gender, and community conflicts as his principal motivations for taking up his pen to complete the work of the anonymous creator of act 1, and he explicitly envisions his *tragicomedia* as a palliative to these social ills as well as a gesture intended to restore direction and reason to a confused and dissolute youth held captive by desire and exploited by 'lisongeros y malos sirvientes y falsas mugeres hechizeras' (7) [flattering and evil servants and false witches].

Peter Russell (1963, 1978), Alan Deyermond (1977), Javier Herrero (1984), Dorothy Severin (1995), and Joseph Snow (1986) have all shown how *Celestina* reifies desire and inscribes it in an anxiety about witchcraft and the supernatural that was an integral part of the social horizons of the late fifteenth century. Each has studied how several fetishistic linking and binding material objects act as crucial metaphors in the work: the skein of thread, Melibea's braided cordon (said to have touched all the holy relics of Jerusalem), and especially the golden chain given to Celestina by Calisto, which are symbolically intertwined with each other and constitute the culminating material images of evil and desire that tie together the notion of human fates and aspirations in the work. Each binding and tying object symbolizes the characters' self-interest and their quests to exploit and overpower each other. Each critic, save Snow, has identified these images as interlaced materializations of the diabolical forces of desire residing in the circulating objects, imbued with supernatural powers as a result of Celestina's invocation of the Devil (at the end of act 3) in her exertions to conquer Melibea (see Russell 1978). More than an embodiment of supernatural power, however, I would argue along with Snow that, though present, the invocation of magic and witchcraft in the work is subservient to the internal psychological and rhetorical forces that move the characters, and that the invocation of occult forces in the chain serves merely as a device to heighten the clandestine, illicit nature of Celestina's trade and the concealed character of her thoughts.[5] The thread, the braided cordon, and the chain in particular are in fact material objects signifying bondage, luxury, and capital that subsume the connected human motivations of dominance and desire in *Celestina* and comprise the sites where the basic internal drives that move the characters metaphorically coalesce: vanity, sexuality, greed, the will to power, and finally death all pass through those symbolically connected linking objects that culminate in Calisto's golden chain. Like Lacan's linguistic signifiers, the articles as such are symbols; they have no meaning apart from those that human beings invest in them. Their power resides in the motivations and attributions conferred upon them by the characters, and their meaning is derived from their circulation and the transactions in which they serve to mediate individual ambition and desire. In Lacanian terms, the linking, tying, fastening objects dispersed in *Celestina* form a metonymical chain that represents the slippage of the signified from under the signifier, the protean objectification of a desire that cannot indicate its object but can only point to its unconscious presence. *Celestina*'s appeal to sorcery signals the presence of obscure powers in the work, but they are not supernatural powers. As these objects travel through the social economy of *Celestina*, they enact transformations in the narrative of desire, passion, lust, and greed. The magic and the supernatural powers attributed to them are metaphors that stand for concealed forces that change and move the human imaginations of the characters to make things come to pass. More than proof of the efficacy of sorcery (which for Celestina, Pármeno assures us, 'todo era burla y mentira' [56] [And all these were mockeries and lies]), the chain and its binding congeners constitute fetishized objects of human yearning in the down-to-earth drama of inner compulsions that Fernando de Rojas explores through the characters in his work.

The skein, the girdle, and the golden chain all lead to the realization that *Celestina*'s transparently simple plot is transformed into a complex string of linguistic and other figural associations that arise out of all the characters' wishes to identify and grasp the objects of their yearning. But what the work reveals is not simply that the dark object of human desire is protean, nameless, or ineffable, but something that is constituted in strenuous opposition to the subject that pursues it – something that ultimately can only be fully defined in death. In Lacanian terms, desire's movement toward death corresponds to the pursuit of the inaccessible signified – the object of unconscious desire – that resides always out of reach of the chain of signification. The language of desire, like Celestina's skein, is always subject to a metamorphosis, to continuous transformation that can never centre on its true object. When examined closely, then, it is clear that Celestina's thread, Melibea's cordon, and especially Calisto's golden chain make up a string of objects that resist the characters' cravings to possess them and, once gained, become only conduits to death. As they tie and encircle, like the image of the serpent that devours its mate in the act of conception described in the work's prologue, these objects that gird and surround trace the destructive, self-devouring pattern of love, life, and desire in the world:

La bívora, reptilia o serpiente enconada, al tiempo del concebir, por la boca de la hembra metida la cabeça del macho y ella con el gran dulçor apriétale tanto que le mata, y quedando preñada, el primer hijo rompe las yjares de la madre, por do todos salen y ella muerta queda; él quasi como vengador de la paterna muerte. (17)

[The viper, a crawling creature and venomous serpent, at the time of engendering, the male puts his head into the mouth of the female, and she, through the great delight and sweetness of her pleasure, strains him so hard that she kills him. And conceiving her young, the eldest of the first of her brood breaks the bars of his mother's belly, eats out his way through her bowels, at which place all the rest issue forth; whereof she dies, he doing this as the revenger of his father's death.]

The serpent, the very image of deception, is deceived by its own desire, aggressively pursuing the compulsion for generation just to find death in sexual union and conception. The serpent's beginning thus inexorably marks its end.

Calisto's chain in *Celestina* closely parallels what Lacan refers to as the 'signifying chain' of language, especially language as a vehicle of desire. It represents the Lacanian distinction between the Imaginary and the Symbolic orders, where the Imaginary is the order of the specular, mirror stage, and arises from the subject's perception of itself as Other. It is the order of deceptive relations, of ideology and fascination. The Symbolic ultimately is language itself, the systematic, trans-individual order of the signifier, the cultural system or law to which individual subjects are subjected. In the logic of Lacanian desire and the 'signifying chain,' desire is unappeasable, a metonymical movement that extends yearning ever forward without reaching a goal – and a goal that cannot be named, since the desired object is beyond the possibility of being represented, beyond being consciously expressed.

There is a progressive symbolization of desire in *Celestina* through the linking and metamorphosis of images and objects that bind, tie, and encircle: the thread, the girdle, and the golden chain. The chain at the end of the string of objects when placed in the hands of the old prostitute, Celestina, signifies the convergence of Eros and commerce, the point where secular economic and libidinal desire become one, thus multiplying and complicating the representation of value in the work. The lustful impulses of the body and the covetous imagination gather in it. Through its ability to adorn and entangle the body, as well as serve as a medium of exchange in intricate financial transactions, the chain codifies the foundations of the social and sexual imaginary that animates the characters of *Celestina*. It signals the conjunction of compulsive somatic desire and monetary circulation in human motivation. Its prized material transforms wealth into an instrument of libidinal value and consumption that, at the same time, signals desire as the driving force in determining the price of all things. In this way, gold is finally eroticized in Calisto's chain and becomes a visible, tangible thing that contains the potential for acquiring not just sexual enjoyment but indeed all pleasures. It is imagined as the fungible means to all gratification.

Celestina's acquisition of Calisto's golden chain is situated precisely at the point where rapacity can be explained in both spiritual and material terms. The chain becomes the object that epitomizes the enslavement of desire as it promises the possibility of all pleasures, just as it conceals the potential for death. An equivalence of value rests at its centre that confers on it a sense of worth and animates the impulse to appropriate it as a medium for both sexual and economic commerce. The transformation of Celestina's thread into Melibea's girdle, and the latter's final metamorphosis into Calisto's golden chain implies a universe of potentially unlimited transformations and exchanges, a place where language, money, desire, and death may become interchangeable in a circuit of words, power, signification, and material goods. In Lacanian terms, the transformation could be made to stand as an image of the metonymical chain of linguistic signification, illustrating the continual slippage of the signified from under the signifier, the protean materializations of a desire that cannot name or fix its object, yet animates speech and action as it stirs the centre of the unconscious. All this points to the emergence of what Jean-François Lyotard (1993) has called 'libidinal economy.' The golden chain's presence in *Celestina* marks, then, not only the nexus of an exchange of value in a clearly Marxist sense but also an exchange of values in the broadest cultural acceptation of the term and embodies the characters' interconnected lives, destinies, and compulsions. The pure force of the world rests at its core: it becomes the objective correlative of desire, the thing that expresses the fungibility of pleasure, life, and death. It is a coveted thing that moves among the characters and, while it does so, illuminates the personal internal human and public social contexts that it traverses.

We follow the chain and all the other objects that serve to bind and encircle in *Celestina* not for their numinous demonic essence (they are only objects in the material world) but for the meaning that they inscribe in a fetishized trajectory of enticement, as they trace a symbolic economy of human incentive whose driving forces are neither solely capital in the material sense or strictly spiritual in the metaphysical Christian one, but libidinal in the way explained first by Freud and more recently by Marginalist economic theory.

Jean-Joseph Goux, a contemporary Marginalist economist, advances a theory of value and motivation based on human yearning that is not unlike the one that both defines and assigns worth to things in *Celestina*. He notes that

> *desire* is what opens and determines the economic register ... The element of labor plays no role ... Economic value ... is no longer divided between exchange and use; there exists a single desire-value that is in principle subjective, variable, ephemeral ... To create value, all that is necessary is, by whatever means possible, to create a sufficient intensity of desire ... To define value by the intensity of desire or the anticipation of *jouissance* is, in the end, to reduce economic value to attraction value or libidinal value, to press one upon the other until they merge not structurally but substantially. (1990, 202)

Although I certainly do not wish to claim Fernando de Rojas as a precursor of Marginalist economic theory, everything in *Celestina* moves according to these principles. Desire by its nature is infinite and trans-social, everything in the work that is desired is viewed as a commodity, and nothing becomes an object of interest until it is circumscribed, enveloped by desire. The impulse to possess therefore arises from desire and plays itself out as an eminently social activity, relational and dynamic rather than private and passive. All social action is subject to calculations in terms of the relations of means to ends. All things, including love and human polity, seem to be bound up together and have a price – a price defined not in terms of the labour expended to actualize or obtain them but in direct relation to their basic human want. They are all links in a chain of interlocking, ever-expanding ambition and desire. When characters act in the work, they do so always motivated as consumers of coveted objects or things rather than as creators of things.

The link between *Celestina* and the notion of economies of want is thus located in their common grounding in desire, which since the advent of Freud and Lacan has come to be recognized as the key for unlocking and understanding the constitution of human signification, agency, and subjectivity in culture. The Christian Middle Ages, more than any other era, recognized this as well and were characterized by a complex, un-yielding discourse on sexuality and desire that recognized the latter's work as something central to human motivation that exceeded mere car-nal temptation. Since the time of Saint Paul, the pronouncements of the Church on human desire are bound up with a notion of covetousness that surpasses the flesh and were tied to their metaphysical Other, a doc-trine prescribing desire's redirection toward the love of God, whose end is salvation. 'Be not deceived,' Paul thundered, 'neither fornicators, nor idolaters, nor adulterers, nor effeminate, nor abusers of themselves with mankind, nor thieves, nor covetous, nor drunkards, nor revilers, nor ex-tortioners, shall inherit the kingdom of God' (I Cor. 6:9–10) However, it was left to Augustine to take what for Paul was an intuitive understanding of desire and develop it into a spiritual economy and an understanding of human motivation. What began as *concupiscentia carnis* in Paul and the Desert Fathers, and as an interdiction of desire at the level of the body, was transformed in Augustine's imagination into something that ex-ceeded corporality. For Augustine, desire constitutes nothing less than a lust of the intellect. As Peter Brown has noted, concupiscence was much more than bodily lust for Augustine, it 'was a dark drive to control, to appropriate, and to turn to one's private ends, all the good things that had been created by God to be accepted with gratitude and shared with others' (1988, 418). Augustine's emphasis on the psychological momen-tum that propels human desire broke down the barriers that restricted it to sexuality and had been defined in an earlier age. It was now under-stood as a destructive form of yearning that dwelt potentially in all forms of human activity. Drawing upon this ancient understanding of human incentive, Marginalist economic theory and *Celestina* both make explicit that desire is the essential driving force of all human action. All seem to acknowledge the absolute significance of desire in social and cultural processes, and all view desire as an unceasing enterprise in the forma-tion of destinies and identities. In this sense *Celestina* in an astonishingly modern turn grasps how desire and human subjectivity are inseparable. Indeed, the genius of the work resides in understanding that the human beings do not beget desire, but vice versa: that desire is what ultimately animates, creates, and shapes the human subject from within.

Celestina's immediate engagement with desire arises from its roots in the emotive economy of courtly love, a never-ending, always frustrated quest for fulfilment and transcendence that was thought to ennoble the spirit and which, according to Lacan (1988), 'marked the rise to the surface in European culture of a problematic of desire as such' (235). In the work, however, as June Hall Martin (1972) has shown, the desire that moves the courtly lover is rendered banal and absurd. In this fashion, it is reconfigured and fails to find spiritual transcendence as it suddenly spills out and beyond its medieval aristocratic containment to infect in unsuspected ways even the lowliest inhabitants of the world. Pármeno, Sempronio, Elicia, and Celestina, not to mention Areúsa, all aspire to something greater than what they possess, all rise up from radical dissatisfaction to want to be something beyond what they know they are. As Américo Castro noted when he commented upon the poignancy of *Celestina*, its place in fifteenth-century literary history, and the profound changes that marked human social formations at the time it was written, 'lo peculiarmente angustioso de tal historia fue el reiterado intento de *querer ser* de un modo y tener que ser de otro, conflicto que se plantea en el siglo XV con más acuidad que nunca antes' (1970, 121) [the peculiarly anguishing aspect of this story was the reiterated intention (of the characters) to want to be a certain way and have to be another, a type of conflict that arises, as never before, with greatest acuity in the fifteenth century].

Castro's crucial observation on the prevailing sense of estrangement in *Celestina* concurs with an idea advanced by Lacan in his theories concerning the formation and operation of human subjectivity: the notion of *manque-à-être*, or to want to be (where *manque* carries a connotation of lack, absence, or inadequacy). In this way, desire becomes the constitutive feature of subjectivity since we are defined as split subjects constituted by our desires and absences, rather than through any sense of wholeness.

Humans exist in a state of desire to possess something from which they are alienated, which Lacan dubs the signifier. It is in this sense of estrangement that people feel as they negotiate the realm of existence Lacan terms the Symbolic, or the space where the signifier operates, principally the field of language. The sense of alienation and inadequacy that dominates the realm of speech and language can be traced back to what Lacan calls the 'mirror stage,' or the moment of individuation and self-recognition when humans move away from an egocentric position of wholeness into a fragmentary realm of distance and separation; the stage when they move into language. The motivation for the shift is the urge to grasp and possess the absolute signifier, or to gain control over the self and others within the social context; to realize their desire. Rather than a situation that produces gratification, however, it is one that produces only dissatisfaction. Since the object of desire is unattainable, the subject splits within itself and from others. Moreover, the object of desire according to Lacan and Zizek is always perceived anamorphically, as something protean and Other. As Zizek notes, the object of desire 'assumes clear and distinctive features only if we look at it "at an angle," i.e., with an "interested" view, supported, permeated, and "distorted" by desire' (1992, 12). It is in this way an object generated by desire itself since its cause is itself postulated retroactively; it can never be materialized and remains always out of reach, non-existent, since it can be perceived only by a distorted perspective, a gaze warped and informed by desire itself. It is something that fails to materialize for any objective perspective. Desire's object implies a continuous displacement, or *différance*, and it is only in moments of *jouissance* where a direct confrontation with its true object – nothingness – can be experienced.

Desire in this way emerges in *Celestina* in direct proportion to the forces that impede it. The most intense moments of it occur, as we shall see, when Calisto either substitutes a fetish object or imagines Melibea present; when he converts nothing into something. But desire is engendered not only by absences in the usual erotic sense but in the more fundamental sense of the illusion of an original lost object. At its end, in Pleberió's summation, the work suggests that not only erotic pursuits but social ideals, economic ambitions, and human identity itself are based upon such illusions. As Lacan speculates, human identity is forged in the imaginary lure of the mirror stage and through the consequent estrangement of the self in language. This alienation indicates the demise of the thing in itself to give genesis to the desire for what cannot ever be secured.

Desire in *Celestina* manifests itself with an anamorphic energy that transgresses, transforms, and dissolves the constituted forms of social life. However, only insofar as these forms are constituted can transgression have consequence. Because transgression is forbidden, it perpetrates by its very definition violence to the established order. Transgression pushed to its limit animates the representation of the end of desire in the work and constitutes the search for an impossible unity that only death can finally provide. Thus death, trespass, and brutal corporal destruction (Celestina's, Pármeno's, Sempronio's, Calisto's, and Melibea's) express a complicity with the very law that forbids them, resulting in a work that portrays unprecedented forms of violence in the world of the everyday.

Celestina has long been recognized as a profoundly modern work, and it has been a critical commonplace that it marks the passage between the

Middle Ages and the Renaissance, or early modernity in the more current formulation of the term. Most recently, Roberto González Echevarría has sought to explore the question of *Celestina*'s modernity in terms of its almost Nietzschean advocacy of an inherent immorality in the human species, 'a depravity so deep-seated that only through careful suppression or sublimation can social life endure,' the understanding of which leads to 'a shocking, unadorned vision of humankind and of literature itself that it cannot be easily imitated' (1993, 9). The present book encompasses a new approach to the formulation of this critical debate. It centres on the conviction that *Celestina* is not modern because of its portrayal of the delusions of human virtue, its amorality, the rise of the individual, the act of suicide, its interest in low-life characters, its unabashed carnality, or its redefinition or parody of literary styles and traditions (courtly love, sentimental romance, etc.), as the arguments go, but rather on the discovery and representation of something more profound: the reality of non-transcendence, the absence of metaphysical presence, in the face of the human desire to transcend. The latter, as stated in the introduction, is what marks the work's early modernity and, more importantly, the emergence of the modern human subject in the literature of the Spanish-speaking world.

The theory advanced here is that *Celestina*'s uniqueness lies in its exploration of the human subject as something that emerges out of a fundamental reconfiguration and rethinking of desire, and from the trauma of the conclusive awareness that lives lived desiring have no reachable or knowable metaphysical object or foundation. Desire, in both its virtuous and perverse materializations, is its own object in *Celestina* and its end is always itself. It is destined always to be obstructed and obscure. At the end of the chain of yearning that constitutes the human lives of *Celestina*, courtly love and Christianity, the secular and mystical discourses of devotion and the ways of envisioning transcendence, encounter a dead end. It becomes plain that neither paradigm holds any promise of redemption. Desire in the end produces only mourning and melancholia under the perception of futility and the finality of individual death; it fails to animate catharsis or signal the prospect of salvation; its only understanding is despair and, finally, silence.

2 Celestina, Mistress of Desire

Un vieja barbuda que ... a las duras peñas
promoverá y provocará luxuria. *Celestina*
Galeotto fù il libro ...

Dante, *Divina Comedia*

Oh that. That's an old business. You'll get used to that.

Scarface (film, 1932)

When as a student at the University of Salamanca Fernando de Rojas
took up his pen to complete the anonymous manuscript that would become act 1 of *Celestina*, he noted that the latter was something confected
by one of the most 'doctos varones castellanos' (6) [brightest intelli-
gences of learned Castilian gentlemen] comparing it to a weapon of the
strongest steel, which stood out for its 'primor, su fuerte y claro metal, su
modo y manera de lavor, su estilo elegante, jamás en nuestra castellana
lengua visto ni oýdo' (6) [its newness, its subtle artifice, its strong and
bright metal, its means and manner of working, its elegant style, never
before seen or heard in our Castilian tongue]. He remarked also how
after reading it three, four, and more times, with each rereading he continued to delight in the wisdom of the work's aphorisms, the pleasure of
its plot, and the 'delectables fontezicas de filosophía' (6) [delightful
founts of philosophy] that flowed forth from it. These observations on
the artistic and intellectual merits of the anonymous author's opuscule,
inscribed firmly in the discourse of Rojas's own readerly desire, point in
one specific direction: toward the learned, scholarly environment of the
university at the close of the fifteenth century in which Rojas moved,
and to the academic debates that were waged there through most of the

preceding years regarding the place of naturalist philosophy – particularly in its Epicurean and neo-Aristotelian guise – in matters of love, and in the universe of the appetites and human want. In an important monograph and complementary anthology of texts, Pedro M. Cátedra (1989, 2001) has pointed to the complex intellectual matrix and scholarly background that serve as touchstones for understanding this aspect of the work, and for the appearance of *Celestina* in general.

At the same time, the research of scholars like Eukene Lacarra Lanz (1990, 1993, aka María Eugenia Lacarra) has uncovered the discrete social and historical content of *Celestina* against a backdrop of the proliferation of prostitution in Castile, and the measures taken by government and civic groups both to contain and control it, at the close of the fifteenth century. Similarly, the investigations of scholars like Mary Elizabeth Perry (1990) have gone a long way in helping us see why women, whose conduct could be considered either deviant or obedient, became increasingly significant subjects in a rapidly changing society at the end of the fifteenth and the beginning of the sixteenth centuries in Spanish urban centres, where the ways of the old social order appeared to be ever more elusive with every passing day.

If Cátedra's work has helped bring out the theoretical and philosophical arguments that structure *Celestina* and the ethical and moral concerns they engage, both Lacarra and Perry have done as much, or more, to help us achieve a deeper understanding of the historical human circumstances from which *Celestina* emerged, and for the striking novelty – it might even be argued, striking improvisational fashion – in which its characters engage the world in which they live. Fernando de Rojas was doubtless immersed in both the historical and theoretical universe uncovered by these scholars, a world in which the philosophy of love and desire, the reality of prostitution, the presence of working women, and the ever-changing perceptions of gender and gender roles in a vertiginously evolving society were a daily presence and a subject of both learned interest and community concern.

Rojas's book portrays the role of women in society in striking new ways and, as we shall see later in chapter 6, confers upon them a sense of self-awareness rarely seen before in their literary portrayal. The most impressive of these female characters, of course, is Celestina, whose imposing personality and seemingly infinite range of manual and rhetorical arts made way for her name to displace the original title of the book, *Tragicomedia de Calisto y Melibea,* that now bears her appellation. The fact that the book in which she first appeared in 1499 was titled *Comedia,* and that it was later deliberately changed and amplified to *Tragicomedia* in an effort to underscore its dark complexity and forbidding nature, did little to prevent the name of Celestina from taking pre-eminence in the memory of all who came across Rojas's work, or to apply her name permanently to it. The reason for this is simple: literary texts exist to be read or performed, and, as they are read or performed, they take on a life of their own in the imaginations of their public in which the most memorable of their characters stand out, to the point where they often may even eclipse the name and identity of their creators, not to mention their original titles.

By 1535, when the humanist Juan de Valdés composed his *Diálogo de la lengua,* Fernando de Rojas's book and the old bawd were already in Valdés's imagination one and the same. There Marcio, Valdés's chief interlocutor in the dialogue, solicits the latter's opinion of the work by asking '¿Qué dezís de *Celestina?* Pues mucho su amigo soléis ser' (182) [What do you say about Celestina? Since you are very often much her friend], a remark that not only conflates the character with the book but makes them both come alive through the personification Marcio employs to frame his question.[1] So powerful, in fact, is the character Celestina, that since the sixteenth century her name has competed with the words *alcahueta* and *trujimán* [go-between] to become the source of *celestina/celestino,* which is today one of the preferred common nouns in the Spanish language used to denote an individual of either gender who engages in securing special favours, attains secret wishes, and performs every manner of covert and illicit mediation for another person. To be sure, the force of the nominative *celestina/o* was so powerful that it also gave rise to a verb, *celestinear,* which today is employed in common speech throughout the Spanish-speaking world and is understood to designate all manner of mediation and arbitration. The word *celestina/o* and its derivatives in this way indicates a person's unique ability to seek out, mediate, and obtain desires for others, and stems directly from Rojas's character's trenchant reputation for helping others to discover and execute their own.

From the outset, when we first learn of Celestina from Sempronio in his description of her to his master in act 1 of the *Tragicomedia,* she is described as something almost preternatural, as a shaman or magician of desire capable of extending what seem like Orphic powers, as one of the epigraphs to this chapter suggests, to move, persuade, and provoke lust even in unfeeling stone and flinty boulders. Sempronio adds that she is an old bearded woman, introducing two crucial images (her abundant facial hair, suggestive of androgyny, and her advanced age, connoting wisdom and experience) that will form part of a complex rhetorical and visual system in which her assumption of male economic, professional, and erotic prerogatives is first signalled in the text.[2]

Perhaps Celestina's most distinguishing physical feature, however, is the scar that she carries on her face, placed there in the past by the blade of some retributive knife. The latter is singled out repeatedly in the *Tragicomedia* as the key identifying characteristic that differentiates her appearance from all the other personages in the book. Melibea and Lucrecia both mention Celestina's scar in act 4 when they meet her. Lucrecia, in fact, invokes it twice: once, when reluctant to pronounce Celestina's name to Alisa, she circumlocutiously informs her mistress that it is 'aquella vieja de la cuchillada, que solía bivir aquí en las tenerías a la cuesta del río' (110) [that old woman forsooth with the scotch on her nose who sometimes dwelt hard by here in Tanner's Row, close upon the riverside] who has come to call, figuring that her mention of the scar will suffice to identify the visitor; and later when she again comments on the facial mark as the only physical sign of Celestina's appearance resistant to change and to the passage of time: 'Mudada está el diablo,' she says, 'hermosa era con aquel su Dios os salve que traviessa la media cara' (118) [the devil she is; she was fair when she met with him (saving your reverence) that scotched her over the nose], as she expresses astonishment at Celestina's temporal transformation.

To be sure, Celestina's scar is the one indelible sign of her identity; it is the single abiding feature of her individuality that transcends all the transformations wrought upon her body by time, excess, and toil. It is only by means of it that Melibea recognizes and remembers her, when she suddenly marvels at what the passage of a scant two years has done to change the fetching woman she once knew into the old bawd that now stands before her: 'Vieja te has parado ... no te conociera sino por esta señaleja de la cara. Figúraseme que eras hermosa; otra pareces; muy mudada estás' (118) [By my fay, you are an old woman ... I did not know you; neither should I, had it not been for that slash over your face; then were you fair, now methinks you are as it were another woman, now wonderfully altered].

Celestina's scar is a tangible mark of an undefined, multivalent universe of ideas that encompass her complex personality (Lillian von der Walde Moheno [2007] traces its signifying links to physiognomy). More times than not, it represents the permanent sign of bodily transgression, which points to a higher, lasting sense of spiritual misrule and evil-doing.

Figure 2.1 Magdalena Ventura, Her Husband, and Her Infant Son, 1631 José (Juseppe) de Ribera. Museo Casa de Pilatos, Fundación Duques de Medinaceli, Seville. With permission.

Figure 2.2 Brígida del Río, La barbuda de Peñaranda, by Juan Sánchez Cotán, ca. 1590. Museo del Prado, Madrid. With permission.

The repeated mention of her facial disfigurement clearly identifies it as a symbol through which the polyvalent themes of intrusion, violation, and abjection are conveyed. Although the scar is always present, manifesting itself in a variety of ways at different times, its meaning is renegotiated and assigned anew each time the characters in the work notice and confront it. More than sexual sin and bodily trespass, Celestina's facial blemish appears to convey a different meaning to each of the characters who point to it.

Bodily signs are, of course, semiotically charged elements of identity and intention, and they may be used to express either legitimacy or subversion depending on their nature and perception. They may either vouchsafe or challenge social categories and moral standards. In the Middle Ages, the body was considered the surface upon which one could read the signs of the inner personality of an individual (see chapter 7). As such, Celestina's scar is both a material and lasting testimonial of a cryptic, albeit belligerent past, the mysterious, disconcerting brand that blemishes her otherwise solicitous outer personality. Although the history of her facial disfigurement is never specified in the *Tragicomedia*, its possible origins have produced considerable critical speculation. Francisco Márquez-Villanueva (1993), for example, incited to imagine domestic violence at its root, wonders if it may have been given to her by an angry husband, while Peter Russell (1991, 74n.114) and Dorothy Severin (1995, 8) interpret it in specific, nefarious, and historical ways: as the mark of the Devil's talon left as a souvenir on the face of all those who consort with him. Roberto González Echeverría (1993), on the other hand, sees the mark's larger potential for generating meaning and perceives it in more broadly symbolic terms: as the sign of Celestina's fiendish monstrosity (5). Although the etiology and precise meaning of Celestina's knife scar remain unspecified, its very ambiguity and lack of specificity suggests all these things and a great deal more.[3]

Beyond any discrete history, Celestina's scar stands as a multivalent, tangible trace of both her social and spiritual transgressions, a mark on her body that points to contradiction, to something hidden, to the crossing of boundaries, to infamy, aggression, abjection, and wrongdoing. Like the scars she leaves on the repaired maidenheads she crafts, it both conceals and commemorates some form of trespass and penetration. It is both a sign and a cover-up of something secret, the vestige of a breach that fails to hide or heal completely an earlier intrusion. Celestina's scar is a violation of the body that indicates the larger, more fundamental, inner breach of her soul. It stands as both a reminder and a screen for some offence; it is a healed wound, yet one that recalls all the wounds and traumas Celestina inflicts and, like a closed door, prevents us from seeing what is hidden immediately behind it. Celestina's scar commemorates some dark event and suggests the presence of a real yet inscrutable absence; of something visible, something there, something confounding, sinister, yet hidden. It is a richly productive image, the mark of an unknown that she bears with her but that, like the nature of her intentions, remains enigmatic, inscrutable and out of reach.

In its fullest sense, Celestina's disfigurement is the semblance of misconduct and lawlessness. Its multiple mentions in the text identify it as an emblem that produces both recognition and anxiety in everyone she meets. It is a sign whose discrete initial referent has vanished, but one that remains sufficiently connotative to make it, like her beard, a crucial and suggestive part of who she is. Although the mark on her countenance is a sign without a context, like a name on a map, the scar conjures something real; it recalls something in time and space. Precisely because it is a closed wound, however, it can only generate intimations of violence, pain, unruliness, and transgression; suggestions of a series of vanished libidinal intensities that once possessed immediate meaning and painful resonance, but which are now concealed, out of sight, lying just below the surface of appearances.[4] Like a riddle inscribed on her body whose origin remains unknown and that can only be imagined, Celestina's disfigurement compels us to guess what it might mean. But it is precisely because its origin must be inferred that the scar serves as such a powerful icon of the turbulent world in which she moves. It moves and motivates the imagination of everyone she encounters.

Perhaps the most complete description of Celestina comes from Pármeno, her wary former houseboy, the son of Celestina's deceased partner and revered mentor Claudina (see Snow 1986), who through his employ as Calisto's second servant has sought to flee childhood infamy by moving up. As Pármeno attends to the door to let Celestina in to meet Calisto, he paints a murky portrait of the old bawd intended to dissuade his master from falling into her grasp, as much as to keep Celestina from exposing the details of his own questionable past. Celestina, according to Pármeno, practises several trades: 'labrandera, perfumera, maestra de hazer afeytes y hazer virgos, alcahueta y un poquito hechizera' (52) [a laundress, a perfumeress, a former of faces, a mender of cracked maidenheads, a bawd, and had some smatch of a witch]. Under the guise of selling cosmetics, notions, herbs, and yarn, she gains access to the homes of women to deliver messages, bring news, and open their hearts and hopes to fantasies of desire. As the consummate go-between, she sees herself performing a much needed, worthy service in society. Her penchant for wine does not seem to cloud her wicked intelligence; she relies always upon the latter and her long experience to master the unwillingness of others and probe the weaknesses of the most obstinate resistance. She is a master of persuasion, but not beyond making imagined pacts with the Devil, the one spectre she must privately consult to assuage her rare misgivings and occasional doubt.

Celestina passes also as a physician – an expert therapist of the indispositions of the body – with a specialty in youth. In this way, she gains entry to the houses of the town (on the suspect nature of women healers and their association with witchcraft, see Perry 1990, 28–30; and Dangler 2001). Referring to her success as a go-between in the traffic of virgins, Pármeno elaborates upon her ability to restore torn maidenheads by sewing them with silken thread, and to how her reputation for this special craft extends her deft reach to 'las más encerradas' (52) [your very Vestals]. Her fame for covering up the very desires she helps realize is such that she serves all the townspeople at large, men and women alike – 'venían a ella muchos hombres y mujeres' [both men and women came unto her] – whom she fleeces down to 'el pan do mordían' (56) [a piece of bread where they had bit it] in exchange for her essential but forbidden services. Both women and men look to her for her knowledge and ability to mediate and realize their compulsions and desires. Finally, Celestina, according to Pármeno, turns all censure and ill fame aside, practises her trade with pride, and takes enormous satisfaction in the sobriquet of *puta vieja* [old whore], which all creation joins in celebration to ring out as she passes down the lane (50–1).

Later, it is Celestina herself who touts her authority in the commerce of desire. Above all, it is she who displays her skills and takes satisfaction in knowing herself, speaking with confidence and bravado about her professional acumen. When Sempronio first informs her of Calisto's passion for Melibea and the role he has come to offer Celestina in it, for example, she confidently responds 'basta para mí mecer el ojo. Digo que me alegro destas nuevas, como los cirujanos de los descalabrados; y como aquéllos dañan en los principios las llagas, y encarescen el prometimiento de la salud, ansí entiendo yo hazer a Calisto. Alargarle he la certenidad del remedio, porque como dizen, el esperança luenga aflige el coraçón, y quanto él perdiere, tanto gela promete' (48–50) [The winking or beckoning of the eye is enough for me; for as old as I am, I can see day at a little hole. I am as glad of this thy news, as surgeons of broken

heads. And as they at the first go festering the wounds the more to endear the cure, so do I mean to deal with Calisto: for I will still go prolonging the certainty of his recovering of Melibea, and delay still the remedy.
For, as it is in the proverb, delayed hope afflicteth the heart. And the
farther he is from obtaining, the fairer will he promise to have it ef-
fected]. While her reference to *descalabrados* (broken or smashed heads)
conceals a macabre prolepsis of Calisto's headlong fall into oblivion, it
also proclaims Celestina's studied self-confidence in the practice of her
art. Subsequently, when Sempronio appears to understate the range of
her professional success to her, she vigorously rejoins with pique, boast-
ful confidence, and salacious double entendre:

> Pocas virgines, a Dios gracias, has tu visto en esta ciudad que hayan abierto
> tienda a vender, de quien yo no haya sido corredora de su primer hilado ...
> ¿Havíame de mantener del viento? ¿Heredé otra herencia? ¿Tengo otra
> casa o viña? ¿Conóscesme otra hazienda, más deste officio de que como y
> bevo, de que visto y calço? En esta ciudad nascida, en ella criada, man-
> teniendo honrra, como todo el mundo sabe, ¿conoçida, pues, no soy?
> Quien no supiere mi nombre y mi casa, tenle por estrangero. (96)

> [Few virgins (I thank fortune for it) hast thou seen in this city, which have
> opened their shops and traded for themselves, to whom I have not been a
> broker to their first spun thread ... Can I live by the air? Can I feed myself
> with the wind? Do I inherit any other land? Have I any other house or vine-
> yard? Knowest thou of any other substance of mine, besides this office? By
> what do I eat and drink? By what do I find clothes to my back, and shoes to
> my feet? In this city I was born; in it I was bred; living (though say it) in good
> credit and estimation, as all the world knows. And dost thou think then,
> that I can go unknown? He that knows not both my name and my house,
> thou mayest hold him a mere stranger.]

Celestina is known by all, knows everyone, and knows all about everyone
in the city. Although old, she has not lost any of her senses with advancing age. She is attuned to everything, warning those who might seek to
deceive her, or to doubt her abilities, against thinking that 'el oýr con los
otros exteriores sesos mi vejez aya perdido' [with these my other outward
senses, old age hath made me lose my hearing]. To be sure, she boasts of
almost metaphysical powers, of an acute sixth sense: 'Que no sólo lo que
veo, oyo y cognozco, mas aun lo intrínsico con los intellectuales ojos
penetro' (62) [for not only that which I see, hear and know, but even the

very inward secrets of thy heart and thoughts I search into and piece to the full with these my intellectual eyes, these eyes of my understanding]; a faculty that, James Burke notes, permits her to be attuned to a vast universe of 'second intentions,' which, in consonance with memory, 'allow her to understand perfectly the wants and needs of those who surround her and to shape these to her own purposes' (2002, 17).

Complementing her acute intuition and consummate expertise with manlike puissance and airs of dark magic, prior to setting off for Melibea's house, Celestina orders Elicia to bring her a talisman of 'la sangre del cabrón, y unas poquitas de las barvas que tú le cortaste' (104) [the blood of the he goat and a little piece of his beard which you yourself did cut off] to devise a hex for Melibea, alluding to her belief in the supernatural but also indicating the way in which she seizes male symbols of virility, authority, and honour as her own to underwrite her powers of seduction.

Celestina, however, is more than a picturesque old libertine with a reputation for instinctive, fine-tuned mediation. She is an old woman who has traded her spent vitality and youthful hedonism for other forms of cupidity – exchanged the needs of the body for the desires of the intellect and transformed *libido capiendi* into *libido dominandi*, the lust of the body for the lust for power. No longer able to enjoy the pleasures of the flesh, she ruefully forsakes them for the instruments that now offer her the satisfaction that she seeks: gold and money. As she realizes the desires of others, accumulates power and seeks wealth for herself, she is, quite simply, the compelling Mistress of Desire in the universe of the *Tragicomedia*, simultaneously handmaiden to cupidity and master of it; the one who, ever subjected by memory to the pleasures of her youth, has learned to control, identify, distribute, and help execute everyone else's yearning but her own, as she helps herself by helping others and fights against the loss and extinction of her own vitality. Celestina's widowhood, lack of heirs, and mastery of masculine trades all make her a fitting figure for her role as the ambivalent, janus-faced Mistress of Desire, a being who both dominates and is dominated by inner yearnings and compulsions.

The representation of desire in the form of a woman would not, of course, have caused a stir in 1499. From earliest times both the Christian and pagan traditions had figured sexual attraction, transgression, and carnal knowledge in feminine form, as either Eve or Helen of Troy. At the same time, the learned clergy, which held the monopoly on knowledge and learning during the Middle Ages, also continued to trope wisdom, memory, and knowledge in feminine guise, as the ancient Roman goddess Minerva, who sprang full-grown from the head of her father, Jupiter, and like Celestina was a master of the weaving arts. To be sure, Ovid, recognizing Minerva's protean skills, referred to her as the goddess of a thousand works (see Solterer 1995). The feminine representation of aged wisdom, Celestina, is thus the weaver of human ambitions and destinies, and in this way incarnates both the lower carnal and the higher intellectual forms of knowledge and human understanding. Through her rhetorical arts, knowledge of medicine, herbs, astrology, weaving, sewing, and cosmetics (which make things seem other than the way they are) she practises the art of making the suppressed desire of all with whom she comes in contact speak. As Peter Dunn succinctly puts it, Celestina occupies 'a place at the center of the work, where she affects the lives of all the rest of the cast and creates a network of interests which converge upon her; makes her, in short, the vortex into which they are all drawn' (1975, 116).

What remains disconcerting about Celestina is that, while a woman, she is also so clearly figured as masculine in the text; as a character that is both manly and feminine, as well as something in between. To be sure, Celestina occupies, lives, and transits in the in-between; she moves through and beyond all boundaries marked by gender, propriety, and the law uncovering desire where its presence and existence are most emphatically proscribed or vigorously denied. As she practises her trade, she is beyond limits and authority and breaches the social, sexual, and physical bulwarks that distinguish order and civility in the world that she inhabits, to discover and realize the power of desire in the intimate recesses of the lives of everyone she touches. Privy to the secrets of both men and women, in her androgyny, like some latter-day Tiresias, she reveals her knowledge of the suppressed realities and secrets of both sexes, making them materialize and speak, allowing them to say what must usually remain unspoken.

Celestina knows well all the characters she meets, making even the most reticent and resistant of them, like Pármeno, discover and concede their hidden thoughts and wishes, buried, as we shall later see, even in the high-pitched titters of a nervous laugh. She knows the human body and the mind and traffics in the appetites of both: covetousness, sex, the will to power, and domination. She is as powerful as any man, yet she is a woman, and in this way provokes anxiety as she materializes all that is held unstable and subversive in the patriarchal world.

The belletristic antecedents of Celestina have been traced back to the go-betweens of Plautus and other Roman comedians (see Lida de Malkiel

1970), as well as to the Ovidian tale (see Schevill 1913), the fourteenth-century Castilian *Libro de buen amor*, and other medieval Latin, Italian, and Arabic congeners, i.e., in Aeneas Silvius Piccolomini's *Historia de duobus amantibus* and Boccaccio's *Elegia di madonna Fiammeta* and *The Thousand and One Nights* (see Ruggerio 1966, Rouhi 1999, Hamilton 2000, and Armistead and Monroe 1999). Although doubtless patterned on these literary models, thanks to Rojas's unprecedented ability to construct three-dimensional characters and redefine the representation of well-worn literary and cultural paradigms, Celestina and all the other characters in the work are *sui generis*. They possess an acute sense of awareness of one another and are portrayed as desiring subjects who see the human objects of their gaze as thinking subjects who are endowed with psychological depth, intention, feeling, motivation, and agency, multifaceted characteristics that mark the modernity of the their portrayal. Constituted as real-seeming participants in uninterpreted and unmediated dialogue, which heightens the illusion of their actuality, all the personages in *Celestina* are point-of-view characters, who as they speak regard, sense, and judge their interlocutors and deliberate about the events that happen to them and around them. Like Celestina herself, each character in the work is intricately complex, possesses thought and discernment, and undergoes change, so as to surprise the reader at every turn, as in the striking case of Pármeno, who declares himself Calisto's loyal servant, only to reveal later that his allegiance to his master is a cover for an unsavoury personal past. Far from stereotypical, each of the characters in *Celestina* emerges unencumbered by textual antecedents: although they spring from recognizable literary types (*servus*, *lena*, *meretrix*, lady, and courtly lover), they possess unique imaginative attributes that lead us to perceive subtle distinctions and even contradictions in their constitution. As they speak directly, they strike us as singular and believable. They provoke revision, or the need for the reader not just to consider, but later to reconsider the characters' words and actions so as to unveil initially unrecognized forces and surreptitious, as well as buried, motivations in their words and deeds, eventually altering the manner in which they were initially perceived. In this way, the reader or audience – which includes the very interlocutors of the characters in the work – remains continually engaged, and is compelled to exercise memory, returning to an action or a word uttered by one of them to give new consideration to its underlying thought or opinion.

Although inspired by a long line of literary forebears (Roman, medieval Latin, Castilian, even Muslim), Celestina is her own person, far from just another shadow of a literary go-between: she has a past, a present, and yearns for a secure future, and like no other of her literary ancestors she sees her identity vested in, and feels the need to facilitate, the propagation of desire. Once a public woman, too old now to exercise her trade, she dedicates her daily efforts to arrange privately the realization of everyone else's secret wishes. And, in the city where Celestina lives, desire is everywhere to be uncovered, so she seems omnipotent and omnipresent as she methodically goes about her work. Rather than a connection to literature, Celestina appears to confirm a larger link to history, to Caludia Opitz's assertion in her study of historical women in the late Middle Ages that 'if a poor woman became unwilling or unable to continue earning a living as a prostitute – usually because she was too old – begging or procuring remained as last resorts' (1994, 307).

Always on the move, always planning and watching, Celestina recognizes that desire lurks in every human heart, ready to manifest itself ecstatically with the slightest spur or provocation. When Sempronio asks if there is really hope for her to conquer Melibea for Calisto, Celestina not only assures him that there is, since all women once they have tasted love capitulate entirely to it, but does so by advancing the memory of her own feminine experience and invoking the continuing pulsations of her own aged sexuality. Although Celestina's observations on the matter are long, they are worth examining since they vividly portray from first-hand knowledge her understanding of a woman's initial encounter with the realization of desire. As much a description of what occurs in others, her words amount to nothing less than a personal confession. The surety of her analysis is guaranteed by the force of her own memory and her wistful nostalgia for the moment:

Aunque esté brava Melibea, no es ésta, si a Dios ha plazido, la primera a quien yo he hecho perder el cacarrear. Coxquillosicas son todas, más después que una vez consienten la silla en el envés del lomo, nunca querrían holgar: por ellas queda el campo; muertas sí, cansadas, no. Si de noche caminan, nunca querrían que amaneciesse, maldizen los gallos porque anuncian el día, y el relox porque da tan apriessa. Requieren las cabrillas y el norte, haziéndose estrelleras; ya quando ven salir el luzero del alva, quiéreseles salir el alma. Su claridad les escurece el coraçón. *Camino es, hijo, que nunca me harté de andar; nunca me vi cansada, y aun assí vieja como soy. Sabe Dios mi buen desseo; quánto más éstas que hierven de fuego.* Catívanse del primer abraço; ruegan quien rogó; penan por el penado; házense siervas de quien eran señoras; dexan el mando y son mandadas. Rompen paredes, abren ventanas, fingen enfermedades. A los cherriaderos quiçios de las puertas hazen con azeytes usar su officio sin ruido. No te sabré dezir lo mucho que obra en ellas aquel dulçor que les queda de los primeros besos de quien aman. Son enemigas todas del miedo, contino están posadas en los estremos. (100, emphasis added)

[For though Melibea brave it, and stands so high upon her pantofles, yet as God have it is not she the first that I have made stoop and leave her cackling: they are all of them ticklish and skittish; the whole generation of them is given to wincing and flinging: but after they are well weighed, they prove good highway jades, and travel quietly; but after that they have once consented and yielded to their riders, suffering themselves to be saddled in the opposite part to their reins and to be strongly girzed in the inside of their loins, they will never be made to give over: the field must be theirs; you may kill them, but never tire them. If they journey by night, they wish it may never be morning. They curse the cocks, because they proclaim it is the day; the clocks, because they go too fast: they lie prostrate, as if they looked after the Pleiades and the North star, making themselves astronomers and star gazers; but when they see the morning star arise, they sigh for sorrow, and are ready to forsake their bodies; and the clearing of the day is the clouding of their joy, hearts. *It is a journey, my son, whereof as yet I had never my fill; me thought I could not perform it so often, nor was I ever in all my life tired out therewith. And yet, as old as I am, God he knows my desire is as good as it ever was.* Then, how much more those that flame without fire? They are captivated even on the very first embracement. And above all, it is worth the while to note how quickly they change copy, and turn the cat in the pan; they entreat him, of whom they were entreated; they endure torment for him, for whom before they had tormented; they are servants to those, whose mistresses they were; they leave of commanding and give leave to be commanded; they break through stone walls, they open windows, feign sickness; if the hinges of their doors chance to creak, they anoint and supple them with oil, that they may perform their office without any noise. I am not able to express unto thee the great impression of that sweetness, which the primary and first kisses of him they love, leaveth imprinted in their hearts. They are enemies of the mean and wholly set upon extremes.]

Men, we learn from Celestina, are no less vulnerable to passion and fall into it as hard. Responding to Sempronio's description of Calisto's extreme urgency to find a remedy for his passion, she recognizes that the longer Calisto desires, the better her chances to convince him of her efficacy, and thus ensure her final victory over him. 'No es cosa más propia del que ama que la impaciencia', she soothes Sempronio, 'toda tardança es tormento; ninguna dilación les agrada. En un momento querrían poner en effeto sus cogitaciones; antes las querrían ver concluýdas que empeçadas' (93) [There is nothing more proper to lovers than impatience, every small tarriance is to them a great torment; the least delay breeds dislike; in a moment what they imagine must be fully effected; nay, concluded before begun]. Sure of her ultimate conquest of Calisto, she understands the need to defer his capitulation, and tells Sempronio that it is required that she, like every good solicitor, 'ponga de su casa algún trabajo, algunas fingidas razones, algunos sofísticos actos; yr y venir a juyzio, aunque reciba malas palabras del juez' (94) [colour his plea with some feigned show of reason; that he press some quillet or quirk of law; to go and come into open court, though he be checked and receive some harsh word from the Judge's mouth].

Celestina's mere presence can call forth hidden yearnings from the recesses of any human heart. There is an immanence to her that provokes the emergence of desire in her all interlocutors. Before they are touched by her, all the characters sense the stirrings of a lack, yet only possess vague feelings and misunderstanding regarding what they feel and seek. However, when Celestina intervenes, their thoughts and emotions suddenly take form; they are recognized, they are transformed into knowledge and self-awareness by her, and they are manifested in irresistible impulses and reified in deeds. Recognized instantly as the mediatrix of desire, Celestina recalls how her presence even in church is capable of igniting desire, stirring the forces of sexuality even as the pious are solemnly dedicated to their rituals of divine devotion:

> En entrando por la yglesia vía derrocar bonetes en mi honor como si yo fuera una duquesa. El que menos avía que negociar conmigo, por más ruyn se tenía. De media legua que me viesen dexavan las horas; uno a uno y dos a dos venían a donde yo estava, a ver si mandava algo, a preguntarme cada uno por la suya. Que hombre avía que estando diziendo missa en viéndome entrar se turbavan, que no hazían ni dezían cosa a derechas. Unos me llamavan señora, otros tía, otros enamorada, otros vieja honrada. Assí se concertavan sus venidas a mi casa, allí las ydas a la suya. Allí se me offrescían dineros, allí promesas, allí otras dádivas, besando el cabo de mi manto, y aun algunos en la cara por me tener más contenta. (240)

[When I came to a church my foot was no sooner in, but I had presently as many bonnets vailed unto me as if I had been a duchess; he that had least acquaintance, least business with me, was held the most vile and basest fellow. They spying me almost a league off, they would forsake their most earnest occasions, their divine service one by one, two by two, and come to me, to see if I would command them any service; and withal, ask me severally, how his love, how his mistress did? When they saw me once pass by, you should have such a shuffling and scraping of feet, and all in such a general gaze, and so out of order, that they did neither do nor say anything aright. One would call me mistress, another aunt, others their love, others honest old woman. There they would consent when they should come to my house; there they would agree when I should go unto theirs; there they would offer me money; there they would make me large promises; there likewise present me with gifts: some kissing the lappet of my coat, and some other my cheek, that by these kindness they might give me contentment.]

Celestina in this way is the human catalyst of passion, the one who makes desire's discovery, realization, and understanding possible; she helps form it into words, into language, into discourse, and then finally into action. As her path intersects with that of others, the latter become agitated and increasingly conscious of the nature and dimensions of their want. This is made especially clear in Celestina's second interview with Melibea. In their first encounter, Celestina had exhorted charity, asking the young woman – who resisted all mention of Calisto's name – for her cordon as a remedy for a young man's painful ailment, a youth whose identity Celestina feigned reluctance to pronounce (161). When she returns on her second visit to Melibea, Celestina knows enough to understand that Calisto is the one word that will set Melibea's heart into combustive motion, that its utterance is enough to produce a revelation, an overwhelming recognition and admission of the young woman's yearning:

CELESTINA. No desconfíe, señora, tu noble juventud de salud; [que]
quando el alto Dios da la llaga, tras ella embía el remedio. Mayormente
que sé yo al mundo nascida una flor que de todo esto te delibere.
MELIBEA. ¿Cómo se llama?
CELESTINA. No te lo oso dezir.
MELIBEA. Di, no temas.
CELESTINA. Calisto. O, por Dios, señora Melibea, ¿qué poco esfuerço es
éste? ¿Qué descaescimiento? ¡O mezquina yo; alça la cabeça! ¡O

malaventurada vieja, en esto han de parar mis passos! Si muere, matarme
han; aunque biva, seré sentida, que ya no podrá sofrir[se] de no publicar su
mal y mi cura. Señora mía, Melibea, ángel mío, ¿qué as sentido? ¿Qué es de
tu habla graciosa? ¿Qué es de tu color alegre? Abre tus claros ojos (256)

[CEL: Lady, let not your noble youth be diffident of recovery: be of good
cheer; take a good heart to you; and doubt not of your welfare. For where
God gives a wound, there He gives a remedy; and as it hurts, so it heals;
and so much the sooner, because I know where the flower grows, that will
free you from all this torment.
MEL: How is it called?
CEL: I dare not tell you.
MEL: Speak and spare not.
CEL: Calisto ... O madame! Melibea! Ah! Woe is me! Why woman, what
mean you? What a cowardly heart have you? What a fainting is here?
O miserable that I am, hold up your head, I pray lift it up! O accursed old
woman! Must my steps end in this? If she goes thus away in a swoon, they
will kill me: if she revive, she will be much pained; for she will never endure
to publish her pain, nor give me leave to exercise my cure. Why, Melibea,
my sweet lady, my fair angel! What's the matter, sweet heart? Where is your
grief? Why speak you not unto me? What is become of your gracious and
pleasing speech? Where is that cheerful colour, that was wont to beautify
your cheeks? Open those brightest lamps, that ever nature tinded: open
your eyes, I say, those clear suns, that are able to give light to darkness.]

Hearing the name Calisto, Melibea loses consciousness just as she
achieves new forms of it. Her swoon stands as the body's mute response
to the overwhelming acknowledgment of her passion for him, a not dissimilar reaction to that of others in the work when Celestina goes about
her business. Just as all creation sings out *puta vieja* [old whore] when
Celestina passes by, so too all the characters seem to intone an admission
of desire when they encounter her. At certain critical moments,
Celestina's presence becomes crucial to the full revelation and perception of the emotions that lie submerged beneath all the characters'
facades.

Despite their best efforts to resist, as we shall later see with Pármeno,
whose secret thoughts are betrayed by a snide snicker, Celestina knows
that they protest too much, and so strives on to conjure even the most
hidden, contumacious of the characters' wishes. To be sure, Celestina
intuits forms of yearning that have not yet been publically acknowledged

or transmuted into language, uncovering their traumas close to the body and at the margins of human communicability: in involuntary gestures, giggles, half-heard sighs, and other seemingly non-referential things that on first inspection appear not to signify in any way like speech. Nervous laughter, fainting, insomnia, anxiety, and anguish are all understood by her and all materialize the moment she appears. After her encounter with the characters who exhibit them the latter can never be the same. Taken by surprise, they discern through her presence something that they knew and yet ignored, spurred on now by Celestina to venture forth in blind pursuit of the objects of their desire. It is only after Celestina touches them that the action and the plot move forward; that motivation manifests itself and provides a reason for all the characters to set trajectories for their yearning. After being taken unawares by the old bawd, each recovers from their revelation of desire to declare intentions, to make their passions known, and thus impose themselves upon the lives of others.

Once touched by Celestina, none of the characters in the book can cease articulating want. They expatiate on their conditions, they relate every perception, they can only say now what they feel and feel what they need. Although Celestina never ceases to speak, to probe and to persuade, the actual onslaught of desire emerges unexpectedly, often, as in the case of Melibea, via a single, crucial word that she strategically lets drop. She can suddenly halt the onrush of her practised rhetoric, block it with a name like Calisto or one like Areúsa, whose unexpected invocation in act 1 crushes Pármeno's resistance, signals his temptation, and makes him fall in league with Celestina and Sempronio to betray and to despoil his master. Celestina, the master rhetorician, knows how and when to restrain all rhetoric, to get to the point and provoke an anagnorisis of yearning in all her victims. In her method, it is especially important to note her use of names and the characters' reactions to them. This is because names incarnate, they incite and validate desire; they make people and things visible and palpable, and urge their subjects to pursue the embodied objects that they represent. At crucial junctures in the text, through the intonation of a single name, Celestina illuminates the most obscurely hidden object of a character's want. At these sudden turning points of consciousness, the level and intensity of the action accelerates: when Celestina informs Pármeno that his secret passion for Areúsa is within reach, we reach the point of no return, the betrayal of loyalty and principle that leads to everyone's dark end; when Celestina reaffirms Melibea's interest in Calisto, he readies for war, organizing nocturnal armed excursions in his exertions to breach the real and the symbolic wall of his beloved's garden; when Celestina names Calisto, Melibea faints yet agrees to see him, knowing well, as we shall later see, the consequences that await her. Celestina quite simply compels desire, and desire impels the plot, toward hopeless scenarios of imagined fulfilment, then on toward death, toward its own, and toward the *Tragicomedia*'s, inevitable end.

Once the characters have confessed their desire to Celestina, they act at heightened levels of knowledge and understanding, they suddenly know that they desire and confess that they perceive the image of desire. Yet this new discernment takes them unawares because it forces them to confront what is forbidden and say and do what is proscribed. The characters of *Celestina*, perhaps with the exception of Calisto, are rarely able or willing to identify their hidden wishes; they at first cannot name the objects of their desire. It is Celestina who makes them come to words, gives their want a name, and renders it visible. When she identifies their yearning, the characters perceive the enunciation of their want in her voice and undergo a transformation, since it is actually their own desire that they hear made audible through Celestina's voice. She is the medium that precipitates and accelerates the externalization of desire in all.

Just as Celestina can reveal desire in others by means of single words or the interpretation of sounds like laughter, however, a single word couched ironically as a diminutive fatally incites and illuminates the presence of her own dark aspirations. Celestina's most hidden compulsions are betrayed in the small details of language, in contrivances that seek to endear or to make nothing out of something; yet they prove devices that ultimately seal her fate. Although she wistfully recalls the sensuality of her youth to all around, revelling in the memories of her early gambols, Celestina is loath to admit or to invoke the names now given to time's transformation of her youthful yearnings: greed, cupidity, and avarice. Yet their presence in her signal her own continuing subjection to desire and are uncovered by her exertions to efface them and make the large seem small, the significant insignificant. To be sure, it is on account of her own linguistic strategies that she herself is taken by surprise, murdered unexpectedly at the hands of her associates, whom she seeks to cheat out of their equal parts of Calisto's tributes.

The initial inklings of Celestina's perfidy and greed are manifested in the subterfuges of her speech, as in act 5, when returning hurriedly to Calisto's house after her first visit to Melibea she runs into Sempronio in the lane. Sempronio greets her and they set off together to deliver triumphantly the news of her progress to Calisto. On the way, Celestina insists she must claim full credit for what has been achieved, although Sempronio can surely expect 'alguna partezilla del provecho' (142) [parcel of the profit], letting slip the first fatal diminutive that marks her covetous intent to defraud him of the spoils. Sempronio's reaction is immediate: '¿Partezilla, Celestina? Mal me parece esso que dizes' (142) [What? Are you at your parcels now? ... I tell you plainly, I do not like this word, that I do not. And therefore parcel me no more of your parcels]. Catching her blunder, Celestina attempts to emend it by means of another diminutive, whose intention is now endearment directed at assuagement: 'Calla, loquillo, que parte o partezilla, quanto tú quisieres te daré. Todo lo mío es tuyo; gozémonos y aprovechémonos, que sobre el partir nunca reñiremos' (142–4) [Go to, you little fool; hold your peace, be it part or parcel, man, thou shalt have what thou wilt thyself. Do but ask, and have; what is mine is thine; let us laugh and be merry, and benefit ourselves the best that we can rather than thou and I should fall out about dividing the spoil]. However, Sempronio's suspicion is irreversibly aroused, and it will lead to murder.

In the previous chapter, the symbolic significance of the gold chain Celestina had received from Calisto to compensate for her services was noted. It serves as an image of bondage, avarice, fate, and language in the work; it symbolizes the final transmutation of the thread Celestina spins to tangle and entwine the destinies of all the characters in the book. Conflict between Celestina, Pármeno, and Sempronio over the chain leads to Celestina's slaying, reifying the latent, fateful impulses of desire, transmuted now into greed, that lie hidden in its golden links. In act 11 Celestina meets Calisto at the Church of the Magdalen, an ironically appropriate spot to inform him that Melibea has capitulated to her desire and will see him. Indeed, she tells him that Melibea is so smitten that she will receive him even on her knees ('aun de rodillas' [270]). Overcome by emotion with the news, Calisto takes the golden chain from round his neck and rewards Celestina with it, as he says 'toma esta *cadenilla*; ponla al cuello, y procede en tu razón y mi alegría' (266, emphasis added) [take this *little chain*, put it about your neck]. There with Celestina, Pármeno comments on the excess of Calisto's gesture in an aside directed at Sempronio. In it, he lays claim to his share of the value of the chain and questions his master's better judgment: '¿*Cadenilla* la llama?' [Call you that a little chain?] he asks incredulously as he observes the value of the chain, '¿No lo oyes, Sempronio? No estima el gasto. Pues yo te certifico no diesse mi parte por medio marco de oro, por mal que la vieja reparta' (266) [Heard you him, Sempronio? This spendthrift makes no reckoning of it; but I assure you, I will not give my part thereof for half a mark of gold, let her share it never so ill]. All present are stunned by the disparity between Calisto's contempt for the great value of the object, marked by his use of the diminutive. Although she does not utter the word *cadenilla*, Calisto's use of it produces a profound effect on the old whore as he confers the chain upon her. Its disconcerting impact upon her is marked by nervousness, immediate recognition of its value, and an urgency to leave after receiving it, a reaction noted by Pármeno, who laughs disdainfully at Celestina's haste. When Sempronio questions his laughter, Pármeno answers that it arises from seeing 'la priessa que la vieja tiene por yrse; no vee la hora que haver despegado la cadena de casa; no puede creer que la tenga en su poder, ni que se la han dado de verdad' (270–2) [what haste the old trot makes to be gone; she thinks every hour a year, till she be gone clear away with the chain; she cannot persuade herself that it is as yet sure enough in her hands].

Later, in act 12, all the momentous diminutives previously mentioned gather. They are recalled and subsumed in just one small new word – yet another diminutive – *palabrilla* [little word], which sounds the prelude to Celestina's death. Wary of her deception, Sempronio announces his intention to go to Celestina's house to claim his share of the chain before she finds the opportunity to exclude him from the take ('quiero yo yr a Celestina a cobrar mi parte de la cadena' [292] [I will get me to Celestina's house, and see if I can recover my part of the chain]). Pármeno agrees and accompanies him, suggesting that they secure their part by frightening the old bawd. Knowing that Calisto has given Celestina enough wealth for her to distribute, Sempronio confronts Celestina and deliberately exaggerates the losses he and Pármeno supposedly sustained while defending Calisto during the night outside of Melibea's garden. He demands that Celestina indemnify them fully. Questioning Sempronio's sanity, Celestina laughs in disbelief at his demand for payment and stresses that such matters are Calisto's responsibility, not her's. She mocks Sempronio for doubting her sincerity and recalls the suspicion he expressed in his reaction to her use of *partezilla* [little part] in their earlier conversation, when she employed it to describe the share of spoils she would offer him: 'A osadas, que me maten', she says with dark irony, 'si no te as asido a una *palabrilla* que te dixe el otro día viniendo por la calle, que quanto yo tenía era tuyo y que en quanto pudiesse con mis pocas fuerças, jamás te faltaría, y que si Dios me diesse buena manderecha con tu amo, que tú no te perderías nada' (296, emphasis added)

[Let me be hanged or die any other death if thou hast not took hold of *a little word*, that carelessly slipped out of my mouth the other day, as we came along the street; for as I remember, I then told you, that what I had was yours, and that I would never be wanting unto you in anything to the utmost of my poor ability; and that if fortune did prosper my business with your master, that you should lose nothing by it]. Celestina then proceeds to diminish linguistically the value of the coveted chain, calling it a *cadenilla* [little chain], and begins to fabricate conflicting explanations about its whereabouts, averring, among other things, that 'di a esta loca de Elicia, como vine de tu casa, la *cadenilla* que traxe para que holgasse con ella y no se puede acordar dónde la puso, que en toda esta noche ella ni yo no avemos dormido sueño de pesar, no por su valor de la cadena, que no era mucho, pero por su mal cobro de ella y de mi mala dicha' (271, emphasis added) [As soon as ever I came from your house and was come home, I gave the (little) chain I brought hither to this fool Elicia, that she might look upon it, and cheer herself with the sight thereof; and she, for her life cannot as yet call to mind what she hath done with it; and all this live-long night neither she nor I have slept one wink for very thought and grief thereof, not so much for the value of the chain (for it was not much worth), but to see that she should be so careless in the laying of it up, and to see the ill luck of it]. All of Celestina's deft explanations prove useless as Sempronio, incensed by them and the dismissive diminutives, condemns her scheming avarice, 'O vieja avarienta, garganta muerta de sed por dinero, no serás contenta con la tercera parte de lo ganado?' [O thou old covetous crib, that art ready to die with the thirst of gold! Cannot a third part of the gain content thee?]. To which Celestina insistently responds, '¿Qué tercia parte?' (302) [What third part?], words enough to make Sempronio and Pármeno fall upon her and stab her to death. As she masters desire in the lives of others through the details of deceptive speech, desire ends by mastering Celestina through the same illusive wiles of language, subjecting her, as it ever does, to its own fatal end.

Beyond Fiction

Celestina's ability to unleash the forces of desire provoked effects beyond the pages of the book that took her name as much as in them. Since she burst upon the scene in Salamanca during the closing years of the fifteenth century, she has continued to exercise her powers of seduction upon readers, and it is doubtless for this reason that generations of them when they speak of the book best remember her and call it by her name. The character Celestina is the overpowering presence in that text, the one in whom all the hidden threads that bind the lives of everyone – characters and readers alike – intertwine and coalesce. Even after she has ceased to exist, gone to her death at the hands of Pármeno and Sempronio, she continues to cast a tempting shadow and have a presence that to this day still pulls mortals toward her. Celestina's murder fails to interrupt her role as the consummate enabler of desire, even beyond the pages of the fiction that contains her. When Pármeno and Sempronio slayed her, it was already too late to detain what she had set in motion in the world. Desire was in the open, unleashed, circulating, moving, rushing both characters and readers of the eponymous book ever forward, searching for its end.

It is clear that Celestina's powers to uncover and incite desire extended, indeed continues to extend, beyond the written page, and that she is capable still of unmapped forms of seduction. In her roughest and most elementary form, we know that she seduced a law student at the University of Salamanca and persuaded him to spend a sleepless holiday with her. To be sure, shortly after that encounter, she learned Italian, German, Dutch, French, English, and even Neo-Latin and continued to seduce the greater portion of the readership of early modern Europe. This is a fact that stands as a testimonial to her numinous power to elicit, compel, and set in motion the synergies of want that transact the spaces between words, texts, the human imagination, and the 'real,' external world of living readers.

Rojas elaborates upon Celestina's ability to incite intellectual enticement and seduction in perhaps the most revealing moment of self-disclosure in the work. In the prefatory 'Carta a un su amigo' [The Author to a Friend of His] referring to his reaction to the opuscule of the *antiguo auctor*, he confesses his own fascination with it, and how 'leylo tres o quatro vezes, y tantas quantas más lo leya, tanta más *necessidad* me ponía de releerlo y tanto más *me agradava*, y en su proceso nuevas sentencias sentía' (6, emphasis added) [I read it three or four times, and the more I read it, the more *necessity* I had to reread it and the more it pleased me, and in the process I understood new meanings]. In his first encounter with the bawd, Fernando de Rojas concedes his attraction for the partially completed, inconclusive fiction, admitting to its beckoning, irresistible pull, and to the strange pleasure he took in it by means of his repeated readings. He acknowledges his feeling of a need for more, envisioning the text in what can only be the terms of as yet unrealized forms of his own personal want. Nowhere is this more palpable than in Rojas's use of the word *necessidad* [necessity] to describe the compulsion that he felt to read on and to justify the imperative to complete – to discover and to realize – what was both hidden and promised in the text, which only continued to produce more discourse, more words, more revelations, 'nuevas sentencias' [new meanings], a longing for more and the search – the desire – for a satisfactory end for the compelling need of his imagination.

The initial culmination of Rojas's quest for the gratification of this desire ended in fifteen added acts and the semblance of a conclusion of his yearning with the publication of the *Comedia de Calisto y Melibea* in 1499. Celestina, however, continued to incite expectations of more, but now among its readers as well as in its author. The book provoked such desire that it reached its climax in the five additional acts of the more comely *Tragicomedia*, which shortly would be fully personified and known as *Celestina*.

In the additions to the text, completed in the years between the *Comedia*'s first appearance in 1499 and 1502 (the date that marks the first recorded reliable attestation of the publication of the twenty-one act *Tragicomedia*), after Rojas introduced the first of his major revisions starting in act 14, Calisto is made by him to utter the following revealing soliloquy: 'O bien sin comparación, o insaciable contentamiento, ¿y quándo pidiera yo más a Dios por premio de mis méritos, si algunos son en esta vida, de lo que alcançado tengo? ¿Por qué no estoy contento?' (322) [O incomparable good! O insatiable contentment! And what could I have asked more of heaven in requital of all my merits in this life (if they be any) than such which I have already received? Why should I not content myself with so great a blessing?]. The early placement of these words in Rojas's interpolations suggests that they signal a fundamental meditation on the dissatisfaction that not only continued to push Calisto toward his end, but the one that obliquely reflected the urgency Rojas felt to flesh out further both his own and his audience's desire for more before reaching the climactic end.[5] Both Calisto and Rojas doubtless continued to feel a discontentment, to realize an insatiable yearning for something more, as well as the need to say something more about Calisto's yearning, all immediately after three striking incidents in the unfolding of the plot: the murder of Celestina, the execution of Pármeno and Sempronio, and Calisto's and Melibea's consummation of their passion. It is as if Rojas and Calisto both speak together in act 14, simultaneously surveying 'lo que alcançado tengo' [that which I have already

received] accompanied by the realization of an 'insaciable contentamiento' [insatiable contentment] that then leads to a confession of radical dissatisfaction, an understanding that, despite everything, nothing
has been achieved, that the end has not yet come, and that perhaps desire is its own untranscendent end.

Quite aside from the fact that in the universe of *Celestina*/Celestina
desire continually reanimates itself and prospers from dissatisfaction,
what remains important at this juncture is how desire materializes both
consciously and unconsciously through words mediated by the pen of
the author. What Rojas seems to have understood in the rewriting of
Celestina as he reworked, refashioned, and refined his characters' desiring is a heightened awareness of the 'insaciable contentamiento' [insa-
tiable contentment] that overcomes Calisto after obtaining what he
believed to be the very object of his desire, the possession of Melibea.
In the process of transforming the *Comedia* into the *Tragicomedia*, Rojas
seems fully to have understood the radically unquenchable nature of
desire and found himself, consciously or unconsciously, affected by it as
much as the very characters that sprung from his imagination.

The readers' parts in desiring more of love and Celestina also played
no small part in its ontogenesis. Confessing to his readers' demands,
Rojas writes about his writing as if it were some compulsion spurred on
by their demands. Responding to his readers' wants, he says 'miré a
donde la mayor parte acostava y hallé que querían que alargasse en el
proceso de su deleyte destos amantes, sobre lo qual fui muy importu-
nado, de manera que acordé, aunque contra mi voluntad, meter segunda vez la pluma en tan estraña lavor y tan agena de mi facultad' (18)
[I had an eye to mark whither the major part inclined, and found that
they were all desirous that I should enlarge myself in the pursuit of the
delight of these lovers; whereunto I have been earnestly importuned in
so much that I have consented (though against my will) to put now the
second time my pen to this so strange a task and so far estranged from
my faculty]. He recognized that what his audience desired was nothing
more than an increase of desire, and that the book and the character –
that *Celestina* and Celestina – incited the desire for more in all who came
in contact with it, with her. This realization, followed by the capitulation
to his readers' desires for more, of course, arose from his own experience; from his own seduction by Celestina and her ability to incite an
unconquerable desire for more. *Celestina*/Celestina unleashed the forces
of desire across the space that is reputed to divide fiction from experience; it is a text that not only nourishes the imagination of its readers,

but one that is nourished by the forces and demands that it uncovers and ignites within them. Neither Calisto, Rojas, nor the book's readers could achieve full satisfaction of their expectations.

To be sure, Rojas's thoughts on his revisions in the prologue to the *Tragicomedia* continue to reflect the rationale for them and the experience of the *Comedia*'s reception, which he there shared with his public. Glossing further upon Heraclitus and the role of strife in all creation that opens the prologue, he masterfully applied it to the human forces that governed the genesis of his text: 'estos papeles [pelean] con todas las edades. La primera los borra y rompe, la segunda no los sabe bien leer, la tercera, que es la alegre juventud y mancebía, discorda' (18) [these papers (engage in struggle) with all ages. The first blots and tears them; the second knows not well how to read them; the third (which is the cheerful livelihood of youth, and set all upon jollity) doth utterly dispute them]. The radical dissatisfaction engendered by the encounter with *Celestina*/Celestina only produces conflict, he notes, amidst incessant cries for more. Discord reigns, yet all continue reading, imagining, yearning for more. His readers, it would seem, besieged him, importuned him, clamouring for more; yet each wanted something different, incompatible with what the other desired. They looked upon him as if they looked upon Celestina; they saw him as the medium for the realization of their readerly desire; as the discoverer of the misrecognized objects of their yearning, and as the translator of the hidden wishes of their imaginations.

Celestina's powers of seduction over all who have ever come in contact with her have not waned. The book, according to Keith Whinnom (1980), remains the only early, modern 'best seller' in Spanish of the sixteenth century still read today. The power of *Celestina* as a book, and Celestina as a character, to uncover undisclosed regions of the human imagination remains forceful, dynamic, and intact. Her ability to ignite desire has not been extinguished. In the sixteenth century, she gave birth to a thousand daughters (see Heugas 1973). Copied, imitated, painted, set to music, brought to the screen, and present in the colloquial utterances of the Spanish language for more than five centuries, as this very book attests, she continues to discover, incite, provoke, and mediate the human desire for more.[6]

3 Calisto's Hunt: The Pursuit of Carnal Knowledge

La caza de amor
es de altanería:
trabajos de día,
de noche dolor.
Halcón cazador
con garza tan fiera,
peligros espera.

Gil Vicente

In the Book of Genesis (2:9) the Tree of Knowledge, located in the Garden of Eden, and from which God forbade Adam and Eve to eat, is directly implicated in carnality and in the distinction between Good and Evil. Violation of God's prohibition to eat the Tree's fruit led to humanity's Fall from Grace. As a result, Adam and Eve 'knew' each other, saw their nakedness (Gen. 3:6–7), understood shame, and were cast out of the Garden of Eden into the mortal, fallen world, where they were forced to live a life of physical pain and survive by the sweat of their brows (Gen. 3:19–24). Since the time of Genesis, with its invocation of the Tree of Knowledge, the human desire for knowledge has been implicated in the material world, in the world of the senses, of instinct, and of mortal flesh. Its pursuit is in fact often figured as a search that seeks to discover an understanding of the world and its microcosm, the human body. As a result, knowledge was often associated directly with carnality and termed *cognitio carnalis* by medieval philosophers, theologians, and jurists. From earliest times, then, the discovery of knowledge and its pursuit was semiotically associated with the material world, the lower instincts, and the body, especially through metaphorical connections and tropes that linked the thirst for knowledge to searching, hunger, hunting, and desire.

In his anthropological history of epistemic and evidential paradigms, Carlo Ginzburg has alluded to the intimate ties that unite the human hunger for knowledge with the metaphors of hunger and the hunt. He notes that the experience of the hunt in particular doubtless lies at the heart of the history of the conception, discovery, and production of knowledge in human society: 'Man has been a hunter for thousands of years. In the course of countless chases he learned to reconstruct the shapes and movements of his invisible prey from tracks on the ground, broken branches, excrements, tufts of hair, entangled feathers, stagnating odors. He learned to sniff out, record, interpret, and classify such infinitesimal traces as trails of spittle. He learned how to execute complex mental operations with lightning speed, in the depth of a forest or in a prairie with hidden dangers' (1989,102). Through the association of the myriad small clues of the hunt, humans built a storehouse of knowledge and learned to construct in their imaginations the appearance of animals and things upon which they had not yet laid eyes. Knowledge, especially the desire for knowledge of the unseen, was thus first associated with, and acquired from, the experience of the chase. By deciphering traces of tangible evidence of what was unknown, humans could be led in the direction of the known, to believing the objects of their quest to be within their grasp and to satisfying their physical hunger through their hunger for knowledge – a drive Freud terms *Wisstreib* – and the acquisition of worldly understanding. However, as Freud points out, on an epistemological level the desire from the drive to know remains intrinsically insatiable, always making its object unattainable, leaving the thirst for knowledge unquenched until it can be stilled only by death (1953–74; 'The Rat Man,' *SE*, 10: 158–249)

The prologue to *Celestina* forges a close link between humans, the animal world, the pursuit of beasts, and the pursuit of knowledge.[1] In it, Creation is portrayed as a continuous struggle, a process presided over by a confounding discord likened to the rapacity and brutality of the hunt. Borrowing from Petrarch's *De remediis utriusque fortunae* and Pliny's *Naturalis Historia* as mediated by the latter, the prologue calls forth Heraclitus to authorize the ubiquity of strife and pursuit in the cosmos, and to portray conflict in everything that makes up the created universe: 'Todas las cosas ser criadas a manera de contienda o batalla, dize aquel gran sabio Eráclito en este modo: "Omnia secundum litum fiunt"'(14) [It is the saying of that great and wise philosopher Hercalitus that all things are created in manner of a contention or battle. His words are these: 'Omnia secundum litem fiunt']. Using Heraclitus's statement as its thesis, the prologue then extends it to apply to the animal kingdom, hinting that the rule can be stretched even further, all the way to the highest order of the animals: 'Pues entre los animales ningún género carece de guerra: pesces, fieras, aves, serpientes, de lo qual todo una especie a otra persigue. El león al lobo, el lobo a la cabra, el perro la liebre y, si no paresciese conseja tras el fuego, yo llegaría más al cabo esta cuenta' (14–16) [Besides among your brute beasts there is not any one of them that wants (lacks) his war, be they fishes, birds, beasts, or sepents, whereof every kind persecuteth and pursueth one another: the lion, he pursue the wolf; the wolf the kid; the dog the hare. And, if it might not be thought a fable or old wife's tale, sitting by the fireside, I should more fully enlarge this theme].

In the prologue to *Celestina*, existence is in this way depicted as an incessant pursuit among the beasts, a hunt that becomes the focal point for drawing a broader analogy to human relations, in which the ceaseless battle and the ubiquitous chase of Creation is also reflected. According to the prologue's interpretation of Petrarch, humankind not only participates in this cosmic pursuit but serves as both protagonist and victim of it: 'los tiempos contra tiempos contienden y litigan entre sí, uno a uno y todos contra nosotros' (16) [times with times do contend; one hing against another,and all against us]. And it is precisely in strife and dissension where the intimate bond between humankind, nature, and the quest to know is most pronounced and most contested, as it projects conflict and contention into the very human search for knowledge and understanding: 'para saber la secreta causa de que proceden [los elementos naturales], no es menor la dissención de los filósofos en las escuelas, que de las ondas en la mar' (14) [to know the secret cause from whence they (the elements of nature) proceed, no less is the dissension of the phiolsophers in the schools than the waves of the sea].

The prologue to *Celestina* thus posits a universal struggle in the natural world for dominance and knowledge by exemplifying it through an encyclopedic catalogue of animals which dwells on their mutual pursuit and the conflicts that beset each kind, even humankind. The evidence presented all points to an inherent discord in the world, to a brutal chase impelled by instinct, to ceaseless conflict between the species, to omnipresent fear and strife, and to the ubiquitous violent struggle of the individual against the overpowering forces of nature and the elements. The fish of the sea, the fowl of the air, and the serpent, the lion, the wolf, the dog, and the hare, all take part in a strife caused by cease-less struggle, desire, flight, and pursuit. Nothing can provide protection or refuge from this cosmic warfare and the struggle for power. The ele-phant's dread for the lowly mouse offers a striking sign of the conflict and the inability for creatures to defend themselves and flee from the battle and contradiction that preside over the world. Its example belies every expectation of power and dominion in relation to size and energy, as noted in the prologue: 'el elefante, animal tan poderoso y fuerte, se espanta y huye de la vista de un suziuelo ratón y aun de sólo oýrle toma gran temor' (16) [The elephant, that is so powerful and strong a beast, is afraid and flies from the sight of a poor silly mouse, and no sooner hears him coming but he quakes and trembles for fear]. Indeed, even mutual attraction and the act of generation among the species only en-sures a clash that culminates in violent coupling in which desire and death serve as the driving forces of courtship and pursuit. This is illus-trated in the wooing of vipers, whose physical ardour at conception only guarantees annihilation, as we saw in the previous chapter.[2] Relying on the lore of beasts as conveyed in the *Naturarlis Historia* (filtered through Petrarch), the prologue to *Celestina* thus demonstrates the universal reign of conflict, struggle, and pursuit moved by the desire of capture and conquest.

In *Celestina*, as remains to be shown, Calisto is closely linked to the chase and to the animal world. From the outset, he is depicted as a hunter, a searcher in close contact with nature and animal instincts, who through his practice of falconry runs down and seizes his quarry. Through the symbolic association of passionate pursuit and hunting, Calisto is portrayed as an emblematic protagonist in a chase of love, passion, de-sire, and conquest, an image that is widespread in early European vernacular literature. It is, according to Marcelle Thiébaux, 'this dis-tinctively medieval figure, arising both from the books men read and emulated and from the life they saw, that provides us with a means by which we may seek to comprehend the earthly love that concerned them' (1974, 246). This commonplace image used in the representation of courtship in medieval love literature constitutes the hunt of love, which Edith Rogers in her study of it in the in the ballad tradition succinctly defines as the 'pursuit of a girl translated into the terminology of hun-ting' (1974, 143). The figure of the chase of love stands for a life close to and in accordance with instinct, an existence in line with a more primi-tive, impulsive being that, like Carlo Ginzburg's prehistoric hunter, fig-ures in the quest for carnal knowledge.

However, Calisto is not the only character to be associated with the hunt in *Celestina*. The image is in fact pervasive in the work and becomes a controlling, central metaphor that applies at one time or another to all the characters from the work's beginning to the end. Calisto's hunt, punctuated by the fortuitous loss of his falcon and restated with climactic irony in his ravishing of Melibea,[3] is transformed throughout the *Tragicomedia* into the violent hunt of human wills that Pleberio ultimately invokes in his final summation of events during the anguished closing moments of the work: 'Cévasnos, mundo falso, con el manjar de tus delytes; al mejor sabor nos descubres el anzuelo; no lo podemos huyr, que nos tiene ya caçadas las voluntades … ¿Cómo me mandas quedar en ti conociendo tus falsías, tus lazos, tus cadenas y redes, con que pescas nuestras flacas voluntades?' (396–8) [O thou false world! Tho dost cast before us the baits of thy best delights, and when we have swallowed them, they seeming unsavory unto us, then thou dost show us the hook that must choke us. Nor can we avoid it, because together with us thou dost captivate our wills].

The Textual Genealogy of the Courtly Hunter

The opening scene of *Celestina* has been amply commented upon, although only a few studies have sought to probe the possible deeper meanings embedded in the episode in which Calisto loses his falcon and chances upon Melibea. Moreover, none has addressed the larger context or the symbolic coherence of the chase imagery, which serves as an overarching metaphor that encompasses the events, and none has examined the falcon's literary ancestry or the role the bird plays in the medieval courtly tradition.[4] Martin de Riquer (1957) noted a similarity between Calisto's and Melibea's first encounter and *Cligés* (6349–84), in which Bertrand, searching for his strayed hawk, stumbles upon a couple and 'Soz l'ante vit dormir a masse/ Fenice et Cligés nu a nu' (*Les Romans de Chrétien de Troyes*, 194) [he saw Fenice and Cliges sleeping together side by side]. María Rosa Lida de Malkiel (1970), on the other hand, suggested a more immediate connection with Lope García Salazar's Castilian *Bienandanzas y fortunas* (composed between 1471 and 1476) in which the author, recounting his genealogy, tells how an ancestor and his brothers 'perdieron un falcón, e andándolo a buscar, llegaron en la Çerca donde viuia Martín Ruyz … E veyendo allí aquellos cavalleros de Salazar, convidólos a çenar por los fazer onrra, e la ventura que trae las cosas así como son ordenadas de Dios, vna donzella fija de aquel Cavallero, enamoróse de aquel Lope de Salazar, que era de XIX años e mucho loçano e fermoso; e así como se enamoró él de ella, ca era moça e fermosa, por manera que durmió con ella secretamente (cited in Lida de Malkiel 1970, 201n.3) [lost a falcon, and searching for it arrived at the wall behind which lived Martín Ruyz ... and the latter, seeing those gentleman of the Salazar clan, invited them to dine so as to honour them, and as fortune brings things as if ordained by God, a maid and daughter of that gentleman fell in love with Lope de Salazar, who was nineteen and very handsome and vigorous; and he fell in love with her, since she was a maid and beautiful, and slept with her secretly].

Charles Faulhaber (1977), on the other hand, has hypothesized that both the anonymous first author of *Celestina* and Fernando de Rojas may have been inspired by Boncompagno da Signa's *Rota Veneris* [Wheel of Venus], a thirteenth-century treatise on *dictamen* that parodies courtly conventions in epistolary form. Although Faulhaber's observations are especially provocative because he proposes a specific textual source, his conclusion that both Rojas and the anonymous author were in fact familiar with Boncompagno's opus remains only a hypothesis. As demonstrated by him, the bibliographical history of the *Rota Veneris* is indeed linked in some instances to that of Andreas Capellanus's *De Amore*, an important source of act 1 (see Deyermond 1961). However, the fact that da Signa's work includes an episode with a hawk not unlike the one in *Celestina*, and that the *Rota Veneris* could well originally have been bound with the *De Amore*, does not necessarily mean that both authors of *Celestina* had access to or were even familiar with the now lost Strassburg edition (1473 or 1474) in which the *De Amore* and the *Rota Veneris* described by Faulhaber were jointly published.[5]

Regardless of the actual textual source of the episode that opens *Celestina*, the falcon is, as Lida de Malkiel remarks, something that 'sabe ... a roman courtois, con claro sobretono erótico' (1970, 201) [smacks of courtly romance, with a clear erotic overtone], and can in fact be traced to a long tradition of symbolism reflected in medieval French and German romances, European balladry, iconography, and folklore, as well as to Andreas Capellanus's *De Amore* itself. Both the original authors of *Celestina* and Fernando de Rojas were doubtless conscious of the bird's iconic significance and its symbolic role in the tradition of the hunt of love, and seized upon the image with definite purposes in mind. It is within the larger context of the allegory of the hunt of love and the search for carnal knowledge that Calisto and his hawk must be located.

Of the commonest cynegetic images developed in medieval literature, falconry is perhaps the most replete with illicit, carnal, and erotic connotations (see Friedman 1989). The bestiaries of the Middle Ages portray the hawk as a bold, determined, clear-sighted bird that takes its name, *accipiter* (robber), from *accipiendo* (taking), related to *capiendo* (seizing), because it snatches greedily from others (McCulloch 1962, 123–4). Moreover, according to Ramiro Pinedo's study of the iconography of Spanish medieval sculpture, the falcon was construed as an allegory of the evil, lascivious mind of the sinner, the animal protagonist in a simulacrum of the pursuit of carnal knowledge. In the cloister at Silos, Pinedo observes that the hunting hawks depicted ravaging a group of hares (a symbol of feminine wantonness) clearly convey this significance (1930, 111). B.F. Weinberg confirms Pinedo's observation and remarks that the falcon stands as 'a traditional symbol for rapine, appetite and destruction'(137), while E.O. James characterizes it as an emblem that signifies masculinity and fecundity (1958, 118). In the early European literary tradition the bird is closely identified not only with these aggressive, primitive, and sometimes evil tendencies, but also with the loss of volition, and deadly, passionate desire, the same desire – the desire for carnal knowledge – that is at the heart of *Celestina* and that ultimately consumes Calisto, Melibea, and all the other characters around them.

In the textual genealogy of the chase of love, the allegorical link between hunting, falconry, and passionate pursuit is first proposed and skilfully developed by Andreas Capellanus in the *De Amore*. To be sure, the predominant image Andreas employs throughout his treatise on love involves the pursuit or hunt of one kind of creature for another: falcons and hawks metaphorically prey upon partridges and pheasants, while dogs chase boars and other beasts. For Andreas, the imagery of falconry best reflects the strategies employed by gentlemen of the middle class who incorrectly pursue noble ladies. In a scene from the second dialogue of the *De Amore* whose imagery and context proves instructive for understanding the differences that probably separate Calisto and Melibea, a lofty-born noblewoman rebukes her commoner suitor and indignantly asks:

Quis ergo tu es, qui tam antiqua conaris temerare statuta et sub amoris commento maiorum praecepta subvertere tuique generis tanta niteris praesumptione metas excedere? Nam si adeo mei sensus obliviosa manerem, ut tua verba me cogerent his, quae dicis, annuere, cor tamen tuum non esset tam grandia tolerare sufficiens. Numquid enim lacertiva avis perdicem vel fasianus sua potuit unquam superare virtute? Falcones igitur vel astures hanc decet capere praedam non autem a milvorum pusillanimitate vexari. Tua igitur est multum fatuitas cohibenda, quod alti generis indignus tibi quaeris amantem. (20–1)

[Who do you think you are, then, to try and violate such long-standing laws and the overthrow of our ancestors' commands under the fiction of love; to strive with such confidence to trespass the bounds of your class? Even if I were to take leave of my senses and be persuaded by your words to agree to your proposal, your heart could not cope with such lofty tasks. Could a kestrel ever prevail over a partridge or a pheasant by its own strength? This booty is suitable for falcons or hawks to seize. It should not be disturbed by a petty spirited kite. So severe restraint should be imposed on your unworthy foolishness in seeking for yourself a lover of exalted family.]

The commoner meets the lady's objections by responding with a comparison taken from falconry, noting that kestrels and sparrowhawks are noble because of their courage and not their species. He observes that 'multos aspicimus nobiles et marinos falcones vilissimos pertimescere passeres et lacertiva saepe ave fugari. Si ergo milvus et lacertiva avis arditus reperitur et audax et a suis degenerare parentibus, asturnina ett falconia est dignus pertica honorari et militari laeva deferri. Si me igitur noveris a meis degenerare parentibus, non contumeliosa milvi appellatione vocandus reperior, sed honorabili falconis vocabulo nuncupandus exsisto' (25–6) [we see many noble falcons and peregrines frightened by the lowliest of sparrowhawks, often made to take flight by a kestrel. So, if a kite or a kestrel is found to be spirited and bold, diverging from its parents' class, it deserves to be honoured with the perch of the goshawk and the falcon, and to be carried on the forearm of a knight. Thus, if you acknowledge my divergence from my parents, I am clearly not to be given the insulting label of kite, but to be given the honourable title of falcon]. The lady, however, fails to relent and affirms that her suitor's bravery and good character have nothing to do with nobility, and even less with his admissibility as a lover.

In the same aristocratic milieu of the Court of Champagne where Andreas conceived and wrote the *De Amore*, there was continued, widespread use of hawks and hawking as metaphors for love's pursuit. Like the later *Cligés*, which has been noted, the earliest of Chrétien de Troyes romances, *Erec et Enide*, also shows an awareness of the erotic connotations of falconry. Probably written before he came under the influence of Marie de Champagne (Andreas's likely patron as well), Chrétien's *Erec* uses the hawk as a focal image that links sensuality with the trials of passionate of love. To be sure, Mario Roques has suggested that from the outset of the work the falcon becomes the image of *Erec*, the animal double for the warrior lover, just as the white stag represents the vulnerable Enide (Chrétien de Troyes 1952, xxi–xxii). When the hero enters Lalut, the place he meets Enide and does battle for her love, he is immediately surrounded by knights and ladies all feeding and tending falcons. The episode of *la conquête de l'epervier* [conquest of the sparrowhawk] that follows constitutes a symbolic representation of Erec's love for Enide, a test to confirm their ardour for one another.

Medieval German romances likewise identify hawks and falconry with furtive, sexual love and carnality. In Gottfried von Strassburg's *Tristan und Isold* (1930), an early thirteenth-century tale linking love and death, Isot is depicted as the predatory force that causes Tristan to lose his will and drive headlong toward their mutual annihilation. Gottfried characterizes her as 'der Minnen vederspil Isôt' (150) ['Isot, love's falcon'], while Tristan himself, the narrative tells us, embarked upon his fateful journey in a quest to find hunting hawks (see Hatto 1957, 302–3). Wolfram von Eschenbach's *Parzival* (ca 1215; 1961, 1962, 1965) also associates the bird with love's suffering and destructiveness. In Eschenbach's narrative, one of King Arthur's falcons strays and attacks a white goose. Three drops of blood fall from the fray and stain the snow. It is at the moment that he contemplates this image that Parzival is overcome with grief and sadness, suddenly recognizing Kondwîrâmûrs' enticing beauty, and capitulates to desire (1:281).

Finally, in the medieval English romances, falconry serves to adumbrate impending doom in tales of tragic sexual love. This is the case, for example, in Chaucer's *Troilus and Criseyde*, where Troilus is portrayed as a hunter who

> In tyme of trewe, on haukyng wolde he ride,
> Or elles honte boor, beer, or lyoun;
> The smale bestes leet he gon biside.
> And whan that he com ridyng into town,
> Ful ofte his lady from hire wyndow down,
> As fressh as faukoun comen out of muwe,
> 　　　Ful redy was hym goodly to saluwe. (Cited in Gardner 1977, 121)

When placed in a broad historical literary context, the symbolism of the chase that opens *Celestina* leads, then, to a better understanding of the initial relationship of Calisto to Melibea, since the encounters in the tradition of the hunt of love usually fail to portray a prior acquaintance between the hunter-lover and the lady. They are sudden occurrences shrouded in mystery, as in the *Romance de la Infantina*, or concealed in wonder, as in *De Amore* (2, 8), where a knight out hunting chances upon a beautiful maiden immediately before winning in battle King Arthur's Hawk of Victory, the allegorical guardian of the thirty-one rules of passionate love. The cynegetic imagery that marks the beginning of *Celestina* thus makes otiose the speculation that the 'original' version of the work – the one composed by the first author and completed later by Fernando de Rojas – might have been prefaced by a scene in which the two lovers had previously met. Indeed, in the courtly chase of love, scenes portraying the precipitous onslaught of desire are the rule rather than the exception. The opening scene of *Celestina* conforms to this pattern in every way.

The falcon and falconry, then, as metaphors for the pursuit of carnal knowledge are usually associated with the larger symbolic context of the hunt of love and are chronologically and geographically widespread throughout the late medieval European courtly literary tradition. Within the Hispanic world itself it is pervasive and usually appears with pronounced tragic, or potentially menacing, overtones. Specifically, the loss of a falcon was considered particularly ominous in late medieval Castile. The mid-fifteenth-century Italian humanist Giovano Pontano mocks Spaniards for believing in this superstition: 'Sed quid de aniculis et puellis loquor: qui scia[m] deos solicitari quotidie a principibus uiris ubi falco lo[n] guia euolauit ubi equus pedem contorsit: quasi aucupes dii sint qui acciptru[m] cura[m] habeant aut tanq[uam] fabri ferrarii equoru[m] contusa et morbos curent act[ue] ex hoc quaestu rem familiare[m] augeant' [But why do I speak of old women and girls, when I know that every day powerful men appeal to the gods when their falcon flies off far away or their horse twists a foot. As if the gods were fowlers who look after hunting birds, or, like blacksmiths, they care for the injuries and illnesses of horses and increase their income by that trade!] (cited in McPheeters 1954, 334n.3). The loss of hunting falcons in the Castilian ballad of 'Rico Franco' (Solalinde 1958) corroborates Pontano's belief, since the event foreshadows the deadly encounter between the protagonist of the ballad and the daughter of the Lord of Maynes. As the leader of a band of unsuccessful hunters, Rico Franco arrives at Maynes castle looking for his lost falcon. There he is smitten by the lord's daughter, whom he abducts and, before he can violate her, she tricks him into giving her his dagger and she stabs him to death. Similarly, in the ballad

was tending to his master's horses ('[estaba]curando de estos caballos' [26] [I am here, sir, about your horses]). Sensing something wrong, Calisto asks how it is that Sempronio emerges from the parlour and not the stable ('Pues, ¿cómo sales de la sala?' [26] [how haps it then that thou comest out of the hall?]). Caught in a lie, Sempronio offers a telling response that calls attention to the unruliness of Calisto's hawk, which flew off its perch in the parlour: 'Abatióse el girifalte y vínele a endereçar en el alcándara' (26) [The gerfalcon bated, and I came to set him on the perch].

Perhaps the best reader ever to peruse act 1, Fernando de Rojas was quick to associate Calisto's desire with that of the aroused falcon whose instincts even in captivity are difficult to tame. In act 2, composed entirely by Rojas, Rojas clearly seized upon the earlier image of the agitated falcon in the parlour as an augury of things to come, when Pármeno attributes the sequence of events leading to the fateful intervention of Celestina to Calisto's wilful hunting hawk:

> Señor, porque perderse el otro día el neblí fue causa de tu entrada en la huerta de Melibea a le buscar; la entrada, causa de la veer y hablar; la habla engendró amor; el amor parió tu pena; la pena causará perder tu cuerpo y el alma y hacienda. Y lo que más de ello siento es venir a manos de aquella trotaconventos, después de tres vezes emplumada. (86)

> [Thus, sir, your losing of your hawk the other day was the cause of your entering into the garden where Melibea was, to look if she were there; your entering the cause that you both saw her and talked with her; your talk engendered love; your love brought forth your pain; and your pain will be the cause of your growing careless and retchless that you will destroy both of your body, soul and goods. And that which grieves me most is that you must fall into the hands of that same trot up and down, that maidenhead monger, that same gadding to and fro bawd, who for her villanies and rogueries in that kind hath been three several times implumed.]

Fernando de Rojas's interpretation of the falcon is, in the end, deliberate, portentous, and tied to tragic causality; and it is closely linked to the images of hunting he develops throughout the work. He was doubtless conscious of the bird's symbolic significance and its connotation of lustful desire and fatefulness, and he was aware of its pervasive use in courtly literature. In *Celestina*, elaborating on the anonymous author's early allusion to it in act 1, he would develop it fully as a harbinger of the deadly consequences of unrestrained desire and include it in the opening summary that precedes act 1.

To be sure, the hawk emerges in the work as Calisto's animal double, the sign or icon of his impetuosity and the animalistic coordinates of his desire. The old bawd Celestina certainly understands this. In act 3, she explicitly compares Calisto to a hawk when she answers Sempronio's query regarding her lack of haste in tending to Calisto's embassy after receiving one hundred gold coins from him. The anxieties of desire, Celestina notes, increase with delay; and by lagging, she hopes to incite Calisto's impatience into more impetuous rewards, comparing the ardour produced by her planned deferral to the blind eagerness of the apprentice falcon who, eager for the completion of the hunt, strikes at the training lure (*señuelo*), unable to distinguish a decoy from real prey. She claims to know well and have mastered 'Estos novicios amantes que contra qualquier señuelo buelan sin deliberación, sin pensar el daño quel cevo de su deseo trae mezclado en su exercicio y negociación para sus personas' (140–1) [These new lovers, who against any luring whatsoever, fly out to check, they care not whither, without any advisement in the world, or once thinking on the harm which the meat of their desire may by over gorging occasion unto them].[6]

Medieval lore on the training of hunting falcons stresses that the bird must first suffer from intense physical hunger to respond to its master's commands. In order to instruct hawks to be used in the chase, the birds must first submit to their master's wishes by way of deliberately induced regimens that alternate starvation with carnal temptation. Don Juan Manuel's fourteenth-century *Libro de la caza* provides striking insight into Celestina's knowledge of falconry and the way she uses it to speak of Calisto and his pursuit of Melibea:

Luego que los falcones son tomados brauos et son bien mansos et non an ningun reçelo de los omnes, deuen los desçender mucho de las carnes, pero non tanto por que pudiessen venir a muerte o a dolençia. Et desque fueren desçendido en la manera que entendiere el falconero quel cunple asaz et que esta el falcon muy fanbriento, deuen encarnar el sennuelo con dos tetiellas o con dos piernas de buena gallina et llamar el falcon a la mano et amostrar le el sennuelo todo. Et desque veniere a la mano y se asentare en el sennuelo, deuen le dar a roer de aquella buena carne y poner le el capirote, et poner aquel sennuelo mismo en tierra çerca del falconero que tiene el falcon, et entonçe tirar le el capirote et mostrar le aquel sennuelo bien encarnado; et el falcon, con la grant fambre que ha et por que ya vino al sennuelo a la mano del falconero, por fuerça saltara en el sennuelo en que vee estar la carne. (537–8)

[After the falcons have been taken in the wild and are well tamed and show no fear of men, their flesh should be much diminished, but not so much as to occasion death or illness. And once they have been reduced in the manner in which the falconer knows that the falcon is very hungry, they should bait the lure with two breasts or legs of good quality hen and call the falcon to hand to show him the whole lure. And after coming to hand and setting upon the lure, they should let him gnaw on that good meat and then hood him, and then put that lure on the ground close to the falconer who has the falcon, and then remove the hood and show the falcon that lure well baited with flesh; and the falcon, with great hunger because he had been at the hand of the falconer, will be compelled to jump at the lure where he sees the meat.]

The role played by privation in provoking physical hunger for flesh is notable in Don Juan Manuel's description of the training of hunting falcons and provides insight into the significance of the chase imagery in *Celestina*. The metaphor Celestina employs to explain her delay to Sempronio in act 3 displays an immediate knowledge of the strategies used to train hunting falcons, just as it reveals her position of mastery over Calisto. Through it, we inescapably come to see Celestina as the mistress of the hunt. On a symbolic level, she is the master manipulator of the process that provides the overarching image that runs throughout the work. As if he were a novice falcon, Celestina recognizes the need to provoke Calisto's submission by prolonging his yearning through the pursuit of the counterfeit objects of hunger and desire. There is a clear reciprocity between the technique of temptation and withdrawal used to direct the hunger of the falcon and the strategies Celestina employs to guide Calisto's pursuit of Melibea. As if he were a hungry falcon, Celestina first entices Calisto by tempting him with Melibea's cordon – the string-like belt or girdle to which she is metaphorically tied – simultaneously bringing the promise of her seduction nearer to him through the display of this item of her clothing while keeping Melibea herself hanging at a tempting distance.

In act 3, with the image of the impulsive novice falcon imprinted on her mind, Celestina governs temporality in relation to Calisto's yearning, simultaneously seeking and putting off its consummation through the lure of Melibea's girdle. Calisto's demanding passion thus runs headlong into Celestina's calculated dallying, which turns gratification aside in order to increase his want. From this point on, the plot moves toward staging the anguish of impossible possession, playing out Calisto's object of desire as a multivalent, protean metonymy. Realizing the importance of deferral, and that Calisto's passion will only continue to grow with every interruption, Celestina amplifies it through the enticement offered by a fetish, or an artefact that, like the falcon's lure, signals both the promise of reward and the immediate disappointment of a ruse.

By means of bait composed of an alluring object of Melibea's clothing – her cordon or girdle – Celestina at once offers and witholds from Calisto that part of Melibea's anatomy the object normally entwines. Calisto's courtship of Melibea is thus mediated by a fetish, manipulated by the bawd as a sort of striptease, promising a progressive and seemingly unending unveiling of Melibea's body according to the impulses of desire, which cannot seize their object until it is too late, until the consummation that marks death and the end to all desiring.

The entire drama of Calisto and Melibea is played out in a vast universe involving images of pursuit, luring, deferral, and hunger that harks back to a long tradition of learned literary texts and symbols: to the hunt of love and to the desire for carnal knowledge. In a moment of heightened awareness into the deepest nature of his longing for Melibea, Calisto alludes to the fate of a pair of legendary doomed lovers, Pyramus and Thisbe, hoping that his love will not end tragically like theirs: '¡O piedad celestial, inspira al Plebérico coraçón, por que esperança de salud no embíe el spíritu perdido con el desastrado Píramo y de la desdichada Tisbe' (26) [O heavens, if ye have any pity in you, inspire that Pleberian heart therewith, lest my soul, helpless of hope, should fall into the like misfortune with Pyramus and Thisbe]. The tale of the fated lovers from Ovid's *Metamorphoses* revolves around another cynegetic image and serves as yet another touchstone for understanding the basic thematic tensions at the heart of *Celestina*. It points symbolically to Calisto's death as well as to the carnal, bestial nature of his passionate desire.

The myth of Pyramus and Thisbe provides important analogies to the plot of *Celestina*, combining forbidden desire, blind knowledge, and carnal passion in a way that casts light on the latter's interplay in the story of Calisto and Melibea. Pyramus and Thisbe, two lovers forbidden to marry by their parents, plan to meet one night by the tomb of Ninus, located near a fountain. Thisbe arrives first and is frightened off by a lioness, who out hunting had come to the fountain to quench her thirst. In Thisbe's haste to escape, Thisbe drops her scarf, which the lioness ravages with her bloody paws. Upon arriving for the tryst, Pyramus discovers the bloody scarf, takes it as a sign of Thisbe's demise, and falls upon his own sword from grief. Recovered from her fear, Thisbe returns to the fountain to find Pyramus dead and, overcome with sorrow, she kills herself with his sword, still warm with the blood of her lover.

Although a minor figure in the myth, the lioness plays a pivotal role in Ovid's text around which the themes of knowledge, desire, the chase, and carnality revolve. Like Calisto, the lioness is a hunter, who comes to quench her thirst at the fountain, a sign of yearning at the level of the body that parallels Pyramus's and Calisto's sexual appetites. Although the lioness fails to kill Thisbe, Thisbe leaves behind an article of clothing that transfixes Pyramus and comes to substitute her in his imagination. Stained with blood, the garment stands as both talisman and souvenir of Thisbe. Thisbe is thus both present and absent to Pyramus in the memento of the scarf. Her life is subsumed in the fetishized object, since Pyramus, blinded by desire and consumed by guilt, concludes that Thisbe is dead. He casts all blame upon himself and commits suicide. The destructive and bestial nature of the lioness is transferred onto Pyramus, all the while paralleling Calisto's own desire, who, as a result of his actions, remains the ultimate cause of Melibea's death in the penultimate act of *Celestina*. In a real sense, by invoking Pyramus and Thisbe, Calisto demonstrates a paradoxical insight to his own plight: though blind to the implications of his own longing, on a symbolic level he intuits and simultaneously compares his suffering to that of others who endured similar pain, even though apprised of their tragic end.

The literary images of animality in *Celestina* continue to devolve upon Calisto and overflow from Sempronio's conversation. In act 1, in an aside, Sempronio invokes more animals to embroider upon the nature of the desire that drives his master to despair: 'O soberano Dios, quán altos son tus misterios ... Su límite pusiste por maravilla. Paresce al amante que atrás queda; todos rompen, pungidos y esgarrochados como ligeros toros, sin freno saltan por las barreras' (32) [Oh God, how high and unsearchable are thy mysteries! ... Thou has set his bounds as marks for men to wonder at: lovers ever deeming, that they only are cast behind, and that others still outstrip them, that all men break through but themselves, like your light footed bulls, which being let loose in the place and galled with darts, take over the bars as soon as they feel themselves pricked]. In this telling comparison, Sempronio likens Calisto to a raging bull that, through brute force, smashes the barriers erected to contain its fury. When Calisto corrects Sempronio and states that his desire for Melibea is like that for God, Sempronio is quick to remind him about the nature of the gods he may actually refer to: '¿No has leýdo de Pasife con el toro [Have you not heard of Pasiphae, who played the wanton with the bull?], adding an intentional grotesque malapropism, 'de Minerva con el can?' (34) [of Minerva, how she dallied with the dog?]. Pasiphae, mother of the monstrous Minotaur, who was half man half beast, similarly suffered from immoderate desire, and yearned to couple with a bull. The mythological references to beasts and bestiality have notable human parallels in *Celestina* since through them both Calisto and Melibea are drawn into a common calculus of physical desire: in act 1 Calisto is compared to the bull with whom the all-too-human Melibea will couple. Sempronio, however, does not fail to embellish his exposition on the nature of Calisto's passion with further mythological and legendary illustrations of animal ardour. He conjures more, going so far as to apply them to Calisto's own genealogy: 'Lo de tu abuela con el ximio, ¿hablilla fue?' (34) [and that of your grandmother and her ape, that's a fable too?] he queries snidely, adding deep insult to injury. As James Burke points out in reference to this malicious disclosure, it relates directly to medieval and early modern theories regarding generation and conception, and insinuates that if Calisto's grandmother had in fact indulged in sexual relations with an ape, 'simian features and characteristics could have been incorporated into her line and transmitted to her descendants' (1998, 123). Calisto is therefore circumscribed and defined by bestial references that point to bestial passions: first through the hawk's predatory instincts and sharp sight, then by means of the lioness that stalks the bloody legend of Pyramus and Thisbe, followed by the raging bull that couples with the gods, and then finally through the ape whose legacy of wantonness likely courses through his very veins.

The hawk, however, remains the animal with which Calisto is most closely identified. From the opening scene described in the summary of act 1, in which Calisto's hawk strays into Melibea's garden, he is associated with this image, which stresses his proximity to nature and to the chase. Everything in the scene points to the presence of the instinctive pursuit of desire. To be sure, the illustrators of the first edition of the *Comedia* (Burgos, 1499) clearly understood the human-animal equation. In the woodcut that portrays the lovers' initial encounter: Calisto, leaning on his

Figure 3.1 Calisto, Melibea, and the Wayward Hawk. Woodcut from the Burgos, 1499? edition of the *Comedia de Calisto y Melibea*. Hispanic Society of America, New York. With permission.

walking stick with a phallic-looking sword dangling unusually from be-hind – between his legs – gazes at Melibea as she makes an ambiguous gesture either of greeting or rejection with her left hand, perhaps adum-brating a sinister outcome. At the extreme upper right of the woodcut, Calisto's falcon sits perched in a tree, its sight simultaneously aligned with his, looking intently from on high at Melibea. ·

Used in the chase for its keen eyesight and eager quickness to seize prey, stirred by its carnal appetite, the hawk stands as Calisto's animal double from the very beginning of the work. Through association with the falcon, Calisto is troped as the bestial hunter, and Melibea, as re-mains to be seen in chapter 6, as his not-so-innocent quarry.

Melibea's ostensibly vigorous rejection of her pursuer frustrates Calisto's quest and provokes his turbulent emotions. He internalizes her repudiation as a loss and reproaches himself, to the point that he is subsumed in a gloom that threatens him in grievous ways. Put off by Melibea, he returns home, retires to his bedroom, and suffers the on-slaught of the *aegritudo amoris*, the lover's malady, or the pathology of love.[7] Subsumed in melancholy fear and apprehension, Calisto orders Sempronio to shut out all light: 'Cierra la ventana y dexa la tiniebla acompañar al triste y desdichado la ceguedad. Mis pensamientos no son dignos de luz' (26) [Shut the window, and leave the darkness to accompany him whose sad thoughts deserve no light]. The hawking imagery in this way turns in upon itself, and provides at once a positive and negative double for the dejected Calisto. Rather than seek a more acute perspective on his own condition, Calisto looks for nothing but the darkness, blind now to everything that surrounds him. His hopes dashed, he himself like the hawk has strayed; he has lost the eagerness and lofty clairvoyance of the falcon. He now shuts out the light, which he once believed infused Melibea's divine presence. As he laments the loss of Melibea's beauty, Sempronio reproaches him, pointing out that Calisto's desire debases him and prevents him from seeing the object of his longing with unfettered eyes: 'Posible es, y aún que la aborrezcas quanto agora la amas; podrá ser alcançándola, y viéndola con otros ojos, libres del engaño en que agora estás' (42) [It is possible that you may one day hate her as much as now you love her, when you shall come to the full enjoying of her, and to looking on her with other eyes, free from that error which now blindeth your judgment].[8] As the conversation incorporates comparisons and references to medical knowledge, Sempronio interprets Calisto's blindness as a symptom of melancholia; his master has detached himself from the world and all reality; he remains in his darkened room, failing to distinguish whether it is night or day, displaying a deep decline in self-esteem and an increase in self-deprecation, all signs of the malady of love, clear symptoms of the pathology of desire.[9]

Alluding to his imminent death – the dialogue in *Celestina* is fraught with ironic foreshadowing and prolepsis – Calisto calls upon the two great healers of antiquity, Hippocrates and Galen, to cure his pain. The two physicians, whose theory of the humours was central to medieval medicine, believed the body to be composed of four fluids (blood, phlegm, yellow bile, and black bile). Good health required that the four humours be in balance, since their disequilibrium afflicted not only health but also the emotions and mental disposition. From the conversation and Sempronio's comments, it is thus clear that the cause of Calisto's passion is understood to emerge from the body, and that it can be cured only through physical therapies, especially sexual relations, or the pursuit of carnal knowledge (see Wack 1990).

At Sempronio's urging, Calisto hires Celestina to aid him in achieving his desire to possess Melibea. Instead of choosing a matchmaker wisely, however, the blind Calisto casts aside all warnings regarding Celestina's reputation for trickery and deceit. Far from considering Melibea's well-being, Calisto employs the old whore without weighing the possible results of his actions. Subsequently, Celestina visits Melibea, and in one of the work's pivotal scenes to which we will return in the next chapter, informs the young girl that Calisto suffers from a toothache, a coded corporal reference to a lack of sexual satisfaction (see West 1979 and Herrero 1984). At first Melibea dissimulates and resists the old bawd's cajoling. However, when Celestina invokes Calisto's physical pain, Melibea takes pity on him and offers Celestina the cordon to her frock, an apotropaic talisman that she claims has visited all the holy sites of Christendom. She does this with the hope that its numinous powers will ease the young man's affliction.

When Celestina returns to Calisto and gives him Melibea's garment, he rises from his depression only to topple into exaltation. The cordon blocks his memory and, unable to recall the traumatic event of his rejection by Melibea, he displaces his adoration of her onto this inanimate material object. The cordon, much like Thisbe's scarf, becomes a fetish, and Calisto responds not to Melibea's goodwill, but rather to the meaning he perceives in the article of her clothing. Emotionally addressing the cordon, he takes it for Melibea, who becomes simultaneously present and absent by means of the object that Calisto now holds as if it were a sacred relic. Melibea's sash in this way supersedes its own value over the animate person to whom it belongs, and Calisto, by wishing to wrap himself in it, assumes a feminized role. Time, memory, reality, desire, and gender all collapse onto this inanimate object as Melibea becomes lost in the distance of language through the excesses of Calisto's speech.

Carnal Knowledge and The Pursuit of the Unseen

Calisto's encounter with Melibea's cordon in act 6 makes it clear that the portrayal of language in *Celestina* in more than one way offers its readers a semblance of the subconscious mechanisms of desire, which point to a unique new way in representing and understanding desire at the end of the fifteenth century. Traditionally, literary criticism has privileged courtly love as the dominant medieval discourse of the emotions and sentimentality. In his influential book on the subject, C.S. Lewis spoke of courtly love's idealization and remarked that it comprised several inter-related elements: 'Humility, Courtesy, Adultery, and the Religion of Love. Hopeless for a sign of recognition from his lady, the courtly lover

is always abject. Obedience to his lady's slightest wish, however whimsi-
cal, and silent acquiescence in her rebukes, however unjust, are the only
virtues he dare claim. In the etiquette of courtly love, there is a service of
love closely modeled on the service which a feudal vassal owes to his lord'
(Lewis 1959, 2–3, cited by Moi 1986, 12). Pierre Le Gentil in his analysis
of the representation of courtly love in Iberian poetry at the close of the
Middle Ages subsequently expanded upon these themes to include the
notion of opposites and contradiction as a key elements in the ritual of
love (1949–52, 126–7). Le Gentil emphasizes the sublime aspect of the
courtly lover's yearning – the dissolution of the opposition between joy
and suffering – that points to love and to desire as totalizing, multifaceted discourses that, as we shall see, disintegrate into excess in *Celestina*,
especially in Calisto's speech.

In her book on Aucassin, Troilus, and Calisto as courtly lovers, June
Hall Martin has underscored parody in *Celestina*, carried out through the
caricaturesque dimensions of Calisto's exaggerated discourse. By means
of her analysis, it becomes clear that Rojas intended to undermine ironically the rhetoric of courtly love by contrasting its rhetorical idealizations
with Calisto's carnal passions and appetites, which lie barely concealed
below a copious yet transparent veneer of words. Martin notes that the
high-flown register of Calisto's discourse constitutes a thinly disguised
attempt to dissimulate the sexual desire that drives it:

> Calisto's essential problem lies within his own nature, and the constantly
> shifting tone of his language is a clue to a certain baseness in his character.
> His words lack the sincerity essential to the ideal courtly lover. His love lacks
> the power to ennoble him. And desire, rather than being refined as it grows
> stronger, tends to become coarser. As though attempting to conceal the
> base nature of his desire for Melibea, he relies heavily on the love religion.
> His worship appears almost from the beginning excessive (Hall Martin
> 1972, 101)

While Calisto appears at first not to recognize, or at least to admit to, the
carnal coordinates of his passion, performing a *méconnaissance*, or mis-
recognition, in Lacanian terms, of the object of his desire, there is more
to his exuberant language than veiled carnality propelled by mere parody. His lovesickness, or melancholia, results from a simultaneous lack
and proliferation of knowledge (or a concurrent 'seeing and not seeing'), which, as remains to be shown, manifests itself in language, fetishism, and an intuition of death. The sheer abundance of words that flows

from Calisto's mouth indicates an excess, a veritable plethora, of speech that, as it increases and multiplies in intensity, loses its ability to signify anything beyond itself. When Calisto speaks, he is transformed into a torrent of empty signifiers that indicates a gap between his thoughts and the meanings of the myriad of words he utters. It is this breach in Calisto's speech that provides an important clue to the atemporal, nihilistic dimensions of language in *Celestina* as the words of all the characters in it point to the death of language, or, as Roland Barthes puts it, a circumstance where 'there is no longer a language on the other side of these figures (which means, in another sense: there is no longer anything but language)' (Barthes 1975, 6–9). Thus, while Calisto's language does indeed parody courtly love's sublimation of carnal desire, and it does indeed speak to the purpose of the *Tragicomedia* stated in its beginning, at a subconscious level it also signals the prolongation and delay in the pursuit and identification of the object of his desire, which on the surface of his discourse appears only as the carnal possession of Melibea.

In Calisto, as well as all the other characters of *Celestina*, language itself is transformed into a fetishized object that is secured in order both to conceal and to delay an ultimate encounter with what lies beyond it, death. The characters of *Celestina* all appear to postpone death through incessant, copious speech, and in this way they embody the modern psychonalytical postulates regarding the intimate relationship between death, language, and desire formulated by Freud and Lacan.

The conjunction of death, language, and desire in *Celestina* is often obliquely intuited by the characters themselves. In act 6, observing Celestina's effect upon Calisto as she protracts telling the news of her visit to Melibea, Pármeno conjoins the three in an aside that underscores a fatal presence in the conversation and foreshadows Calisto's sure demise in the pursuit of his desire. 'Temblando está el diablo como azogado; no se puede tener en sus pies; su lengua le querría prestar' [He shakes and quivers like a fellow that hath had his senses over-touched with quicksilver. Look, he cannot stand on his legs; would I could help him to his tongue], he says, 'para que hablase presto. No es mucha su vida; luto avremos de medrar destos amores' (150–2) [that I might hear him speak again; sure he cannot live long Every man his mourning weed, and there's an end].

A close reading of the remainder of act 6 reveals just how the representation of language in it marks the transformation of the word into a festishized, empty object, and how language takes on an anamorphic, protean cast that is altered reflexively by the speaker into its own solipsistic expression of unquenchable, unattainable desire. Calisto's words there constitute their own end, in the end creating the very object of desire he seeks to articulate through them, signifying nothing but themselves as they disguise the ever-present threat of annihilation. As he speaks, Calisto's subconscious transforms his initial wish to possess Melibea physically into a proliferation of speech and verbal overabundance that serves as a screen to conceal the menacing presence of the Real, or that which pursues every desiring subject, according to Freud and Lacan.

Jean-François Lyotard, as he explores the theories of Freud and Lacan, elaborates upon the Lacanian notion of the impossibility of representing the Real through language in the conjunction of desire, *jouissance*, and death, and how speech constitutes a flight from an encounter with it. He notes that 'desire cannot be assumed, accepted, understood, locked up in names, nomenclatured, because these intensities we desire horrify us, because we flee them, because we forget them ... in fleeing jouissance-death, we meet it head on, unrecognizable, immediately recognized, *un-heimlich* because *heimlich*, different, not willed by a deliberate decision, on the contrary avoided, fled from in panic and nostalgic terror, and therefore truly desired (*Wille*), unassumable' (Lyotard 1993, 20). Lyotard's observations emerge from his attempt to combine semiotics and psychoanalysis in his inscription of the body and libidinality in an economy of human want. As he effaces the binary nature of the Freudian death wish, Lyotard incorporates language into the synergies of desire and sees language as a metalinguistic performance of lack.

Following J.L. Austin's theory of speech acts, in her discussion of Molière's *Dom Juan* Shoshana Felman discovers a not disimilar paradigm from the one outlined by Lyotard. Felman identifies an erotics of language characterized by a constant distancing and deferral and concludes that 'The desire of a Dom Juan is at once desire for desire and desire for language; a desire that desires itself and that desires its own language. Speech is the true realm of eroticism, and not simply a means of access to this realm. To seduce is to produce language that enjoys, language that takes pleasure in having 'no more to say'. To seduce is thus to prolong, within desiring speech, the pleasure-taking performance of the very production of that speech' (Felman 1983, 28). Using as a point of departure Lyotard's observations on the unspeakable nature of desire plus Felman's analysis of seduction as a process that extends the search for pleasure by means of the prolongation of speech, it is possible to proceed with an examination of act 6 of

Celestina and toward a better understanding of the complexities of Calisto's discourse in it.

The Latin root of the word *seduction* in itself implies distance, separation, remoteness, estrangement. The Latin *seducere* is a compound of *se*, 'astray, aside, away,' and the verb *ducere*, 'to lead': it thus signifies to be led away or astray. Therefore, it is not far-fetched to extend the notion of drift and breach to Calisto's language in his search to 'know' or to seduce Melibea, and indeed beyond Calisto to the representation of attraction and separation between all the characters in *Celestina* from the objects of their desire. On the surface, the parody in Calisto's discourse emerges from the tense distance created by the courtly register he employs and the sexual energy that clearly drives it. The abyss between his words and the things they seek to indicate is continually pointed out in his conversations with his servants, Celestina, and later, of course, Melibea herself during their night in the garden. To be sure, in act I Sempronio brutally exposes the duplicitous nature of Calisto's words when in exasperation he impulsively utters the remedy for his master's suffering. Referring to Melibea, in order to still Calisto's passion he blurts out that 'traérgela he hasta la cama' (42) [I shall bring her to his bed]. Sempronio's prescription, however, is met with continued resistance by Calisto, and we understand that Calisto suffers less from hypocrisy than from blind self-deception. Sempronio and the reader see that Calisto's rhetoric, though moved by his libido, fails to find the signifying authority in his speech, so that the true object of his want remains unknown, deferred, out of reach, and out of sight. Calisto's words are thus animated by a form of unattainable, protean desire. His speech constitutes both a presence and an absence that through reiteration perpetuates the gap between the speaking subject and the wanted object. In its unfolding Calisto's discourse produces more words that, in the end, themselves come to constitute a fetish, or an autonomous activity that becomes a substitute – a decoy, as it were – for the direct gratification of his desire.

As stated, however, it is in act 6 that Calisto's linguistic self-seduction takes full shape. It is there, in his conversation with Celestina, who has come to regale him with the details of her visit to Melibea and to deliver the latter's cordon, where Calisto's desire for carnal knowledge is fully reified and invested in a tangible, material fetish: Melibea's girdle. Impatient, Calisto urges Celestina to stop rambling and to get to the point of her visit: 'si no quieres, reyna y señora mía, que desespere y vaya mi ánima condenada a perpetua pena oyendo esas cosas, certifícame brevemente si no ovo buen fin tu demanda gloriosa y la cruda y rigurosa muestra de aquel gesto angélico y matador' (154) [If thou wilt not, thou that art sole queen and sovereign of my life, that I die desperate, and that my soul go condemned from hence to perpetual pain (so impatient am I of hearing these things) delay me no longer, but certify me briefly, whether thy glorious demand had a happy end or no? As also whether that cruel and stern look of that angelical face whose frowns murder ... sorted to a gentle entertaining of thy suit?], he says, revealing an erotic investment in his urgency to know the outcome of Celestina's embassy. At the same time, Calisto's extravagant need to know is implicated metaphorically in his own death and damnation, since death, he says, is preferable to the anguish he feels from not knowing the outcome of Celestina's visit to Melibea: 'Madre mía, o abrevia tu razón, o toma esta espada y mátame' (150) [Good mother, either cut off thy discourse, or take thou this sword and kill me] he cries out as he offers his sword to Celestina.

Although there can be no quarter from Calisto's compulsion to know, his desire to know will be thwarted from its outset and transformed into frustration, since, as Freud and Lacan agree, desire always exceeds the capacity of its objects to satisfy it. As noted, Calisto's passionate desire for knowledge constitutes what Freud characterizes as *Wisstreib* (1953–74, vol. 10, 245), translated by Toril Moi as 'epistemophilia' (1989, 203), a dangerous impulse that leads easily to annihilation, since it is inherently always frustrated. Freudian theory suggests that the drive to search for knowledge is profoundly implicated in sexuality, and that the investigative gaze becomes fixed on fetish objects like Melibea's cordon, an item of clothing that Calisto addresses and caresses as if it were her very body.

Melibea's presence is invoked by a piece of clothing, the girdle that points to the part of her body that it normally encircled while it held up the apparel that was intended to conceal her nakedness. Overcome with anxiety, Celestina perceives the recklessly extravagant nature of Calisto's desire and incites it even more, handing him Melibea's girdle as she waits for him to topple further into the abyss of desire. 'Da espacio a tu desseo; toma este cordón, que si yo no me muero, yo te daré a su ama' (166) [afford thy desire some time; take unto thee this girdle: for if death prevent me not, I will deliver the owner thereof into thy hands], she says, as she expects the predictable reaction and both she and Calisto ominously foreshadow the presence of death in their dialogue. His response to the girdle is one of exultation:

¡O nuevo huésped, o bienaventurado cordón, que tanto poder y meresci-
miento toviste de ceñir aquel cuerpo que yo no soy digno de servir! ¡O nudos
de mi passión, vosotros enlazastes mis desseos! Dezíme si os hallastes presentes en la desconsolada respuesta de aquella a quien vosotros servís y yo
adoro, y por más que trabajo noches y días, no me vale y provecha ... ¡O mi
gloria y ceñidero de aquella angélica criatura, yo te veo y no te creo! O cordón, cordón, ¿fuísteme enemigo? (166)

[O new guest! O happy girdle which hast had such power and worth in thee
as to hedge in that body and be its enclosure, which myself am not worthy
to serve. O ye knots of my passion, it is you that have entangled my desires;
tell me if thou wert present at that uncomfortable answer of fairest she,
whom thou servest and I adore. And yet the more I torment myself for her
sake, mourning and lamenting night and day, the less it avails me and the
less it profits me ... O thou glory of my soul, and encircler of so incomparable a creature; I behold thee, and yet believe it not. O girdle, girdle, thou
lovely lace! Wast thou mine enemy too?]

Apostrophized, Melibea's cordon constitutes a reified metonymy, an object which gives a lifelike presence to the previously unseen and un-
nameable part of her body ('Aquella proporción que veer yo no pude,
no sin dubda por el bulto de fuera juzgo incomparablemente ser mejor
que la que Paris juzgó entre las tres diesas' [42] [The proportion of
those other parts which I could not eye, undoubtedly (judging things
unseen by the seen) must of force be incomparably far better than that
which Paris gave his judgment of, in the difference between three god-
desses]) which it was intended to conceal. Its presence in Calisto's hands
suggests that it is not now covering Melibea, and that, as he holds the
girdle, those parts it wrapped are apprehensible, undraped, visible, and
approachable. Though absent, Melibea is present, invoked by means of
an item of her clothing. The cordon or girdle, a mere accessory object,
becomes a titillating fetish, a source of erotic pleasure that is transformed by Calisto into an emotionally charged, anthropomorphized
substitute for Melibea. Lost in a world of words and anxieties, Calisto
falls headlong into self-induced obsessions that undermine the possibility of his knowing the world at all. He constructs a solipsistic universe of
permutations, of substitute objects – of words and of things – that occlude the prospect of ever acquiring the very knowledge that he seeks:
to 'know' Melibea.

The eagerness of his exchange with Celestina reveals Calisto's search for an opening through which to express his intense urges and flesh out the concupiscent impulses that subtend his discourse. When Celestina appears, Calisto's libido transforms her words into a linguistic fetish constituted by the very act of her own telling and the narration of her encounter with Melibea. He needs to hear it all – he is in fact 'dying to hear it all' – and wishes for her narrative to continue, not to stop. As Barthes notes, a told text may often taken on a type of morbid sensuality, a pleasure that is felt at the level of the very body of the listener who hears it or the teller who tells it (Barthes 1975, 51). Calisto's eagerness to listen to Celestina will thus become a self-sufficient instance of desire in which he finds an almost pathological, ecstatic pleasure as he submits to the mystical effect that her words have upon him. On his knees before Celestina, Calisto urges the old prostitute to tell him everything as he nervously awaits her 'suave respuesta' (136) [sweet answer]. Overcome by impatience, however, he interrupts her with a series of exclamations, verbal ejaculations that end in the revelation of his wish to have been there, under Celestina's skirt, listening attentively as the old whore performs her own linguistic enticement of Melibea: '¡O gozo sin par, o singular oportunidad, o oportuno tiempo! ¡O quién estuviera allí debaxo de tu manto, escuchando qué hablaría sola aquélla en quien Dios tan estremadas gracias puso!' (158) [O joy beyond compare! O singular opportunity! O seasonable time! O that I had lain hid underneath thy mantle, that I might have heard her but speak, on whom heaven hath so plentifully poured forth the fullness of his graces!].

Calisto's repetitive, exclamatory diction betrays a profound urgency, as if he had caught a glimpse of the mortal dangers that stalk extravagant desire, and he had seen that his earlier plea to die rather than wait to be given the news of Celestina's embassy was more than mere metaphor. Metaphorically dying to know, he is perhaps as frightened by his morbid want as he is attracted to Melibea, simultaneously affirming and rejecting the prospect of *jouissance* offered by his contact with the object of his desire through the voice of Celestina. In the end, Calisto cowers, preferring to hide under the old whore's skirt, a space which marks a voyeuristic middle ground between the realization of his drive for carnal knowledge and the safety afforded by distance and clandestine observation. Calisto revels in the possibility of becoming inconspicuous, effacing himself amidst Celestina's underclothing, listening attentively to Melibea's voice – close to her but barely out of reach.

In act 6 we perceive in the morbid grain of Calisto's voice the intersection of words with pleasure, supported by a certain awareness and subterfuge of death that in Barthes' terms is characterized by 'an erotic mixture of timbre and language' whose end is not the clarity of the message spoken or the representation of the emotions felt, but the 'pulsional incidents, the language lined with flesh, a text where we can hear the grain of the throat, the patina of consonants, the voluptuousness of vowels, a whole carnal sterophony: the articulation of the body, of the tongue, not that of meaning, but of language' (Barthes 1975, 66–7). Calisto's discourse revels in its own incarnate nature, it takes self-reflexive – even onanistic – pleasure in its own oral/aural constitution and, in conjunction with Melibea's cordon, acts as a substitute for her physical body until the latter is ultimately – and anticlimactically – surrendered to him in act 14.

Celestina in her own right is the incarnation of linguistic duplicity, mistress of the cult of doublespeak as she embroiders and recasts the events that transpired during her visit with Melibea to prolong Calisto's yearning and wring even greater compensation from him. Her first laconic mention of Calisto's name to Melibea is recreated by her for him, told now in terms of a physical blow against her flesh that culminates in Melibea's seduction, provoking 'mil amortescimientos y desmayos, mil milagros y espantos, turbado el sentido' [swoonings and trancings, making many strange gestures, full of fear and amazement, all her senses being troubled] upon the penetration of 'aquella dorada frecha que del sonido de tu nombre le tocó' (160) [that golden shaft, which at the very voicing of your name had struck her to the heart]. Celestina's words are purposefully chosen to incite Calisto's carnal desire as she turns his name into the golden arrow that penetrates and wounds Melibea at the level of the flesh. She deliberately inscribes the effects of Calisto's name in somatic terms, evoking at the level of Melibea's own body the physical symptoms his name provokes when she pronounced it to her. The rhetorical exploitation of Melibea's body increases Calisto's desire for her, to the point where he refuses to permit Celestina to take leave with Melibea's cordon. 'Dame licencia, que es muy tarde, y déjame llevar el cordón, porque, como sabes, tengo dél necessidad' (172) [give me now licence to take my leave of you; for it grows very late; and let me have the girdle along with me], Celestina says, which is met by Calisto's anguished cry: '¡O desconsolado de mí, la fortuna adversa me sigue junta! Que contigo o con el cordón o con entramos quisiera estar esta noche luenga y oscura' (172) [O disconsolate that I am! My misfortunes still pursue me; for with thee, or with the girdle, or with both, I would willingly have been accompanied all this dark and tedious night]. Celestina's departure signals the end of his revery, the end of the pleasure he takes in hearing Melibea's words and in caressing her girdle, which have become metonymical embodiments of the most coveted, unseen object of his desire. The cordon, though only a piece of outer clothing that once entwined Melibea's lower body, allows Calisto to imagine this inanimate object as an extension of her, as the inverse form of what it once bound. Like language in relation to its objects of desire, the girdle makes Melibea present by way of her absence. It becomes the mark of the body that signals arousal, a trace or a fragment of a distant, inaccessible, unseen, unknown coveted object. Calisto's dialogue with Melibea's sash mobilizes his entire imagination, and just as his fantasies on it increase so too does his distance from what it represents, Melibea's body. As he revels in the presence of the cordon, Melibea is supplanted first by the material object that girded her midriff and then by the tempest of words Calisto uses to invoke it.

Celestina's deliberate introduction of a fetish – a physical fragment that represents Melibea's body – is not so much transformed into an event that involves a substitute for an impossible 'reality,' as Freud understands fetishism, but into 'the cutting-out from the other's body of a fraction of its surfaces, and the annexation of this to the body of the phantasizing subject' (Lyotard 1993, 75–6). The cutting out and the reintegration of the fetish-object is performed through the transposition of the libidinal energy of the word (although empty of sense as a result of its conventionality) upon the physical object that constitutes Melibea's girdle. It becomes the reification of Lyotard's 'libidinal fold,' located in the precise place, according to Barthes, 'where the garment gapes' (1975, 10).

Calisto's pleasure multiplies with the proliferation of discourse, to the point where, as we have seen, he insists on amplifying his desire by continuing to talk about it with Celestina, attempting to stop her from leaving his presence. The cessation of talk about desire, and Celestina's departure with Melibea's sash, Calisto insists, would lead to his immediate death. He offers 'toda esta casa y quanto en ella ay ... cuanto yo tengo' (162) [my whole house, and all that is in it ... everything I own] solely for the pleasure of hearing the news Celestina bears about Melibea and speaking with her about it, translating his desire into terms of material exchange. It is clear that he believes that the satisfaction of his obsession belongs to a system of substitutions and exchanges, to a fungible economy of libidinal desire that can be negotiated and stilled by barter and transactions in kind.

The accounts offered by both Calisto and Celestina during their encounter in act 6 (Celestina as accomplice in the seduction of Melibea and in Calisto's own hypnotic verbal self-seduction) occupy a space doubly removed from the object of Calisto's desire, where his words invoke Melibea's cordon, which invokes her imagined encircled, embraced body. Involving a series of substitutions, Calisto's observation is conducted from a momentarily safe distance that impedes his direct contact with, or knowledge of, the object that he covets. Through this mediation, oblivious to the stalking presence of death in the conversation, Calisto enjoys only a fleeting but evermore energizing, oblique glimpse of the desired object, at the spot where, to repeat the striking way Barthes puts it, 'the garment gapes' (Barthes 1975, 10). When Calisto lingusitically collapses Melibea and her girdle in his imagination, he tropes the object as prosopopoeia, as if it were Melibea herself, seeking to make present the absent, unseen object of his want. The girdle, like a linguistic sign, is thus a metonym and a metaphor for Melibea's body, a signal of Calisto's desire to pursue it, to know it, and to possess it. This performance of displacement and substitution gives rise, in Lyotard's words, 'to a voluminous place, to the theater, to the substitute sign, to interiority put in the place of exteriority, of the thing lost' (Lyotard 1993, 22). When Calisto attempts to conjure the spirit of Melibea's sash so that it might reveal to him his fortune with her, he exceeds the power of all language and verbally transforms the object into a talisman: 'Conjúrote me respondas por la virtud del gran poder que aquella señora sobre mí tiene' (166) [I conjure thee that thou answer me truly, by the virtue of that great power which that lady hath over me], he entreats it. Bewitched by the fetish, the cordon becomes 'the sign [that] at the same time screens and calls up what it announces and conceals,' just as it metonymically erases the object that it substitutes. The thing signified in the sash and in Calisto's words in this way appears solely as a constellation of signs, occluding and effacing the presence of the Real. Although not explicit, however, the presence of death remains implicit throughout his encounter with Celestina. The sash stands as an object that represents the desire of the transcendent; something material that signifies the immaterial; an object in which, according to Lyotard, 'the material is immediately annihilated ... where there is a message, there is no material;' all of which leads to the 'infinite postponement ... of the signifier' (Lyotard 1993, 43).

Calisto, like the examples of Hugo and Richard of St Victor Lyotard offers in his study of libidinal economy, valorizes both aesthetically and economically 'that aspect of things which denies them the code.' Instead, 'they love the negative of the code in the message, they value the labor of this negative, the text, the dissimilitude of things, and find beauty in it' (Lyotard 1993, 49). Calisto is seduced by the very pleasure and delight he takes in words, substitutions, and exchanges; a torrent of signs and signals that simultaneously produce delectation and frustration, the presence and absence of the flesh of his lover by means of her girdle, and the presence and the absence of the Real meaning of the object of desire.

Celestina, tired of hearing Calisto's rant, cuts him off. However, it is Sempronio's scathing but incisive observation that cuts to the quick and provokes his master's momentary return to understanding and to anger: 'Por holgar con el cordón, no querrás gozar de Melibea ... Que mucho hablando matas a ti y a los que te oyen' (168) [rejoicing in this girdle cannot make you enjoy Melibea ... talking and babbling so much as you do, you kill both yourself, and those which hear you], Sempronio remarks, ironically raising the spectre of death, which lurks in the folds of the girdle and lies in wait in the depths of Calisto's speech. The warning, however, goes unheeded, as Calisto falls back into hypnotic revery, whimpering 'no tengo sofrimiento para me abstener de adorar tan alta empresa' (170) [I have not the power to abstain from adoring so great a relic, so rich a gift!], unable to resist the compulsion to worship Melibea through the words he utters and the sash he runs between his fingers. 'Que muero por oýr palabras de aquella dulce boca' (170) [I die out of longing, for to hear the words which flow from so sweet a mouth], Calisto croons, as he again comes perilously close to transforming metaphor into experience, transmuting the substitute into the Real. A slave of desire, Melibea, he says, 'me tiene ligado y puesto en dura cadena' (172) [hath she bound me in so hard and strong a chain, that I must fore ever remain her prisoner], instantly conjoining the images of Celestina's thread, Melibea's cordon, and the golden chain that seals his fate and Celestina's. Melibea is fairer than Polixena, more beautiful than Helen, whose stunning beauty led to the destruction of a nation and the death of a million men, obliquely troping through mythology his own impending doom.

In one of his best known seminars, 'Anamorphosis' (number 11, titled *The Four Fundamental Concepts of Psychoanalysis*) Lacan (1981) analyses *The Ambassadors* (1533), a painting by Hans Holbein, in order to explain the ever-present blindness of the human subject to the menace of ubiquitous death and decay. The painting allegorizes the essential limitations

Figure 3.2 The Ambassadors, by Hans Holbein the Younger, 1533. National Gallery, London. With permission.

of human perception and understanding in the presence of death, underscoring humankind's ephemeral presence in the macrocosm. Although now prominently on display in the National Gallery in London, the painting was originally intended to hang in an unsuspecting place, a stairwell, so that people ascending the stairs from its left would be taken by surprise by the sudden emergence of the skull that is anamorphically embedded in the picture's foreground as they changed their upward angle of movement. Through the spectator's sudden perception of the graphically embedded skull that lurks hidden from the august human subjects who look out unawares from the painting – emissaries to Henry VIII who remain immersed in the signs of power and worldly authority that envelop them – Lacan draws an analogy to desire's ability both to represent and to obscure the presence of the Real through sight and the language of signs.

For Lacan, Holbein's painting illustrates the split – the Freudian *Spaltung* – caused by the encounter of a signifier with the Real. In Lacan's ontology of the subject, the Real takes the form of what he calls the 'gaze,' or the fleeting consciousness of an eye that seems to look back, watching from outside the field of vision. In Lacan's interpretation, the blurred skull in Holbein's portrait points to the crucial role played by oblique perception in relation to the presence of the Real, without which the subject's assertion of its existence cannot be sustained, even as the subject remains incapable of recognizing that presence (1981, 88–9). In this sense, the distorted skull is the trace of an unattainable kind of knowledge for the conscious subject; a perception that can only be fleetingly represented at the most liminal margins of subjectivity.

In Holbein's oblique image of death, Lacan perceives a trompe l'oeil construction that captivates the onlooker's gaze and conjures both absence and lack in the spectator. By approaching the language of act 6 in *Celestina* from a similarly oblique, anamorphic angle, by looking at what goes mostly unnoticed – the seemingly innocuous deathly metaphors of courtly love – the almost undetectable presence of death amidst the interlocutors in this dialogue centring on the pursuit of desire emerges clearly. Although in Calisto's reverie and Sempronio's and Celestina's response to it in act 6 mortality remains but a metaphorical undertone, as the action proceeds it will become dominant and lead to the final multiple crescendos marked by Celestina's, Sempronio's, Pármeno's, Calisto's, and Melibea's actual death, punctuated by the final anguished realization of death's palpable ubiquity in Pleberio's concluding lament. The menacing presence of the Real, as it is depicted analogously in Holbein's painting, resists symbolic representation. So too in the language of *Celestina*, and the seduction by language implicit in Calisto's reverie with Melibea's fetishized cordon. Calisto's words and the coveted object permit the Real's deferral, yet they do not hide completely what cannot be seen directly from being perceived askance, anamorphically. Direct contemplation would be petrifying; death must remain in the shadows of discourse as the hunt goes on.[10]

In *Celestina*, the intimate bonds between love and death are invoked as both pursuit and avoidance, the presence and the absence of a desire that never can quite speak its name nor quite attain its object. In act 6 we see Calisto, a prisoner of his desire, at the edge of the abyss, yet blind to the spectre of annihilation as he languishes in the seductive powers of

Figure 3.3 Anamorphic Death's Head, detail from *The Ambassadors*, by Hans Holbein the Younger, 1533. National Gallery, London. With permission.

his own words and seeks his pleasure in an object that only underscores his mortal subjection. Calisto displaces his desire by investing it in linguistic fetishes, reifying its presence while simultaneously exhibiting his inability to grasp and conquer the absolute, unseen signifier of his yearning. Calisto's rhetoric multiplies, extends itself, and becomes a supplement that supersedes all desire for Melibea. In Derridean terms, Calisto's libido sharply deviates toward words because 'pleasure itself, without symbol or suppletory, that which would accord us (to) pure presence itself, if such a thing were possible, would be only another name for death' (Derrida 1997, 155). Calisto's pleasure is a counterfeit: his absurd, dramatically physical, untranscendental death in act 19 after a heated night of passion remains inevitable. In the end, his brutal physical demise ('su cabeça está en tres partes' [320] [his head is split in three parts]) will stand as a striking example of the futility of seeking to guard against the sudden, final confrontation of Eros with Thanatos in a universal cycle of violent pursuit, death, annihilation, and blind human desire.

4 Yearning to Look: Desire and the Pleasure of the Gaze

'Lucerna corporis tui est oculus tuus.'

Matt. 6:22

'Omne quod est in mundo concupiscentia carnis est et concupiscentia oculorum et superbia vitae; quae non est ex Patre, sed ex mundo est.'

I Johan. 2:16

'La admiración concebida en los ojos desciende al ánimo por ellos.'

Sempronio, Act 5

'Werfen wir zunächst einen Blick ...'

S. Freud

Calisto's very first words in *Celestina*, 'En esto veo, Melibea, la grandeza de Dios' (24) [In this, Melibea, I see God's greatness], mark the critical importance played by both vision and the gaze in the development of the action and the characters in the work. From its starting point, the plot emerges from the possibilities and the frustrations of seeing. Using Calisto's invocation of sight as their point of departure, three studies have underscored the prominence of this faculty as a constitutive element of all the characters. Emilio Blanco (1993) has stressed the pervasiveness of metaphors dealing with sight and misapprehension in *Celestina*, emphasizing how the characters are aware of the deceptive nature of the things they perceive, and the need for careful discernment. In his book *Fernando de Rojas and the Renaissance Vision*, Ricardo Castells specifically locates *Celestina* within the current of late medieval and early modern medical lore and belief tied to the phenomenon of the malady of *amor hereos*, or the disease of love. Concretely, Castells associates Calisto's description to the dreamlike state produced by the disease and shows how the action in the work may be interpreted as the phantasmagorical dreams and visions of a melancholic lover. Another study, James F. Burke's *Vision, the Gaze, and the Function of the Senses in* Celestina, traces the presence of late medieval optical and visual theory in the plot; a theory that in many ways may be seen as a precursor of modern psychoanalytic object relations theory and its effect on the human subject (see Kernberg 1986). Emphasizing how sight belongs to an all-encompassing sensorial sphere that extends itself into the realm of the Evil Eye, Burke shows how vision is imagined as a reciprocal process between subjects and objects and comes to configure and determine both human motivation and conduct in the world of *Celestina*. Burke demonstrates how the medieval theory of sight becomes a sustaining intellectual pillar upon which to build an understanding of the characters. In both instances, Castells and Burke conclude that vision and the gaze are the key mechanisms through which the human subjects that are portrayed orient themselves and influence each other. Vision, Burke finds, was the medium that 'more than anything else, was understood as basic to the process of the constitution of the subject, [and] the self, as this entity was perceived in the medieval world' (33; see also Sanz Hermida 1994).

Notwithstanding the important insights offered by Blanco's, Burke's, and Castells's studies, however, there is yet another dimension of vision in *Celestina* that remains to be studied and that affects desire and the psychological and sexual representation of the characters in the work. I am referring to the prevalence of voyeurism in the text and the scenes where the will to see, and even to hear, furtively is represented as the mobilizing force of the characters' longings and desires. In *Celestina* everyone is driven by a need to see, a compulsion to grasp the objects of desire with the eyes, that is portrayed as an extension of the erotic imagination, a need to apprehend visually and thus possess what is caught by the field of vision. Seeing, hearing, but especially looking in *Celestina* are highly charged lubricious acts that stimulate desire, intensify the appetites, and compound passion. The gaze is configured as the conductor of desire and as the mainspring of sexual energy. *Celestina* is a work that fleshes out the erotic properties of the senses and the sensory imagination, above all in the acts of seeing, hearing, and observing without being observed.

In his *Three Essays on the Theory of Sexuality*, Freud (1953–74) argues for the primacy of an erotically invested visual relation to the world in all human subjects. What he calls scopophilia, or the libidinous pleasure of looking, is one of the 'component instincts' that make up human desire and sexuality from earliest childhood. The erotically invested instinct or drive to look is closely related to the instinct or drive for knowledge (*Weisstreib*) examined via Calisto in the last chapter. Epistemophilia, or *Weisstreib*, and the compulsion to look are both constructed on models of frustration because the desires to see and know always exceed the capacity of objects of sight or knowledge to satisfy them. The drive to possess, often troped as the desire to see, is closely linked to the drives to see and know and, like the latter, is destined never to attain its real object, often playing itself out in extended scenarios of voyeurism.

The portrayal of voyeurism in *Celestina* signals an important psychoanalytical aspect of the work and of the striking psychopathology of its characters. The contest between the psychological and the social – between the private and the public, the intimate and the communal – spheres of their actions in the development of the characters is a constant that is materialized in the continuous fluctuation between direct speech and asides, a perpetual shifting between what is said openly and thought privately, between direct looks and oblique glances that permit us to perceive the presence of dangerous thoughts that cannot be expressed in the ordinary flow of social interaction or conversation. This dialectic compels us to contemplate the continuous concealed presence of socially transgressive thoughts and impulses in the human conduct depicted in the work. What is clandestinely seen and thought in *Celestina* becomes integrated into the fabric of daily life and constitutes a determining factor of the social world in which the characters move.

The role of the eyes as mute accomplices of desire and of the mental incorporation of the Other almost reaches the limits of a pathological voyeurism, which may be defined as morbid gratification achieved through the contemplation of the unattainable, the achievement of pleasure – above all sexual pleasure – in the very act of seeing and gazing at a desired object with the full understanding of its inaccessibility. In this sense, voyeurism hinges upon the scopic impulses of desire – the will to look instigated by the radical separation, and even absence, of a desired object (on scopophilia as a human instinct in the visual world, see Freud, 'The Rat Man,' *SE* 10, 245). Commenting upon the scopophilic nature of the cinema, Christian Metz has sought to define specifically what is voyeuristic about it. He notes that 'The voyeur represents in space the fracture which forever separates him from the object; he represents his very dissatisfaction (which is precisely what he needs as a voyeur). If it is true of all desire that it depends on the infinite pursuit of its absent object, voyeuristic desire, along with certain forms of sadism, is the only desire whose principle of distance symbolically and spatially evokes this fundamental rent' (1975, 61). Voyeurism thus emphasizes the presence of a breach between the observing subject and the observed object where desire both resides and is configured. It is what permits the realization of desire. In this context desire is more than a simple impulse for contact or physical consummation: it is the need to see and recreate imaginatively what is observed as an object of pleasure. Sometimes, however, the will to see in order to gratify becomes reflexive, and in this case it is transformed into narcissism, a modality of voyeurism that consists in the pleasure derived from self-contemplation, or from the knowledge of being observed by another. Frederick Goldin (1967) has explored how not only the myth of Narcissus but also narcissism as an existential symptom are key elements in the constitution of the medieval courtly lover, and how they are part of an erotic dynamic in which the eyes and the gaze play a central role in inciting passion and animating sexual appetite.

In the third book of the *Metamorphoses* Ovid combines the images of visual and auditory reduplication and repetition as key elements of the plot in the tragic story of Echo and Narcissus. Narcissus's rebuff of the nymph is tragically inverted when Echo reiterates it, thus imperfectly rendering Narcissus's negation as an affirmation. Nemesis punishes the vanity of Narcissus with the curse of self-love, instilling reflexive desire in him and producing a fatal fascination with his own inaccessible image. The object of desire is thus situated beyond all possible reach as it is inscribed in a reflexive visual and auditory discourse, transforming the story of Narcissus into the allegory of a pernicious, impossible, egocentric desire and the key for understanding the nature of courtly love as a self-reflexive discursive modality. The entanglement of hearing, passion, and the gaze in the story of Narcissus leads to the realization of the impossibility of consummating self-love and to a frustration that ends inevitably in the self-destruction of the desiring subject.

From the very beginning of the first act of *Celestina*, Calisto visually recreates Melibea through language, imaginatively evoking her person in order to revel in the most intimate and forbidden parts of her anatomy. Everything that is hidden, untouchable, and concealed from his gaze incites Calisto's voluptuosity to recreate through words the obscured object of his desire. What can only be divined from Melibea's outer appearance becomes the visual focus of his inner desire:

Las manos pequeñas en mediana manera, de dulce carne acompañadas, los dedos luengos, las uñas en ellos largas y coloradas, que pareçen rubíes entre perlas. Aquella proporción que veer yo no pude, no sin dubda por el bulto de fuera juzgo incomparablemente ser mejor que la que París juzgó entre las tres diesas. (42)

[Her hands little, and in a measureable manner and fit proportion accompanied with her sweet flesh; her fingers long; her nails large and well coloured, seeming rubies intermixed with pearls. The proportion of those other parts which I could not eye, undoubtedly (judging things unseen by the seen) must of force be incomparably far better than that which Paris gave his judgment of, in the difference between the three goddesses.]

Calisto's passion is anchored in the consummation of his desire through thought and contemplation, in his imaginative pursuit of the unseen, and in seeking what remains out of sight, guarded, and forbidden. The fantasy of Melibea's body allows him to penetrate the most guarded recesses of her intimacy, to violate the enclosures of Pleberio's house with the eyes of his imagination and delight in the unseen parts of Melibea's anatomy while fully conscious of their distance and inaccessibility. To be sure, Melibea's evocation by Calisto achieves its erotic peak when he considers the possibility of beholding her naked body beneath the clothing she wears, to see through her clothes and revel in those anatomical parts that are most hidden from view (on the erotic implications of 'seeing' through clothing, see Hollander 1975).

Calisto's desire to see and know Melibea without being seen or discovered is expressed in extraordinary terms when he interrogates Celestina about Melibea's comportment during the bawd's first embassy to her. Hearing Celestina's relation of the events, Calisto, as we have seen in chapter 3, is overcome with ardour and exclaims, '¡O quién estuviera allí debaxo de tu manto, escuchando qué hablaría sola aquélla en quien Dios tan estremadas gracias puso!' (158) [O that I had lain hid underneath thy mantle, that I might have heard her but speak, on whom heaven hath so plentifully poured forth the fullness of his graces!]. The text thus repeatedly insists upon the need to recreate both visually and audibly the object of the subject's desire in his imagination, whose presence may even be conjured fetishistically by assigning erotic value through the gaze to inanimate objects that come to substitute the object of desire. Obsessed by Melibea's baffling conduct and her mystifying anatomy, Calisto in act 6, for example, transforms her cordon, 'que tales miembros fue digno de ceñir' (164) [that glorious girdle, which was held so worthy to engirt so goodly a body], into the physical object that re-presents the absent image of desire before his eyes. When Celestina places the cordon in his hands, he exclaims heatedly that by means of it 'gozarán mis ojos con todos los otros sentidos' (164) [my eyes together with the rest of my senses will enjoy so great a happiness]. As he continues caressing the girdle, he apostrophizes Melibea, invoking her presence through the object in his hands:

> ¡O nuevo huésped, o bienaventurado çordón, que tanto poder y mesescimiento toviste de ceñir aquel cuerpo que no soy digno de servir! ¡O nudos de mi passión, vosotros enlazastes mis desseos! ... ¡O mi gloria y ceñidero de aquella angélica creatura, yo te veo y no lo creo! O cordón, cordón ... Conjúrote me respondas por la virtud del gran poder que aquella señora sobre mí tiene ... ¿Qué secretos avrás visto de aquella excellente ymagen? ... O mis ojos, acordaos cómo fuistes causa por donde me fue mi coraçón llagado, y que aquél es visto hazer el daño que da la causa. (166)

> [O new guest! O happy girdle which hast had such power and worth in thee as to hedge in that body and be its enclosure, which myself am not worthy to serve. O ye knots of my passion, it is you that have entangled my desires ... O thou glory of my soul, and encircler of so incomparable a creature; I behold thee, and yet believe it not. O girdle, girdle, thou lovely lace! ... I conjure thee that thou answer me truly, by the virtue of that great power which thy lady hath over me ... O what secrets shouldst thou then have seen of that so excellent an image ... O my eyes call to your remembrance, how that ye were the cause of my ill, and the very door through which my heart was wounded.]

Calisto's very words indicate that his desire is rooted in sight and in the pleasure produced by seeing as it is played out through fetishistic objects like Melibea's sash, which he beholds and caresses in his hands as if it were a holy relic. At this point, Melibea's sash, like all fetishes, has become a metonymy of Calisto's desire; it stands as the object that makes present not only Melibea but specific parts of her uncovered body that the girdle fails to name but nevertheless suggests. The presence of her uncovered body is imagined by means of this material object normally used to fasten clothing to the body specifically because it is now not on Melibea's body holding up her clothing to conceal what lies beneath her clothes.

Indeed, Calisto's fetishism is underscored and the extremity of his desire for the absent Melibea is metonymized once again through items of her clothing. He tells Celestina that his desire is so great that he feels he can see Melibea vividly in dreams and in his mind's eye as if she were present, and that he would 'alegre me sería vestir su vestidura' (164) [be glad to see myself clothed with anything that is hers].

It remains clear, then, that the passion to see as well as to do is a fundamental motivator of the actions that Calisto performs, and that the need to contemplate the object of desire is intimately tied to its very absence and in the radical impossibility of obtaining what is coveted. Even inanimate objects may be redefined as they take on an erotic charge when subjected to the power of the gaze of the desiring subject. The imperative to see and to look achieves such intensity that it displaces desire onto the lifeless objects associated with the desired person. When Calisto's eyes fix on Melibea's sash, it is circumscribed by the circle of desire projected by his gaze to displace momentarily the presence of the desired object. And while Melibea's cordon literally stands in for her presence, it remains as a powerful material souvenir, a memory object, that only increases Calisto's desire for the absent Melibea. In this way, Calisto's actions confirm the theory advanced by Otto Kernberg (1986), who observes that voyeurism and promiscuity are manifested in narcissistic personalities by means of 'sexual excitement for a body that "withholds" itself or for a person considered attractive or valuable by other people' (187).

To be sure, Calisto's narcissistic personality is notably underscored when he insists on the pleasure of being seen and observed while making love. Vexed, Calisto resists and objects when Melibea, invoking modesty, asks Lucrecia to leave the scene where she and Calisto will make love: '¿Por qué, mi señora? Bien me huelgo que estén semejantes testigos de mi gloria' (314) [And why madame? I should be proud to have such witnesses as she of my glory]. Calisto's voyeurism and fetishism reveal themselves as they materialize in the form of an immoderate, transgressive auto-erotic arousal: the wish to become the observed object of the lubricious interests and desires of others. In the garden scene, where he first makes love to Melibea, his voyeuristic proclivities are transformed into an auto-erotic exhibitionism in which he derives pleasure at the thought of being watched by Lucrecia. It is clear that his heightened desire to see is at once also symptomatic of the need to be seen and be noticed. At this moment, we become aware that Melibea is merely a projection of what Calisto wants, a substitute for a constitutional lack that he feels. Rojas with striking acuity portrays Calisto's psychopathology, and places him squarely in the realm of narcissistic egoists.

Beyond narcissism itself, Calisto confuses the real with the imaginary and in his mind recreates past experiences of things both seen and heard as he fails to distinguish the boundaries between what he has lived or imagined. The result is the dreamlike state in which he lives and contemplates Melibea in his mind's eye and ear; the way he imagines the pervasive object of his desire. Driven by the aspiration to revisit Melibea after their initial night of love, time cannot pass quickly enough for Calisto. As a result, he invokes his imagination to repeat (literally re-present) audibly and visually the forbidden pleasures of his night with her in the garden:

> tú, dulce ymaginación, tú que puedes me acorre; trae a mi fantasía la pres-encia angélica de aquella ymagen luziente; buelve a mis oýdos el suave son de sus palabras, aquellos desvíos sin gana, aquel 'apártate allá, señor, no ll-egues a mí', aquel 'no seas descortés' que con sus rubicundos labros vía asonar. (324)

> [thou, my sweet imagination, thou who canst only help me in this case, bring unto my fantasy the unparalleled presence of that glorious image. Cause thou to come unto my ears that sweet music of her words, those her unwilling hangings off without profit, that her pretty, 'I prithee leave off; forbear, good sir, if you love me; touch me not; do not deals so discourte-ously with me.' Out of whose ruddy lips, methinks, I hear these words still sound.]

What has been experienced and what is desired thus take on a 'real' pres-ence in Calisto's imagination. Fantasy and reality cannot be differenti-ated, and their lack of distinction produces an instance of what Freud has termed *perceptual identity*, or the subject's imaginative visualization of ob-jects and events linked to the satisfaction of a drive or need (1965, 605).

Voyeurism in *Celestina* is not, however, limited to Calisto. The most in-significant characters in the work are portrayed as voyeurs subject to wants constituted through the interaction of sight and the imagination, driven to desire by what they contemplate. Sosia and Tristán, Calisto's two young lackeys, for example, are portrayed as voyeurs who revel in furtive observation and who spy and comment upon the unobtainable objects of their longings. The voyeurism of the two young servants mate-rializes as, unobserved, they watch Elicia from an elevated window in Calisto's house. The encounter materializes in a dialogue centring on the prostitute's seductive melancholy as she, dressed in mourning to mark Sempronio's death, passes through the street to visit Areúsa after both their lovers' execution. Upon inviting Tristán to set his gaze from afar upon the new 'widow' [la viuda] of Semprino, Sosia sets his own eyes upon her widow's weeds and invokes the suffering Elicia experiences in order to compare it to the lack of pain Calisto feels for his departed servants. Commenting upon his master's insensitivity to the death of his retainers, he says:

> ¿Piénsaste tú que le penan a él mucho los muertos? Si no penasse más a aquella que desde esta ventana yo veo yr por la calle, no llevaría las tocas de tal color ... Llégate acá y verla has antes que trasponga; mira aquella lutosa que se limpia agora las lágrimas de los ojos; aquélla es Elicia, criada de Celestina y amiga de Sempronio, una muy bonita moça, aunque queda agora perdida la peccadora porque tenía a Celestina por madre y a Sempronio por el principal de sus amigos. Y aquella casa donde entra, allí mora una hermosa mujer muy graciosa y fresca, enamorada medio ramera, pero no se tiene por poco dichoso quien la alcança a tener por amiga sin grande escote, y llámase Areúsa. Por qual sé yo que ovo el triste Pármeno más de tres noches malas, y aun que no le plaze a ella con su muerte. (324–6)

> [Dost thou think that he takes any great grief and care for those that are dead? If she did not grieve more, whom I see here out of the window go along the street, she would not wear a veil of that colour as she does ... Come hither and see her, before she be passed. Seest thou that mournful maid, which wipes the tears from her eyes? That is Elicia, Celestina's servant and Sempronio's friend: she is a good, pretty handsome, well-favoured wench, thou now poor soul she be left to the wide world and forsaken of all. For she accounted Celestina her mother, and Sempronio her chiefest and best friend. And in that house, where you see her now enter, there dwells a very fair woman, she is exceeding well-favoured, very fresh and lovely: she is half courtesan; yet happy is he, and counts himself so to be, that can purchase her favour at an easy rate, and win her to be his friend. Her name is Areúsa, for whose sake, I know, that unfortunate and poor Pármeno endured more than three sleepless nights. And I know that she, poor soul, is nothing pleased with his death.]

Yet in addition to pity, Sosia's words on seeing Elicia dressed in mourning also mark a strong sexual attraction. The young servant confesses to being moved by the seductive beauty of the youthful and now lonely prostitute, as well as feeling a strong pull from Areúsa's own voluptuous endowments, whom he evokes hidden just behind the entry door of her house waiting for Elicia's arrival. With a covetous note of envy, Sosia goes on to evoke the 'más de tres noches malas' (326) [more than three sleepless nights] Pármeno had enjoyed with the comely Areúsa. The events of act 14 justify and provide the antecedents for Elicia's and Areúsa's revenge for the death of their lovers, all of which leads to Centurio's intervention and to Calisto's fall. Beyond this, however, Sosia's and Tristán's furtive observation of the two women takes on a lubricious, voyeuristic caste that evokes two well-known, traditional motifs of medieval misogyny upon which the scene in question rests: the strong sexual attraction exercised by the veiled female form, and the proverbial lascivious sexuality of widows (see Vasvári 1992, Jardine 1983, and Weissberger 1996, 209–10).

In traditional folk culture, feminine attributes hidden under a veil, but especially under a veil of mourning, are associated with mystery, eroticism, and forbidden pleasures. The concealing veil or covering garment is, as Malek Allouha points out in his study of the erotics of representation in the seraglio (1986), nothing but a titillating extension of hidden female sexuality. Certain forms of feminine apparel thus emphasize contrast and set in motion a dialectic between a garment and the body it conceals, between what is seen and what is present but remains just out of sight, between desire and its disguise, in order to produce a frisson of pleasure and attraction in the observer, as is the very case in Calisto's description of Melibea.

Anne Hollander (1975), Mario Perniola (1989), and Valerie Steele (1996) have all studied the link between the representation of the covered female figure and voyeuristic sensuality, identifying the phenomenon as a form of fetishism and the expression of socially proscribed longings through their sublimation in material objects. In Elicia's case, however, the sensuality of her portrayal as a covered woman is doubly intensified by Sosia's revelation that she wears widows weeds ('tocas de luto') in recognition of her grief for the departed Sempronio. Her characterization as a widow who stops to wipe away her tears of pain entwine Sosia and Tristán in a scene of sympathy coloured by morbid sensuality and produce a type of voluptuous, imaginative voyeurism. For them, Areúsa's secretly observed widows weeds, just as they conceal the ripe charms of the experienced feminine body behind them, also signal her emotional vulnerability and sexual availability. Made more enticing and desirable by her supposed widowhood and her concealed beauty, Elicia's description evokes the lusty reputation of widows as described in many early modern erotic festive lyrics filled with double entendres, like those collected by Pierre Alzieu, Yvan Lissorgues, and Robert Jammes (1975) in their anthology of risqué Golden Age Spanish poetry:

Viudas de gallardo brío,
si a compasión os movéis,
por vuestra vida me déis,
en que envuelva un niño mío,
que se muere de frío
y a ratos se me desmaya.
Metedle bajo la saya,
si queréis que calor cobre.
¿Si hay quien dé limosna a un pobre,
que, si no lo masca, no lo come?   (Alzieu, Lissorgues, and Jammes 184)

[Widows of buoyant spirits,
if you are moved to compassion,
by your life give me,
a place to enwrap a child of mine,
who is dying of the cold
and sometimes faints from weakness.

Place him under your skirt,
if you wish him to warm up.
Can someone give alms to a poor one?
if you don't chew on it, you'll not swallow it.]

Areúsa's mourning clothes and her evocation as Pármeno's widow thus lend a festishistic frisson to her portrayal and underscore the secret delight of her observers, who scrutinize, imagine, and interpret her in a manner that only emphasizes her beauty and desirability. Rather than focus on Elicia's suffering and pain for the loss she has endured, Rojas makes Sosia's and Tristan's gaze slide into the expression of the desire to possess the lonely prostitute and their reverie in the fantasy of possibly becoming Sempronio's and Pármeno's successors for each of the unhappy whores.

Far from passive subjects in the work, Sosia and Tristán, though minor personages indeed, actively take part vicariously in the sexual adventures of the other characters that surround them. Imaginatively delighting in the sensual pleasures of all the lovers in *Celestina*, their desire is aroused not just by voluptuous sights but by suggestive sounds, like the ones that emanate from Melibea's garden in the shadows of the night. Standing guard for their master Calisto in the dark street, deprived of their ability to see, the two young servants revel in the sounds made by the lovers on the other side of the wall of Melibea's garden. Aroused by the agitated murmurings and muffled groans of Calisto and Melibea's encounter, they impulsively confess their disquietude and heightened emotional state provoked by the couple's anxious fumblings: 'Tristán,'Sosia exclaims, 'bien oyes lo que passa; ¡en qué términos anda el negocio! [Tristan, you hear what passees and how the gear goes!]. To which his callow interlocutor energetically responds: 'Oygo tanto que juzgo a mi amo por el más bienaventurado hombre que nasció; y por mi vida, que aunque soy mochacho, que diesse tan buena cuenta como mi amo' [I hear so much that I hold my master the happiest man that lives. And I assure thee, though I am but a boy to speak of, methinks I could give as good account of such a business as my master]. An affirmation that Sosia enthusiastically endorses with praise for Melibea's seductiveness: 'Para con tal joya quienquiera se ternía manos' (316) [To such a jewel as this, who would not reach out his hands?]. Finally, upon hearing Melibea's pleas for Calisto to be gentle with her, Sosia falls imaginatively headlong into the situation and, as if addressing Melibea, vehemently murmurs under his breath that 'Ante quisiera yo oýrte essos milagros; todas sabés essa oración después que no puede dexar de ser hecho,; ¡y el bovo de Calisto que se lo escucha' (316) [Would that I could hear those miracles; you all know that song, but it cannot be undone, there is no fence for it. But the fool Calisto who listens to it] to express his fantasy of providing a better accounting of Melibea's virginity than his master could possibly offer. Perhaps the two most inconsequential speaking figures in *Celestina*, both Sosia and Trsitán are nevertheless portrayed as furtive sexually active characters who quicken the pulse of their desire through the pleasure they derive from their nosey curiosity, their seeing and hearing the partially hidden sights and muffled noises of the sexual lives and escapades of others.

Erwin Panofsky (1969), one of the most astute historians and critics of early modern culture, has emphasized how even in early modern painting the depiction of the complementarity of sight and sound go hand in hand with the portrayal of desire. In his masterful study of Titian's iconography, he notes that the juxtaposition of seeing and hearing is used to enhance sensuality in a number of the Italian artist's paintings. In Titian's well-known *Venus Enjoying Love and Music*, now in the Prado Museum (Number 420 of the collection), for example, the conjunction of the two faculties of sight and hearing are graphically displayed so as to complement the sensuality the picture is meant to convey, as well as to depict the presence of masculine desire for the female body. In the

Figure 4.1 Venus Enjoying Love and Music, by Titian, ca 1550. Museo del Prado, Madrid. With permission.

painting, a reclining Venus is seen from the front, distracted by Cupid, as a musician on the left plays an organ and simultaneously turns his head back toward her, craning his neck in order to gaze rapt at the goddess, absorbed by the beauty of her naked form.

Panofsky comments that, beyond the figure of Venus herself, the real protagonist of the painting is in fact the musician, whose nimble fingers blindly fleet across the keyboard while his envious eyes remain fixed upon the goddess' *os pubis.* The inclusion of the leering onlooker in the scene is calculated to evoke the energizing role played by sound in tandem with sight in the mobilization and increase of masculine desire. The scene thus captures the early modern preoccupation with the conjunction of, and competition between, the senses. Panofsky concludes that Titian's painting of Venus and the musician is nothing less than a pictorial 'subject calculated to stimulate the carnal passions' (1969, 121). Seeing and hearing are in this way considered indispensable elements in the body of ideas that make up Renaissance erotica, and point toward a theory of desire whose foundation rests firmly upon the audiovisual faculties.

Modern psychoanalytical theory maintains that voyeurism in both its visual and aural manifestations is a phenomenon circumscribed principally to the realm of masculine desire since the great majority of clinical instances of it are found mostly in men (*Encyclopedia of Psychology*, vol. 3, 312). In an analogous way, art history locates visual perspective and its aesthetic configuration in a setting and field of vision that privileges the male gaze, identifying it always with the exercise of power in the conventions that govern representation in western art. In his *Ways of Seeing,* John Berger summarizes the notion of the male gaze and its dynamics when he explores the portrayal of nudes in painting. In the synergies that go into nude representation, Berger observes,

> *men act* and *women appear.* Men look at women. Women watch themselves being looked at. This determines not only most relations between men and women but also the relation of women to themselves. The surveyor of woman in herself is male: the surveyed female ... In the average European oil painting of the nude the principal protagonist is never painted. He is the spectator in front of the picture and he is presumed to be a man. (1972, 47, 54)

Consequently, Calisto's, Sosia's, and Tristán's voyeurism should not be a surprise. They are masculine subjects that constitute the object of their desire through the power of their eyes, their male gaze expressive of their longing for a woman. Their constitution as characters thus fits the expected manner in which they see women and the latter's traditional correlation to gender. What does surprise, however, are the number of repeated instances in which Rojas explicitly inscribes and mobilizes desire in these personages by means of sight and the need to see and hear. The representation of Calisto, Sosia, and Tristán as furtive observers and the mediation of their desire through the auditory and visual faculties underscore the intense sensuality of their passions and the almost morbid pleasure each derives from contemplating what they want. In Calisto's portrayal the highly eroticized, almost salacious nature of the masculine gaze becomes explicit, as when he invokes what he imagines to be present under Melibea's clothing in his description of her ('Aquella proporción que veer yo no pude, no sin dubda por el bulto de fuera juzgo incomparablemente ser mejor que la que París juzgó entre las tres diesas' (42) [The proportion of those other parts which I could not eye, undoubtedly (judging things unseen by the seen) must of force be incomparably far better than that which Paris gave his judgment of, in the difference between three goddesses]).

In addition to the studies by Berger (1972) and Panofsky (1969), numerous other critical investigations into the construction of perspective in the visual arts have emphasized the pervasiveness of the voyeuristic gaze and how, indeed, it reigns in composition as the dominant way of regarding objects in painting, literature, and other forms of mimetic representation. Painting, literature, photography, and cinema all constitute themselves around what are called phallocentric perspectives, or male-oriented gazes that tend both to propagate and reinforce a patriarchal depiction of human social relations and the nature of the economies of power in them (see Spearing 1993, Bal 1991, Weissberger 1996, Mulvey 1989, and Kuhn 1982). In the arts from antiquity into modern times, the depiction and observation of the female as the object of desire of the masculine gaze remains at the centre of the Western imaginary. The medieval rhetorician Matthew of Vendôme, for example, notes that in the praise and depiction of a woman 'one should stress heavily her physical beauty,' and immediately adds that 'this is not the proper way to praise a man' (1980, 46), reflecting his belief in the premise that in the representation of people it is men who look at women. Indeed, the male gaze is firmly ensconced and fully sublimated in the symbolic unconscious of the West and has in large part determined the conventions of the representation of human forms in narrative and visual culture.

Yet in *Celestina* there is a striking instance in which the conventions of masculine perspective are transposed and inverted, overtly locating sexual desire in a feminine gaze that mediates an intense homoerotic attraction of one woman for another. This is the case when Celestina, seeking to convince Areúsa to sleep with Pármeno, visits her former protégée in her lodgings and encounters Areúsa at the moment she is undressing to retire to her bed for the night. The scene constitutes one of the most salacious moments in Rojas's work – a calculated depiction of hedonic delectation – that, as Dorothy Severin notes in her edition with unwarranted vacillation, 'revela, quizá inadvertidamente, un interés lesbiano por parte de la vieja' (1989, 202n.25) [reveals, perhaps inadvertently, a lesbian interest on the old woman's part]. To be sure, the scene portrays more than a passive, inadvertent incursion into sapphism. From its very outset it is charged with a voluptuous homoeroticism that, when closely examined, can only be interpreted as detailed and deliberate. In responding to Areúsa's query,'¿Quién anda aý?' [Who's there?], Celestina identifies herself as 'una antigua enamorada tuya, aunque vieja' [a lover of thine from past times, though now I am old], alluding to something greater than a vague, unintended trace of prior sexual intimacy between mistress and pupil. The old procuress's suggestive response to Areúsa unfolds in a highly charged erotic atmosphere that highlights Celestina's androgyny, as noted by Burke (1998, 45–6) and others, and subsequently materializes in the lewd, eye-beaming looks and comments that Celestina directs at the alluring, youthful courtesan.[1] At the instant Celestina descries the naked Areúsa seated on the edge of her bed, the old bawd admits to the strong, seductive sexual pull of what she contemplates, comparing Areúsa to a siren (201), the ancient symbol of the temptations of dangerous and forbidden pleasures. But there is more to Celestina's simile than tragic foreshadowing or the invocation of taboo: Areúsa's comparison to a siren, the ancient feminine mythical being that joins the lower half of a beast to the upper body of a woman, symbolizes the presence of the lower, animal instincts in Celestina's vivid mental image of her. From this point forward, the episode develops along strictly corporal and sensorial lines, in a deliberately titillating synaesthetic manner that, in addition to the visual, portrays the encounter through the olfactory, tactile, and gustatory faculties.

Areúsa's sliding into bed provokes a lubricious response from Celestina, as the latter contemplates the young prostitute's naked body and perceives the aromas that flow forth from the bedclothes that surround her. The sensual vapours emanating from Areúsa's movements in the sheets, saturated with the fragrances of her recent amorous adventures between them, provokes a lustful exclamation from the old go-between:

> ¡Ay cómo huele toda la ropa en bulléndote! ¡Aosadas, que estará todo a punto; siempre me pagué de tus cosas y hechos, de tu limpieza y atavío; fresca que estás! ¡Bendígate Dios, qué savanas y colcha, qué almohadas y qué blancura! ... Verás si te quiere bien quien te visita a tales horas; déxame mirarte toda a mi voluntad, que me huelgo. (190)

> [O how sweetly everything smells about thee, when thou heavest and turn-est thyself in thy bed! Well have I always been pleased with all thy things and doings! You will not think, how this neatness, this handsomeness of yours doth delight me. O how fresh dost thou look! What sheets! What quilts be here! What pillows! O how white they be! ... See whether I love you or no, that I come to visit you at this time of night! Let my eye take its fill in beholding thee; it does me much good to touch thee, and to look upon thee.]

From Areúsa's immediate reaction to Celestina's ejaculation, we know, too, that the crone's provocative words are accompanied by even bolder deeds, as Celestina attempts to trace manually what she visually admires with the tips of her fingers, which now run below the covers that wrap the seductive Areúsa. The compelling audacity of Celestina's desire for Areúsa is underscored through her choice of words, all anchored not just in the visual but in the tactile and olfactory senses. Feigning annoyance, Celestina's words and deeds produce a sense of unaccented displeasure in Areúsa: 'Paso, madre, no llegues a mí, que me hazes coxquillas y provócasme a reýr, y la risa acresciéntame el dolor ... Que no soy tan viciosa como piensas' (190) [Careful, mother, don't touch me, you are tickling me and make me laugh, and laughter doth but increase my pain ... I am not so much given to vice as thou thinks] (on the transgressive connotations of laughter in *Celestina*, see chapter 5). In spite of Areúsa's tepid rebuff, Celestina forges ahead with lascivious determination, libidinously groping Areúsa's abdomen and lower parts under the pretext of relieving the young prostitute's discomfort from wandering womb ('mal de madre'). During her dissembled diagnostic probing, Celestina utters the following suggestive words:

¡Bendígate Dios y el señor Sant Miguel Angel, y qué gorda y fresca que estás; qué pechos y qué gentileza! Por hermosa te tenía hasta agora, viendo lo que todos podían ver. Pero agora te digo que no ay en la cibdad tres cuerpos tales como el tuyo en cuanto yo conozco; no paresce que ayas quinze años. ¡O quién fuera hombre y tanta parte alcançara de ti para gozar tal vista! Por Dios, pecado ganas en no dar parte destas gracias a todos los que bien te quieren. Que no te las dio Dios para que pasassen en balde por la frescor de tu juventud debaxo de seys dobles de paño y lienço. (192)

[God help thee and Saint Michael the Archangel! O how plump and fair is thy flesh! What clear skin! How fresh to look too. What a breast is here! What sweet swelling paps! What beauty! What fine feature in every part! I did evermore hold thee fair and beautiful, seeing but that which all men might see, but now I must needs tell thee that there are not in all this city three such sweet bodies as thine. Why, here is flesh that no man living can judge to be much more than 15 years of age! O that I were a man and might gain so great a part of thee as this to glad my sight. Now by God, daughter, you are to blame, and I tell you it is a sin in you, that it is, not to impart these good graces and blessings which God hath bestowed upon you, to as many as wish you well; for God did not give them you in vain that you should let them wither, and lose the flower of your youth under six linings of woollen and linen.]

Aroused by what she sees, touches, and smells, invoking Areúsa's physical charms, Celestina attempts to stimulate sexually the comely courtesan, just as she chastises Areúsa and counsels her against the foolishness of masturbation, reminding her that 'tú no puedes de ti propia gozar' (192) [Since thou canst not take any pleasure in thyself]. As a result of Celestina's literal manipulation of Areúsa, Celestina convinces her to receive Pármeno, and invites him to make love to her former pupil as she looks on from the shadows in the corner of Areúsa's bedroom; but not before grasping the young servant and visually inspecting his own physical endowments, as she shamelessly pulls Pármeno toward her and provokes him with the following words: 'Llégate acá, negligente, vergonçoso, que quiero ver para quánto eres antes que me vaya. Retócala en esta cama' (198) [Come hither, Modesty. Come hither you bashful fool, for I will see before I go what metal you be made of. Come play the wag a little with her, and tickle her as she lies in bed]. This happens just as Celestina has met Areúsa's expression of second thoughts with an emphatic censure: '¿Qué es esto, Areúsa? ¿Qué son estas estrañezas y esquividad, estas novedades y retraymientos? Parece, hija, que no sé yo qué cosa es esto, que nunca vi estar un hombre con una mujer juntos, y que jamás passé por ello ni gozé de lo que gozas, y que no sé lo que passan y lo que dizen y hazen' (200) [Why, how now, Areúsa, what's the matter with you? Whence comes this strangeness? Whence this coyness of yours? This niceness? Why, daughter, do you think that I know not what this means? Did I never see a man and a woman together before? And that I know not all the tricks and devices? What they say, and what they do?]. When Celestina finally abandons Pármeno and Areúsa in the midst of their ardent coupling, she confesses the need to leave not as an act of modesty but one compelled by the intense frustration she feels from the conflict of her desire to participate in the action and her inability to do so because of the ravages of old age. 'Quedaos a Dios,' she says with resignation, 'voyme solo porque me hazes dentera con vuestro besar y retoçar, que aún el sabor en las enzías me quedó; no le perdí con las muelas' (200–2) [And so good-night, for I will be gone. I will get me away by myself. You do but set my teeth on edge with your kissing, your smacking, your tickling; for I have some inward feeling still in my gums, the taste sticks in my mouth still, as old as I am, I have not lost that touch together with my teeth].

Sight, touch, taste, and smell all criss cross and intermingle with androgyny, homoeroticism, and onanism throughout this scene of female voyeurism to set off an encounter charged with sexual tension that is inscribed in the margins of a series of doubly proscribed social and linguistic taboos. Although Celestina's brazen words and salacious deeds are performed by a female, they portray a sexuality not limited by the boundaries of male-female desire. While they emphasize the arousal of the old bawd's yearning for another woman, her clear association with masculinity places the old voyeuse in a phallocentric position of enunciation. Celestina's perspective is thus both masculine and feminine. In this way, her simultaneous articulation of both male and female inclinations, like a latter-day Tiresias, transform her into the epitome of desire.

Yet, despite all this, aware of the transgressive nature of her urge, Celestina suddenly desists in her groping of Areúsa and refrains from her prurient impulse to possess her – and all that she sees, touches, and smells of her – with a revealing exclamation that propels Celestina's desire toward surrender and the realm of resignation: '¡O quién fuera hombre ...!' (192) [O that I were a man], she exclaims, conceding that she is not without a profound sense of abnegation. Through sight, sound, and smell, Celestina embodies a protean sexuality that repudiates repression and all the social boundaries that circumscribe gender and desire.

Beyond the portrayal of Celestina's homoeroticism, Rojas continues to subvert the traditional medieval phallocentric depiction of the discourse of desire, above all desire as it materializes in courtly love. A less surprising but no less disruptive form of feminine desire couched as voyeurism and vicarious delectation intrudes on the scene in Melibea's garden through the figure of Lucrecia, Melibea's maid who accompanies her mistress during the latter's trysts with Calisto. Portrayed as an ardent spectator of, and wistful participant in, Calisto and Melibea's sexual congress, Lucrecia embodies an anxious, aggressive feminine sexuality that borders on an almost uncontainable lust capable of violating every limit set by decorum and propriety. Stirred by what she witnesses in the enclosed garden, a place meant to evoke the *hortus conclusus* and *locus amoenus* of the courtly tradition, Lucrecia is vicariously moved by Calisto and Melibea's sexual encounters, and will vehemently manifest the urge to realize her own desire for Calisto. Moved by undisguised instinct, despite Melibea's pleas for decorum, Lucrecia's erotic impulses ultimately reach a crescendo, quickened by what she hears and sees during Calisto and Melibea's night of love.

The increase of Lucrecia's desire, enkindled by her sense of sight and sound, is first elicited in the suggestive words of the song she sings in the darkness to Melibea as they await Calisto's arrival for the couple's second tryst. Infused with courtly imagery and double entendres, the erotic connotations of the images of the song (see Lecertua 1978) inflame the imaginations of both maidservant and mistress to the point where Melibea, overwhelmed with yearning, interrupts the singing to assert that 'Quanto dizes, amiga Lucrecia, se me representa delante; todo me parece que lo veo con mis ojos' (374) [Friend Lucrecia, methinks I see that which thou sayest , represented most lively unto me; methinks I see it as perfectly with these mine eyes, as if it were before me]. Yet it is Lucrecia who, overcome by her own passionate words and the sights and sounds around her, abandons all self-restraint and is vanquished by desire.

Calisto appears on the scene at the very moment Lucrecia finishes her song, and, overtaken by the sight of him, she impulsively throws herself upon Melibea's lover, torridly kissing him and embracing him. To be sure, Lucrecia's actions make María Eugenia Lacarra's (1990) comments about her and the other underlings in *Celestina* appear like an understatement: 'si los criados desean a Melibea, no menos desea Lucrecia a Calisto' (73) [if the servants desire Melibea, Lucrecia desires Calisto no less]. Moved to anger by Lucrecia's provocative gestures, and protesting her maidservant's boldfaced impudence, the sight of Lucrecia astride Calisto incites Melibea and moves her to express disbelief, questioning the forces that move her servant: 'Lucrecia, ¿qué sientes, amiga? ¿Tórnaste loca de plazer? Déxamele, no me le despedaces, no le trabajes sus miembros con tus pesados abraços; déxame gozar lo que es mío; no me ocupes mi plazer' (376) [Lucrecia? Why, how now, friend. What are you doing? Art thou turn'd mad with pleasure? Let me alone with my love; touch him not, I charge you; do not pluck and hale him from me; do not burden his body with your heavy arms. Let me enjoy what is mine, you shall not possesss any part of my pleasure].

Lucrecia, however, represents far more than the ravages of overwhelming desire. She is, in fact, the character in *Celestina* who is most consistently moved by voyeuristic urges to see and not be seen as she contemplates what is forbidden. A veritable snoop and eavesdropper, she is always furtive and compelled by the need to be privy to everything around her, to hear, to watch, to know, and not be seen. Even in situations not involving sex directly, Lucrecia can be found lurking in the corners, prying and spying and making everything her business. In act 16, for example, she listens in on Alisa's and Pleberio's conversation in which they discuss an eventual marriage for Melibea, just to be surprised by the latter ('¿Qué haces ahí, loca?' (289) [What are you doing here, mad woman?]) as the servant mutters to herself the news of Celestina's death and remarks upon the fateful timing of Melibea's parents' conversation.

However, Lucrecia's desire to see and hear what is proscribed is most intensely mobilized by the desire for carnal knowledge.[2] Although in act 14 she responds negatively to Melibea's question, '¿Asnos oýdo?' (318) [Didst thou not hear us?], and denies having been hidden in the shadows of the garden hearing and watching Calisto and Melibea making love the night of their first rendezvous ('No, señora, que durmiendo he estado' (318) [No, madame, I was fast asleep]), by act 19, stirred by what she sees and hears, she throws shame and caution to the wind, and transforms self-restraint and the need for decorum into sexual licence. While Calisto manhandles Melibea with salacious energy and fumbles to remove her clothing ('Señora, el que quiere comer el ave, quita primero las plumas' (378) [Madame, he that will eat the bird must first pluck the feathers]), Lucrecia, the unnoticed witness skulking in the darkness,

becomes infected by the lover's ardour and, in a an expression of comi-
cal self-pity, acknowledges her own frustration and passion to herself:

Mala landre me mate si más lo escucho; ¿vida es ésta? Que me esté yo des-
haziendo de dentera y ella esquivándose por que la ruegen. Ya, ya, apazi-
guado es el ruydo; no ovieron menester despartidores; pero también me lo
haría yo si estos necios de sus criados me fablassen entre día. (378)

[The devil take me if I hearken to them any longer. Here's a life indeed! O
how I feel myself melt within, like snow against the sun; and how squeamish
my mistress seems, because forsooth she would fain be entreated! So, so!
Now the quarrell is ended, they have need of nobody to come and part
them. I would also have taken part with them myself, if the fools his men
would have asked not the question.]

Finally, on the verge of collapse from her vicarious sexual arousal provoked by what she hears and glimpses in the dark, Lucrecia sighs envi-
ously as she keeps count of Calisto and Melibea's successive couplings:
'Ya me duele a mí la cabeza descuchar y no a ellos de hablar ni los braços
de retoçar ni las bocas de besar' [My head aches with hearing; and yet
their tongues ache not with talking, nor their arms with coiling, nor
their lips with kissing] she says, followed by 'Andar, ya callan; a tres me
parece que va la vencida' (378) [Why this battle was ended with three
blows]. Resistant to hearing the news of Calisto's headlong fall to his
death, Lucrecia remains so sexually excited by what she witnessed earlier
that she fails to listen to Tristán, who comes to tell of Calisto's demise.
Rather, she seizes upon the adolescent and, oblivious to his words, whispers lustfully, 'Tristán, ¿qué dizes, mi amor' (382) [Tristan, what's the
matter my love?].

In conclusion, the energies of pleasure and desire are closely linked to
hearing and seeing in *Celestina*, but most especially to seeing and hearing
what is not meant to be seen and heard. Throughout the work, the eyes
and ears of the characters capture all manner of forbidden words and
deeds, which, because they are so, become the compelling forces that
kindle libidinal energies and the economy of want. In *Celestina*, voyeurism is repeatedly linked to the subversion of traditional representations
of love. In a general sense, this subversion consists of a displacement of
sentimentality, virtue, and propriety, in favour of sexual desire and, as in
the case of Calisto, a drive for self-affirmation. The act of observation in
itself serves to dismantle all pretence and reveal the deeper, animal

desire for sexual contact that characterizes human relations in the work. In his careful portrayal of the stirring effects of looks and sounds in *Celestina*, Fernando de Rojas traced an anatomy of passion in which he placed audiovisual perception at the centre of the domain of all desire. Audiovisual discernment heightens desire and drives the forces of the lower appetites in *Celestina*, and it allows us to contemplate directly those things that could only be suggested or allusively invoked in the earlier courtly tradition. The imperative to see – indeed, the demands of all the senses – in all the characters of *Celestina* not only contributes to the representation of their ardent innermost imaginations, capable of crossing the frontiers of heteronormative sexuality as in the case of Celestina's advances toward Areúsa, but also permits the reader to examine these characters intimately and come to understand the nature of the objects and the forces of the desires that move them. Taken together, the figurations of voyeurism examined here establish a widespread pattern in the portrayal of vicarious pleasure throughout the work, where characters are led to desire by observing the desire of others. The nature of the gaze in *Celestina* thus especially exceeds its medieval theoretical formulations (see Burke 1998) to coincide with the nature of desire itself as outlined in its modern formulations, always allusive, always vicarious, never capable of grasping its object. It seeks perpetually and impossibly to fill in, absorb, or recover something that remains inaccessible or lost. Desire as portrayed by Rojas constitutes a metaphor for difference, or the fundamental lack in being that marks the nature of all human aspiration. A phenomenon observable in both male and female, its persistent presence in *Celestina* offers an imitation of the rhetorical form of the discourse of the unconscious. The desire it expresses is always deferred and fetishized, and cannot be directly named or diegetically presented: it can only be generated by a hidden discourse, which like the discourse of the unconscious, Freudian slips, or bungled intentions disturbs and rearranges the logic of speech and the action of daily life.

The presence of the body of the Other as captured by sight and sound, touch and smell, in *Celestina* inevitably points to the ubiquitous desire for the Other in the work. The senses all point to an erotic investment in an urge for knowledge about the Other that has traditionally been portrayed as masculine. As we have seen, however, *Celestina* dislocates the masculine gaze and shows the immanence of the kinds of desire usually associated with it beyond the anticipated limitations imposed by gender. Rojas installs an epistemology of observation and a drive to see and know in both the men and the women who vie with each other for knowledge, conquest, and domination. The overwhelming desire to perceive and to know is a constitutional component that moves all the subjects that sprang from his pen. Yet, in the end, as we follow their lives and come to *Celestina*'s conclusion, we see that they were all destined to fail in their quest to reach full knowledge, full possession. From the beginning to the end of the *Tragicomedia* they are all obliged to be satisfied with only fleeting, oblique moments of perception in the hunt for the ends of their desire, but that satisfaction remains elusive.

In *Celestina*, Rojas portrays sense perception as the fundamental motors of pleasure and seduction in the human beings that leaped from his imagination. The human gaze is the sign, source, and vehicle of pleasure and desire in all of them, regardless of their gender. With this, he shows his characters to be sensitive psychological, social, and carnal beings who are moved radically to want by the slightest scopic, auditory, tactile, or olfactory sign. To contemplate others or be contemplated by them, to hear others or be heard, to perceive them in every way and be perceived, acquire a crucial importance in the constitution of the complex world in which the characters of *Celestina* live. In the human drama of the work, the spur of passion that strikes the voluptuary imagination is driven by the eyes, the ears, the tips of the fingers, and the nose. Seeing, hearing, and sensing others marks always the first step toward action and, in the world of *Celestina*, the first step toward the urge to dominate and conquer. Attempts at seeing and hearing are nothing less than gestures toward knowing directly, which implies the desire to master and to possess. Sensorial perception in *Celestina* in this way constitutes a touchstone for understanding the formulation and representation of human desire at the threshold of modernity.[3]

5 Complicitous Laughter:
The Sounds of Desire

Celestina, as Dorothy Severin (1978–9; 1989, 63–80), Louise Fothergill-Payne (1993), and María Eugenia Lacarra (1990) have shown, is a work fully capable of making us laugh. Yet it is also one of the few works, indeed perhaps the first work, of early Spanish literature where the sounds of laughter, plus the act of laughing, are audibly, visibly, and prominently recorded in the text. At certain critical moments, laughter in *Celestina* is far from trifling. Indeed, it becomes a meaningful act of signification, a referent of discourse and concealed desire, which performs both a decisive communicative task and a crucial artistic function in the characterization of the personages in the work. Subtly, laughter is almost imperceptively sown throughout *Celestina.* However, upon careful scrutiny, it is clear that it is central to a fuller perception of the elaborate contradictions, emotional subterfuges, connivance, and plots that lie submerged beneath the language of the work. The modes of laughter recorded in *Celestina* are thus essential to its sense as they resound in uncommon variety and capture feelings ranging from the jocular to the scornful, to the conspiratorial and the compulsive.[1]

Laughter is first inscribed in *Celestina* in Sempronio's asides, in which he derisively comments upon the blasphemous nature of Calisto's passion for Melibea and defines the latter as nothing more than lust. It is clear from the context and its dramatic presentation that his laugh is far from an expression of wholesome fun: '¡Ha, ha, ha! ¿Este es el fuego de Calisto: éstas son sus congoxas?' (32) [Ha, ha, ha, this is Calisto's fire! These his intolerable pains!], he mocks under his breath as Calisto proclaims his impious faith in Pleberio's daughter. The servant's sign of scorn is evident in its explicit, albeit oblique, acoustical articulation. In this scene, Sempronio's laughter, though audible to the reader, remains concealed from Calisto. Since it is full of dangerous thoughts, it is furtive and only registered surreptitiously within the context of Sempronio's faithless muttering.

When accidentally overheard by Calisto, Sempronio's insulting laugh is instantly qualified, retracted, or, when questioned, rephrased and palatably explained. His laughter, and his instant recisions of it, mark Sempronio's derision and cautious contempt for his master, while it defines the true nature of his private thoughts. Through laughter, the *antiguo autor* establishes in act 1 the subterfuge of hostility and rancour between Sempronio and Calisto that justifies ironically in the reader's eyes the former's willingness to despoil the latter. Here laughter is both an instrument of characterization and an audible dramatic key to understanding Sempronio's egocentric motivation.

In his rich study Bergson (1937) warns, however, against reducing laughter to a single form. He sees that laughter is a complex human response involving varied patterns and motivations, and that it ranges over a wide assortment of emotional conditions and tones that are at their root often quite different from each other. If we look further into *Celestina*, it is apparent that both the *antiguo autor* and Fernando de Rojas understood this too. There are several more instances where characters laugh outright, yet where the nature of their laughter is quite distinct from Sempronio's scornful rumblings, and far from expressions of clean fun. This laughter, like the demonstration of Sempronio's contempt, also asks to be taken seriously and functions as a crucial referent of a character's authenticity, yet it is more subtle and complex.

Two of the most notable moments where the resonances of a distinct, perhaps more subtly shaped, laughter rouse our attention are also in the first act and signal the presence of sentiments quite dissimilar from Sempronio's plain expression of disdain. Both of these involve Pármeno, Calisto's other servant, who must be persuaded to deceive his master for the plot to continue unfolding. Although on these occasions, as in many others in *Celestina*, it is easily possible to miss the full implications of what seem nothing more than superfluous vocalizations in a text consisting of pure dialogue, upon close inspection it becomes apparent that Pármeno's snickering is in fact semantically charged, and far more eloquent than the words he speaks.

In her first interview with Pármeno, Celestina marshalls the full force of the logic of Scholasticism, the pieties of epigrams, and the rhetoric of the classroom to conquer the young servant's overt resistance to join her and Sempronio in exploiting Calisto. Yet the tempest of rhetoric, the flood of sentiment, and the deluge of erudition she brings forth falter and fail to find a complement in Pármeno's responses. He resists yielding to her importunate reasoning. Probing his opposition, all of Celestina's powers of persuasion, plus her hollow invocations of principled abstractions, misfire – until she hears him laugh. Only a scabrous joke, a final appeal to Pármeno's lower instincts, provokes a response, whose essence is betrayed by laughter. Significantly, it is his giggle that supplies Celestina with the decisive clue to provoking Pármeno's capitulation.

Hearing the laugh, Celestina invokes the example of the natural world and the authority of Aristotelian science, suddenly changing the tenor of the conversation, supplementing her speech with salacious diminutives, provocative questions, and implied physical gestures:

> CELESTINA. ¿Qué dirás a esto, Pármeno? ¡Neciuelo, loquito, angelico, perlica, simplezico! ¿Lobitos en tal gestico? Llégate acá, putico, que no sabes nada del mundo ni de sus deleytes. Mas rabia mala me mate, si te llego a mí, aunque vieja! Que la boz tienes ronca, las barvas te apuntan; mal sosegadilla deves tener la punta de la barriga.
>
> PÁRMENO. ¡Como cola de alacrán!
>
> CELESTINA. Y aún peor, que la otra muerde sin hinchar, y la tuya hincha por nueve meses.
>
> PÁRMENO. ¡Hy, hy, hy!
>
> CELESTINA. ¿Ríeste, landrezilla, hijo? (64)

> [CEL: How can you answer this Pármeno? Now my pretty little fool, you mad wag, angel, my pearl, my honest poor silly lad, come hither, you little whoreson; thou knowest nothing of the world nor of its delights. Let me run mad and die if I suffer thee to come near me, as old as I am. Thou hast a hoarse voice; by thy brizzled beard, and I believe the point of thy primum mobile is no quieter than he should be.
>
> PARM: As quiet as the tail of a scorpion.
>
> CEL: It were well and it were no worse, for that other stings without swelling, and thine swells for nine months together.
>
> PARM: Hy, hy, hy!
>
> CEL: Laugh'st thou, thou pocky rogue?]

Celestina's question is rhetorical. She knows he does – and why. She understands that laughter is an involuntary gesture more immediately connected to the passions than to language, which defends against them. Although usually moved by intuition, upon hearing Pármeno laugh,

Celestina may actually be drawing upon Aristotle's remark that 'when men are tickled they are quickly set a-laughing, because the motion quickly reaches this part, and heating it though but slightly nevertheless manifestly so disturbs the mental action as to occasion movements that are independent of the will' (*On the Parts of Animals*, 3, x). Pármeno's laugh is, in fact, a negation of his spoken words and introduces a new, involuntary code into the conversation while generating, through his comic response, new insight into his character. Hearing it, Celestina grasps that Pármeno's laughter reveals an inverse relationship between his verbal messages and his hidden thoughts. She discerns that Pármeno's unintentional outburst distinguishes an alternate discourse charged with nervous pleasure; that it resonates a deep discrepancy between his public obstinacy and his turbulent private musings. Laughter allows Celestina to see how Pármeno's words fail to represent his inner essence, and that there is discord between his concealed opinions, which harbour the real objects of his desires, and his public resistance to her reasoning amid empty protestations of loyalty to Calisto. Suddenly, the expectations of her ploys for success change, as she senses the true course that will lead to Pármeno's enlistment in her enterprise.

Celestina's initial assumption that rhetoric and moral sophistry will demolish Pármeno's ethical arguments (which in fact are nothing more than unctuous posturing), now veers recklessly toward wantoness as laughter unmasks the hidden compulsions of his private thoughts. The basic incongruity between Pármeno's verbal defiance to Celestina's arguments and the sudden disclosure of his emotions in a lewd giggle triggers her perception of his lingering weakness, a certainty of his unyielding sensuality. His laughter is, she discerns, an unerring sign of his anxious delight at obscenity. She thus concludes that the youth, whom she initiated sexually when he shared her bed in childhood, has not changed and that his laughter signals, in Bergson's words, a 'revival of the sensations of childhood' (1956, 104–5).[2] However, knowing that her age offends him, Celestina recognizes she is too old now to offer herself to him, and hence shifts the conversation to the evocation of sharing lubricous acts with friends – and to the ripe charms of her proxy, Areúsa. Through Pármeno's unanticipated laugh his mere words are exposed to Celestina as scant defence against the onslaught of desire.[3]

Pármeno's grasping bent and his decisive leanings toward conspiracy are exposed yet again in a fleeting giggle at the close of act 1. Overhearing the final exchange between Calisto and Celestina, in which the latter alludes to the efficacy of the former's generosity, he asks Sempronio what the master has given Celestina. Sempronio responds: 'Cient monedas en oro' [a hundred crowns in good gold], which Pármeno greets with a high-pitched 'Hy, hy, hy' (78) capturing his covetous delight and marking a first release of tension and fright.

In act 1 of *Celestina*, hence, in both instances the high-pitched sounds of Pármeno's laughter (his 'hy, hy, hy' as distinguished from Sempronio's 'ha, ha, ha') are clearly appended to covetousness, to sensuality, to desire, and to trepidation. They aggravate rather than relieve the dramatic tension as they connote deception, dissolution, and concealed complicity. Just as they contradict the spoken pieties of language, they betray dark passions and foreshadow tragic reversals in the work. Here the lapse into hilarity is itself not funny. Pármeno's laughter bares his cupidity and the subterfuge of unremitting lust – coupled with wariness – that lie beneath the image of his smug self-satisfaction.[4] Tempted now with both pleasure and wealth, his snickering signals his true seditious disposition and his yet unpublicized proclivity to collaborate with Sempronio and Celestina.

Pármeno's tittering in act 1 corresponds to what Freud characterizes as 'tendentious' laughter, which expresses wishes or forbidden impulses in the face of obstacles opposing the latter's direct expression (1960, 150–3). Initially calculating he will fare better with Calisto than with Celestina and Sempronio, however, Pármeno's giggle is more a momentary truancy in his carefully crafted, self-interested defence against Celestina's eloquence than any demonstration of repressed desire. In fact, his lapse uncovers the studied concealment of his conscious yearnings that cannot be publicly voiced, and thus exposes his hypocrisy and cowardice – his preference to advertise allegiance to his master until he can conclude with certainty where the larger personal advantage lies. Rather than the gratification of subconscious wishes, Pármeno's slip into hilarity serves as a window to his private thoughts and informs Celestina, Sempronio, and the reader of his readiness to join them in plundering Calisto. His giggling conveys the secret agreement of his personal desires with what experience and memory tell him are the bawd's real plans.

After Sempronio's invocation of the 'cient monedas en oro' [a hundred crowns in good gold], firm now in the conviction that the greater gain and pleasure lie in the old whore's scheme, Pármeno, though publicly acknowledging misgivings, requires no further persuasion. Sempronio asks him, 'Pues, ¿cómo estamos?' [How is it, then, with us?], to which he responds, 'Como quisieres, aunque estoy espantado' (78) [As thou wilt thyself. Yet for all this methinks I am still afraid]. Though Pármeno at this point has had the last laugh in act 1, it is clearly Celestina and the passions who have triumphed over fear and wary circumspection. Albeit apprehensive about the ultimate prudence of his decision, the final choice having been made, Pármeno's desire need no longer cloak itself in pretence and hide under the veil of language. He now openly declares it as he proclaims his complicity with Celestina and Sempronio in the conclusive idiom of proverbs: 'Pues dizen, a río buelto ganancia de pescadores. ¡Nunca más perro al molino!' (90) [It is said the best fishing, in troubled waters. I will never any more be a dog in a mill!].

It is clear that Rojas, as both the continuer and as the most alert reader of act 1, fully understood the semiotics of laughter as they were conceived and developed by the *antiguo auctor*. He grasped how a snicker was a referent of discourse, and how it was capable of 'defamiliarizing' the language enveloping it, while throwing spoken words into ironic relief, exposing their hollowness.[5] Recognizing laughter's ability to produce a sharp awareness in the difference of meaning conveyed by it and by the measured sounds of public speech, Rojas saw how laughter cuts across linguistic codes and spoken language – how it casts doubt upon them – and how it may be laden with trenchant, often contradictory, meanings. When he read act 1 he surely discerned laughter's function as a basic element of irony in the dialogue – as a sign pointing to the presence of a double-voiced discourse in the text – and how it was in fact capable of being read as a parallel but dissident code to speech. He recognized it as the heteroglossia of desire and then set out to use laughter in a similar fashion in his continuation, capitalizing upon it in one of the least conspicuous, yet revealing moments, in the work: Alisa's brush with Celestina within the confines of her home.

Indeed, it is through Alisa's laughter that we can begin to unravel some of the mysteries posed by modern critics regarding the nature of her character and the motivations for her behaviour. In act 4, Celestina encounters Lucrecia, the maidservant, at the entrance to Melibea's house. Under the pretence of conveying greetings from Lucrecia's cousin, the prostitute Elicia, she seeks entry, but not without rousing Lucrecia's suspicions, who detects a pretext for some other errand. After querying her, Celestina admits to Lucrecia that she comes not only out of friendship but also out of need. Celestina pleads poverty and tries to sell her thread and notions to the lady of the house. Overhearing the conversation at the door, Alisa calls to Lucrecia and asks after the visitor. Ashamed to invoke Celestina's name, Lucrecia answers with evasions, until Alisa, unable to guess the identity of the caller, demands Lucrecia say her name. Reluctant still to utter it, Alisa scolds Lucrecia and orders her to say it:

> ¡Anda, bova, dile, no me indignes con tu tardança!
> LUCRECIA: Celestina, hablando con reverencia, es su nombre.
> ALISA: ¡Hy, hy, hy! Mala landre te mate si de risa puedo estar, viendo el desamor que deves tener a essa vieja que su nombre has vergüença nombrar; ya me voy recordando de ella. Una buena pieça; no me digas más. Algo me verná a pedir; di que suba (112).

> [Go too, you fool; tell me her name; do not anger me by this your delay.
> LUCRECIA: Her name, saving your reverence, is Celestina.
> ALISA: Hi, hi, hi! I am not able to stand for laughing to see that that the loathing which thou hast of this old woman should make thee ashamed to name her unto me. Now I call her to mind; say no more. A fine piece of work! She is come to beg somewhat of me. Bid her come up.]

In crafting Alisa's portrayal, Rojas gleaned from the *antiguo autor*'s use of laughter, that, as Henri Bergson states, 'laughter always implies a kind of secret freemasonry, or even complicity, with other laughers, real or imaginary' (1937, 6). Alisa's high-pitched giggle invokes, hence, not just the sounds but also the sentiments of Pármeno's response to Celestina's ribald joke. It marks a sympathy between the two. At the same time it refers us to Alisa's more than casual acknowledgment of Celestina's presence. Alisa's laugh acts as a paralinguistic gloss to the exchange with Lucrecia and specifies the former's unequivocal recognition of Celestina, as well as her full appreciation of the nature of the old bawd's forbidden trade.

Beyond Alisa's explicit invitation for Celestina to enter her home, Alisa's snicker also points to her tacit approval of Celestina's presence in the house plus a more than ingenuous awareness of her mission ('Una buena pieça; no me digas más. Algo me venrá a pedir' [A fine piece of work! She is come to beg somewhat of me]). Indeed, it carries a hint of understanding and a whiff of past chicanery; at the very least it betokens curiosity while suggesting, perhaps, Alisa's inner wish to exploit the possibilities of Celestina's visit on behalf of her marriageable daughter.

Recognizing Celestina, as well as ignoring Lucrecia's explicit description of her as 'la que empicotaron por hechizera, que vendía las moças a los abades y descasava mil casados' (110) [she that stood on the pillory for a witch; who sold young wenches to your Abbey Lubbers and that hath marred many thousands of marriages], and, more importantly, indicating by her giggle that she knows full well how she makes her living, after a warm exchange of greetings, Alisa calls Melibea and asks her to attend to their visitor. Suddenly declaring her distress at the lateness of the hour, Alisa turns heel and leaves the two alone, invoking the need to visit an ailing sister, whom she has not seen since yesterday. Till the moment of her precipitous departure, Melibea's mother seems on estimable terms with Celestina, despite her full knowledge of the nature of her business. Indeed, she is on too good terms with the bawd and thus compels us to reach for other motives for her warmth – and for her mischievous giggle and her hasty exit.

Critics have been confounded by the logic of this scene, and have thus attributed Alisa's actions either to stupidity (Gilman 1974, 251) or to the effects of Celestina's witchcraft (Russell 1978b, 57). With the exception of Louise Fothergill-Payne, who maintains that *Celestina* is a rational book rooted in the realities of society as she seeks to discard the importance of magic in the work (1989, 85), Alisa's motivation is always portrayed as essentially irrational. Patricia Grieve sums up the critical response to Alisa's behaviour when, in her discussion of mothers and daughters in sentimental romances, she notes that by contrast to mothers in the latter, 'Alisa ... barely emerges: her seeming obliviousness to the purpose of Celestina's visit to Melibea shows her either to be ignorant or unconcerned, to be guilty of negligence, perhaps, since everyone in the town seems to know the business of Celestina, or to be bewitched by Celestina's diabolical magic' (1990, 352).

Yet, from Alisa's and Celestina's conversation after the former's invitation for the latter to enter the house, in addition to their mutual recognition, we become aware of their long friendship and association prior to Celestina's moving from the neighbourhood (Russell 1989, 157). It is at this moment that mindful readers, signalled by Alisa's earlier risqué snicker, are obliged to suspect something more than sorcery or foolishness afoot. Indeed, framed by the immodest and mischievous connotations of her own and Pármeno's giggling, Alisa's friendly greeting to Celestina allows us to cast for levels of insinuation embedded deep in the text that suggest a shadowy side of her character not unlike the young servant's.[6] Obscured by modern maudlin readings of the work, there are in fact wicked implications in Alisa's cordiality, her snicker, and her 'unreasonable' comportment, all of which are confirmed by literary history, social practice, the plastic arts, and the very text itself.

One of *Celestina*'s richest artistic resources is the fact that all the characters in it lead lives beyond the text itself. Bound together by ties of memory and recognition, as inhabitants of the same space and time, their existence has in the past, in some way, all touched one another (see Severin, 1970). It is for this reason that, placed within the context of her laugh and, as we shall see, Celestina's professional blustering, Alisa falls suspect and raises the prospect of less than altruistic motives in her conduct. We sense that below the surface of her snicker and sudden retreat there lies more guile than witlessness or witchcraft; and that behind her and Celestina's recollections of past acquaintance there abides more than honest amity. Alisa's warmth and naughty laughter, coupled with her sudden exit (is her ailing sister a transparent excuse?) point toward acceptance, toward history, and toward her unspoken complicity in the seduction of her daughter.

Our suspicions of Alisa's unuttered mischief are also corroborated by our own recollections of the text, as Celestina's braggadocio in act 3 echoes in our reading of the encounter with her. There the bawd boasts to Sempronio of her celebrity, her long years of professional prowess; she brags of her enduring monopoly on promiscuity among the citizenry. There she exults in her scrupulous accounting of the maidens of the town, and gloats upon her everlasting skill at cornering the market of virginity. It is there, too, that she evokes her ability to correct with silken threads the infamous slumps in the economy of maidenheads – caused by her very contribution to demand and by her own steadfast prosperity in the trade. Lapsing into the metaphors of commerce, Sempronio takes solace in Celestina's deftness, observing thankfully that Melibea's seduction will certainly not be 'el primero negocio que as tomado a cargo' (96) [the first business thou hast taken in hand]. Offended by the understatement, Celestina rejoins in a tone filled with pique and professional vanity. She takes umbrage at Sempronio's miscalculation of her skill. Brimming with ribald double entente, her response underscores her abiding mastery of the business of pandering plus the unmistakable commercial euphemisms of her vocation:

¿El primero, hijo? Pocas vírgines, a Dios gracias, has tu visto en esta ciudad que hayan abierto tienda a vender, de quien yo no haya sido corredora de su primer hilado. En nasciendo la mochacha, la hago scrivir en mi registro, y esto para que yo sepa quántas se me salen de la red. (141)[7]

[The first, my son? Few virgins (I thank fortune for it) hast thou seen in this city, which have opened their shops and traded for themselves, to whom I have not been the broker to their first spun thread; there was not a wench

born in the world, but I writ her down in my register to the intent that I
might know how many escaped my net.]

Alisa's warm greetings, her snicker at the mention of Celestina's name,
and her impetuous departure thus all point to their prior dealings and
to the spacious arc cast over time by Celestina's net. Put simply, they invoke the checked entry with Alisa's name in the early pages of Celestina's
tattered ledger.

Quite aside from the text's insinuation of Alisa's questionable prior
association with Celestina and her silent complicity with her vis-à-vis
Melibea, folk tradition, plus a string of literary ancestors and successors,
corroborate our suspicions of her dubious character and artfulness. The
redundant peccadilloes of mothers and daughters are traditional in the
Spanish folk patrimony, and are linked to remorse through their association with the rue plant, a symbol of regret. How daughters repeat
their mothers' carnal education (was Pleberio Alisa's Calisto?) is captured in the ó version of the Judeo-Spanish ballad *Una matica de ruda*:
'Madre mí'a, la mi kerida, no yoréš, ni vos ah.arvéš. / Lo ke 'iziteš 'en
gu'estro tyenpo, lo veniteš vos a ver' (Armistead and Silverman 1979,
46) [Mother, my dear mother, do not weep or get excited. / What you
did in your good time, you came to see pass.]

From another perspective Lida de Malkiel, in her discussion of Alisa's
literary forebears, notes that in both Roman comedy and in the *Libro de
buen amor* 'la madre de la enamorada o es su tercera ... o está al tanto de
los deslices de la hija' (1970, 490) [the mother of the beloved is either
her go-between ... or is aware of her daughter's backsliding]. Indeed, in
the *Libro de buen amor*'s reworking of the *Pamphilus* (824–7), the bawd
gains access to Doña Endrina only with the compliance of her mother –
and in a scene not unlike the one in which Alisa receives Celestina.
Calling at Doña Endrina's door, Trotaconventos speaks to Doña Rama,
who, after greeting her warmly and evoking past acquaintance ('¿Cómo
venides, amiga?' [825] [How come you now?]), knowingly absents herself to leave the two alone.[8]

Yet other instances of maternal collaboration in a daughter's seduction can be found in Iberian texts. In the anonymous *Triste deleytación*, for
example, La Señora's stepmother not only conspires to facilitate the latter's rendezvous with El Enamorado, but takes an active part in an illicit
affair of her own that parallels her stepdaughter's. There, indeed, the
adulterous stepmopther takes El Enamorado's friend as her lover and
revels in the betrayal of her husband as she enthusiastically promotes the

trysting of the younger pair. Later in the text, too, the Lady's Godmother (*La Madrastra*'s [the stepmother's] more philosophical and less physically active döppelganger) offers her surprisingly matter-of-fact, even cynical, advice on love and functions explicitly as the mentor in the young woman's sexual and social education.

The collusion of go-betweens and mothers in seducing marriageable daughters is broadly documented outside of late medieval Iberian texts as well: La Vielle in the *Roman de la Rose*, who counsels the Lover (through Bel Acueil) on the usefulness of maternal aid in the corruption of a daughter (vv. 13709–24), provides a salient example. Similarly, Sostrata, Lucrezia's mother in Machiavelli's *Mandragola* (1498), who arranges with Frate Timoteo for Callimaco to lure her daughter, offers a near contemporary parallel to Alisa. In fact, the latter is described by the other characters in Machiavelli's play as having been a 'lively' sort in her salad days, who, despite her present dedication to domesticity, stops at nothing to orchestrate her daughter's 'night of sin.'

As Hanna Fenichel Pitkin (1984) comments in her study of the representation of gender and politics in Machiavelli, in the works of the Florentine statesman, matrons, through their daughters, perform a significant role in transacting institutional power as they become brokers of marriage, lineage, and social influence. They are thus the ones who hold sway over the young maidens; and it is not the youthful women but the older ones who play the chief roles in initiating the former into the politics and social possibilities of adult sexuality. Mothers in Machiavelli, Pitkin notes, are often as, or more, ambitious than the men, particularly when marketing a marriageable daughter: 'Their power to exploit ... sexual concerns,' Pitkin writes, 'takes on legendary proportions ... The older women in Maquiavelli's fiction are very different from their daughters. They are not sexually attractive or seductive, but they often control access to the young women, either blocking or facilitating the men's desires' (1984, 119). Mothers of the loveliest maidens in particular become the duplicitous manipulators of masculine sexuality, and vie to become the silent architects of social power by trafficking in the carnal allures of their feminine offspring. In fact, it is in the Italian Renaissance, in the *Ragionamenti* of Pietro Aretino, where the misogynistic portrait of the complicitous mother finds its most audacious manifestation: Day 1 of part 2 of the dialogues is dedicated exclusively to recording Nanna's brazen advice to her daughter on how to become a successful courtesan.[9]

Finally, a variant of Alisa's mischievous laugh of recognition has a been immortalized in a picture. In a painting completed by Bartolomé Esteban

Murillo (ca 1670) that currently bears the title *A Girl and Her Duenna*, now owned by the National Gallery of Art in Washington, DC (Widener Collection), an innocent-looking young girl and an older woman said to be her chaperone – quite possibly even her mother – gaze adventuresomely out a window at the spectator of the picture, presumably a man who gazes back (see figure 5.1). As the young woman looks out intently with a flirtatious smile of amused pleasure, the older woman behind her, hidden partially by the window shutter, covers the lower part of her face with a scarf to conceal what is a look of delight, or perhaps even to muffle a giggle or a snicker. Prior to its acquisition by Lord Heytesbury and its sale to the National Gallery in 1942, the painting formed part of the collection of the Duque de Almodóvar in Madrid, and there it was popularly known as *Las gallegas*, its earliest known appellation, and one that referred to two notorious seventeenth-century courtesans of Seville at the time Murillo finished the picture, a mother and daughter who came from Galicia. Regardless of the title of the painting, one thing remains clear: it portrays the complicity of the older woman with the younger one, as she delights in her young charge's dalliance with an admiring observer.

A tradition of Dutch moralizing pictures also portrayed wayward young women with their procuresses, who were often said to be their 'mothers' or 'aunts.' Murillo would certainly have been familiar with these works since many of his clients were Flemish and Dutch merchants living in Seville. The Dutch paintings, however, usually contained more overt indications of their subject – the procuress was depicted as a much older and more sinister figure, and they provided other clues to their meaning, like the presence of animals commonly associated with lust. Thus, although Murillo's painting may on first inspection look like an innocent scene in comparison to the Dutch ones, given what we have heard and seen in Alisa's recognition of Celestina, it is more likely that something quite contrary to innocence is depicted in Murillo's picture, something that doubtless casts light as well on the meaning of one of the most misunderstood scenes of the *Tragicomedia de Calisto y Melibea*.[10]

Both the text of *Celestina* itself and the broader context of its classical and vernacular literary congeners, as well as the plastic arts, provide support, then, for the suspicion of Alisa's quiet complicity in compromising Melibea. It is not surprising, therefore, that social history and law offer yet further confirmation of it, as well as insights into Alisa's incentives for welcoming Celestina to her house. Confirming the historical reality of mothers who market, marry, and manipulate their daughters for social

Figure 5.1 A Girl and her Duenna, by Bartolomé Esteban Murillo, ca 1670. National Gallery of Art, Washington, DC. With permission.

and economic advantage in the 1480s in France, the preacher Olivier Maillard in his *Sermones de adventu quadragesimales dominicales* (Lyons: Etienne Gueygnard, 1503), decries women who 'barter' their offspring either for personal profit or with an eye to making advantageous alliances: 'Habemus multa mulieres vendentes filias suas, et sunt lene filiarum suarum et faciunt eis lucrare matrimonium ad penam et sudorem sui corporis' [We have many women who sell their daughters, and they are their procuresses and make money through marriage and the pain and sweat of their bodies] (cited in Rossiaud 1988, 131n.3). By the same token, María Eugenia Lacarra, who has studied the history of prostitution in late medieval Castile in relation to *Celestina*, observes that it was not uncommon to find mothers in league with the 'madame' of a brothel in order to marry off a daughter. Noting that 'unos de los problemas con los que se enfrentaba el legislador es que con frecuencia eran los padres, madres o señores quienes obligaban a sus hijas, siervas o criadas a prostituirse para obtener ganancia de ellas' (1993, 2) [one of the problems legislators confronted often involved fathers, mothers, or masters who obliged their daughters, wards, or servants to prostitute themselves to make money off of them], Lacarra provides both social and psychological insight into Alisa's ambitions for Melibea.[11]

Alisa's insinuated complicity with Celestina spreads new, startling shadows upon her response to Pleberio's urgency to find a mate for Melibea in act 16. His anxieties there, expressed in terms of the legal and moral implications of his daughter's marriage, and cast within the sphere of paternal authority ('Pues en esto las leyes dan libertad a los hombres y mujeres, aunque estén so el paterno poder, para elegir' [344–6] [For in this particular the laws allow both men and women, though they be under paternal power, for to make their own choice]), are met by Alisa's astonishingly abrupt cancellation of them: '¿Qué dizes? ¿En qué gastas tiempo? ¿Quién ha de yrle con tan grande novedad a Melibea, que no la espante? ¿Cómo, y piensas que sabe ella qué cosa sean hombres, si se casan o qué es casar, o que del ayuntamiento de marido y mujer se procreen los hijos?' (346) [What do you mean, husband? Why do you talk and spend time in this? Who shall be the messenger to acquaint our daughter Melibea with this strange news, and shall not affright her therewith? Alas, do you think that she can tell what a man means, or what it is to marry or be married? Or whether by the conjunction of man and woman children are begot or no?]. As all exchanges in *Celestina*, Alisa's and Pleberio's dialogue is dramatically ironic. The reader, uniquely privy to the larger implications of the words uttered by both characters, is the only one in a position to construct the greater sense of the scene. Knowing what the reader knows has transpired, Rojas thus meant to underscore disagreement between Melibea's parents, and intended their encounter to be taken ironically – in terms of Alisa's and Pleberio's opposition to each other. The only issue in play is Alisa's hidden motivation for abruptly revoking Pleberio's apparent good intentions. Rojas, a lawyer whose entire work revolves around the notion of the limits and the persistent transgression of licit conduct, was doubtless alerting his readers not only to the sensitive personal and legal issues evoked in Pleberio's remarks, but also to Alisa's resistance to them, and to her role in their evasion.[12]

If, indeed, Alisa is silently conniving with Celestina, fearing Pleberio's overzealous intervention might impair her daughter's pleasure – not to mention the possibility of yielding an unacceptable husband for Melibea – she would be at pains to induce Pleberio not to raise the marriage question. Hence, her expression of astonishment, amid her emphatic avowal of her daughter's innocence and youth, may just as well camouflage a ruse as signal stupidity or enchantment. Indeed, it is likely that Alisa's retort to Pleberio conceals a legal subtext all its own: by lending a blind eye to Celestina and the unmistakable motive of her visit, Alisa perhaps wishes her daughter's trysting to proceed, hoping that the lovers will eventually be apprehended *in flagrante*, so as to provide the freest choice of mate for Melibea. In the late Middle Ages, as James Brundage (1982) remarks, to be apprehended *in delicto*, followed by a charge of seduction, 'might ironically allow a woman a greater freedom of choice in her marriage than she could otherwise enjoy' (146), since the laws against seduction in late medieval civil and canon law were developed and designed 'to force marriage between the couple' (147). In light of Alisa's complicitous laughter, her words to Pleberio are, to be sure, better read as premeditated feints devised to deflect her husband's aims, and – barring unforseen events – point to the inescapable conclusion of Melibea's affair – marriage to the man she loves.[13] Far from a sign of inner shallowness, or an imprint of the devil's deeds, Alisa's conduct as illuminated by her laughter makes her the more rational and problematical as a character; and, as in the case of Pármeno, it lays bare a complex subjectivity residing behind the mask of language.

In the face of *Celestina*'s textual evidence and literary forebears, critics have persisted in portraying Alisa as something different, invoking the latter's moral probity, her naive trust in her daughter, and her devotion to duty while ministering to the sick, as palliative to her 'perplexing' behaviour. Yet, when closely scrutinized and framed by her mischievous laughter, it seems clear that there is even broader truth to Patricia Grieve's observation that 'On a fundamental level … There is no room in *Celestina*'s world for the favourable portrait of mothers (1990, 353).

The sounds of laughter in *Celestina*, thus, constitute key elements of dialogue and lead to the possibility of reformulating our understanding of some of the more puzzling characters in the work. By looking closely at the internal correspondences and registers of laughter in the text, it is possible to see how laughter functions as the counter-discourse of virtue, and, hence, as a vehicle of concealed desire and conflict. In *Celestina*'s unique verbal universe the conveyance of meaning is never circumscribed to words alone. Words, indeed, serve only to hide thoughts that cannot be openly expressed. However, the portrayal of language and desire in *Celestina* transcends mere words and implies the text's complex relation to a broad system of utterances, discourses, codes, and modes of signification. Both Fernando de Rojas and the anonymous *antiguo auctor* interjected an aural dimension to their dialogue to fashion an idiom that not only serves to relate events through words themselves but captures subtly the tensions and oppositions of desire that subtend human conversation in the fullest way. In *Celestina*'s dialogues words and the sounds of laughter are syntagmatically linked in both complimentary and opposing structures, and recreate the oscillating pattern of parallels and differences that contribute to the richness of human speech. By tracing the tones and forms of laughter in *Celestina*, and by seeking their intricate connections to the words they frame, the text itself begins to generate new instructions for how to read it, and for how to understand the workings of concealed desire in the protean personalities who inhabit its contentious world.

6 Melibea Speaks: Language and Feminine Desire

The medieval literature of courtly love generally falls silent when it comes to expressing feminine desire. In the late Middle Ages, courtly love as represented in literature consisted of an unrequited male passion and a concomitant devotion to a woman that exhibited various distinctive features. Among those features are an inverted gender hierarchy where the male lover suffered physically from lovesickness, wounding, or other corporal ailments, all of which led to melancholy depression, characterized by spiritual pain, despair, and a sense of impotence; the claim that the fetishized, desired, and incomparably beautiful body of the beloved provided the key to fulfilling the lover's yearning and would lead to the healing of his malady, if only the lady dispensed her favours to him, as he knelt before her like a subservient, often abased, vassal who supplicated for mercy from her, who stood as a figuratively empowered, if silent, lord or demiurge who held absolute dominion over the lover; and, finally, a refined art of courtship, mediated exclusively by the masculine voice and highly developed rhetorical embellishments that followed a series of codified rules of social propriety, all of which we have encountered in exaggerated and parodic guise in the figure of Calisto.

Based on these ideas and ideals, the literature of courtly love in the late Middle Ages staged elaborate scenarios of the vicissitudes of heterosexual desire that focused mainly on men at the expense of women; these were textual simulacra that were set in spheres of idealized aristocratic refinement where women had little to say. In the literary universe of courtly love, it was the male voice that dominated discourse, continually asserting masculine power and social standing – the wages that were truly at stake in the enterprise – as men practised and professed the art of love through discursive rituals that made their god-like ladies stand as mute observers of their performances. In a variety of contexts, courtly ladies were portrayed as adored objects in a unidirectional economy of desire that systematically silenced them and occluded their status as desiring subjects.

These courtly attitudes toward love evolved, according to R. Howard Bloch (1991), from a long history of Western misogyny stemming from the Christian patristic tradition, in which women were belittled, caricaturized as lascivious and garrulous, devalued as a product of the legacy of Eve, and were thus condemned to silence. To be sure, in his examination of medieval literary genres in relation to gender, Simon Gaunt has gone so far as to argue that even in the most elegant and moving expressions of courtly love 'it is not always clear whether the poet is taking about his relations with his lady or other men' (1995, 140), seeking to define courtly love exclusively as a homosocial activity, or as an exercise in the masculine display of verbal skill and social dominance in which historical women played little or no part. Since the 1990s, feminist scholarship has argued this case convincingly, revealing from a number of perspectives that, if the woman is the supposed subject of courtly love, she nonetheless remains subjected to social restrictions and regulatory systems that privilege heterosexual men as the sole desiring, speaking, and most visible agents of all authority and, above all, as the masters of amorous speech and comportment. (For feminist approaches to courtly love and chivalry, see, for example, Kay 1990, Weiss 1991, Fenster 1996, and Rasmussen 1997.) Contemporary feminist readings of late medieval courtly love thus frame it as a kind of male-centred wooing or coupling between high-born men and eroticized, idealized ladies. Psychoanalytic critics, following a Freudian paradigm that accentuates masculinity and male potency in the construction of their critical models, have gone so far as to emphasize only the negative role played by the feminine in courtly love, leading them to erase the woman's role completely from their scenarios of courtly desire, often making the lady 'vanish' altogether (see Fisher and Halley 1989, 2–17). According to the psychoanalytical critics, courtly love is fundamentally an expression of repressed carnal or erotic pleasure, in which the woman's role in Western culture is precisely to be absent (for a critique of the Freudian and Lacanian paradigms vis-à-vis women, see Irigaray 1985).

Following the Freudian and Lacanian principles, for example, Jean-Charles Huchet perceives the courtly lady as an entity wholly abstracted from historical particulars, as 'La Femme' in the sense Lacan's *objet à*, or lost object, the unattainable Other that desire can never reach and that erotic discourse cannot fully represent (1982, 13; 1987, 35). According to the psychoanalytical model, the courtly lover crafts an auto-erotic fiction of a resistant lady both sovereign and divine, so that he can then subject himself ceaselessly to her imagined whim, never fulfilling her demands or satisfying the physical cravings of his desire.[1] Even if historical women have no place in these scenarios, the psychoanalytical readings of courtly love have gone a long way toward explaining male fantasy as it is represented through literary language. In either case, however, both the feminist and psychoanalytical models have now far exceeded Paul Zumthor's acute initial insight from 1972 that courtly love was a self-referential discourse involving only male-centred interest, and they have led us to look closely at and question the gendered coordinates of courtly love.

Despite the diversity of opinion, one thing remains clear: the courtly tradition rarely portrays feminine discourse, and with its absence, it implicitly eschews any direct representation of feminine agency or empowerment, let alone the direct portrayal of feminine social or sexual desire. Yet, when judiciously considered, the silence of the female voice in the courtly idiom of love can only be seen as the mark of the socially repressed expression of female desire, and in this way it may be taken as an absence that makes its presence known, and one worthy of comparison when confronted with the emergence of the voices of the feminine characters in works like *Celestina*.

Using this current understanding of courtly love by feminist and psychoanalytical critics as a point of departure, it is possible to expand and refine our appreciation of the portrayal of desire in *Celestina*, to show how the work offers a striking range of alternatives to the courtly tradition, which not only rejected the rigidly gendered stereotypes of the lovestruck suitor and the beguiling, silent lady, but opened a space for representing a broad range of feminine subjectivity at the end of the fifteenth century. In its rich social and linguistic complexity, *Celestina* offers a series of key disjunctive representations of feminine desire, pleasure, and personhood that, in addition to resisting courtly norms through contradiction, move well beyond prevailing social ideas about female language, empowerment, agency, and mastery of the gendered notions of knowledge and wisdom (see Solterer 1995). The women in the *Tragicomedia de Calisto y Melibea*, particularly in their display and discovery of feminine sexuality as a right – and even as a possession and a form of capital that can be exchanged for power – emerge as assertive members of the human community, as individuals conscious of themselves who believe they can both have their say and get their way, although in the end they always encounter obstacles to achieving their desires.

An examination of the representations of feminine desire in *Celestina* yields two important results. It causes us, first, to reconsider the change in the place of female desire in romantic literary love plots in European literature at the threshold of modernity; and, second, it opens new possibilities for understanding the manner in which agency was being reconstructed socially and historically in terms of gender on the part of both women and men at the close of the Middle Ages. While *Celestina* invokes the standard courtly plot of the male-centred social courting/coupling between a high-born man and his eroticized, fantasized, and fetishized god-like lady just to subvert it, the process does not end solely in disruptive parody. To the contrary, other forms of yearning are represented in *Celestina* that offer options to the foolishness of courtly love and the caricatures of misogyny that move women away from being absent, distanced objects of desire or uncomplicated garrulous tarts into roles of speaking persons who redefine, as well as subvert, the ways of understanding feminine subjectivity at the beginning of the sixteenth century.

Disavowing its medieval foundations just as it invokes the idiom and axioms of courtly love, *Celestina*, through all its female characters, dramatizes the feminine subjection to the search for, and the mutability of, passion. Contrary to the courtly tradition, women in *Celestina* are portrayed as self-conscious subjects who transcend the male ego-ideal of courtly love to deny their role as passive objects of masculine desire. To be sure, from the aristocratic Melibea to the comely prostitutes Areúsa and Elicia, on to the crone Celestina and even the marginal, secondary figure of Lucrecia, the text stages an exploration of ambition, the suffering for love, the search for pleasure, and the pursuit of seduction that resides in all these female subjects. It adopts a nuanced, complex cultural attitude toward them that admits their potential for enjoyment outside of and beyond the clichés of medieval misogyny and dominant masculine ideologies. Each of these characters actualizes female impulses for feeling and the quest for enjoyment that reach out beyond the medieval antifeminist aesthetic of bawdy female representation and places their capacity for desiring on an equal footing with that of the male characters in the work. In *Celestina*, the feminine wish for gratification and fulfilment exceeds its obligatory medieval repression or caricaturization ultimately to be candidly exhibited by all the women who populate the text. Melibea, most especially, offers a means for perceiving this reconceptualization of feminine desire, as she turns the hackneyed model of the silent, distant lady overtly on its head, as is clear from the outset of act 1.

A close reading of the initial scene of *Celestina* shows that Melibea's rejection of Calisto is at best ambivalent and that, rather than constitute a definitive foreclosure of desire, it opens wide the door to it under the very cover of propriety. Although the lovers' initial exchange is couched in the hyperbolic idiom of courtly love, Melibea poses her first response to Calisto's effrontery as a spoken question, obliging him to answer, engaging him in conversation and inviting more while implicitly seeking an answer to her query in the dialogue that she seeks. To Calisto's sudden inflated declaration that he perceives the work of God in her, Melibea unflinchingly responds with the simple interrogation '¿En qué, Calisto?' [In what, Calisto?], disclosing that she not only knows who he is but, casting prudence to the wind, that she wishes for him to answer and elaborate on his enticing gambit. Melibea's retort, far from seeking to cut Calisto off and dissuade him from any further interest, bids him to amplify his statement. Without faltering, Calisto answers extolling Melibea's divine beauty, whose contemplation, he says, elevates him to a place higher than that of the saints, who glory in Paradise with the vision of God. He adds that he celebrates the auspiciousness of their encounter 'en tan conveniente lugar' (24) [in a place so convenient], a blissful spot that permits disclosure of his secret passion.

Calisto's sensational response does nothing more than provoke another question from Melibea, framed by her as a contemptuous expression of disbelief. Yet again, her query does nothing more than challenge him and call forth the need for further exposition: '¿Por gran premio tienes éste, Calisto?' [Holdest thou this, Calisto, so great a reward?], she says, followed by a simultaneously hostile and slippery addendum, 'Pues ¡aún más ygual *galardón* te daré yo, si perseveras'! (24, emphasis added) [I shall give thee a reward answerable to thy deserts, if thou persevere]. Melibea's repeated responses couched as interrogatives constitute nothing more than appeals for amplification deployed amidst flirtatious disparagement. They scarcely conceal her indiscretion as she teases Calisto and, using the world *galardón* in her response (a courtly euphemism for sexual favours; see Whinnom 1994, Lazar 1964, and MacKay 1989), she displays her mastery of the circumlocutious, euphemistic lexicon of love, finally rejecting his advances with an emphatic rebuff and condemnation that moves her just a little farther from his reach – a move that only fuels his passion. Melibea baits Calisto to elaborate upon his admiration, finally just to censure him with declarations of resistance that feebly assert her moral superiority while disclosing full knowledge of the true business at hand: illicit love and pleasure. '¡Vete, vete de aý, torpe! que no puede mi paciencia tolerar que haya subido en coraçón humano conmigo el ilícito amor comunicar deleyte' (26) [Go, wretch, begone out of my sight, for my patience cannot endure that so much as a thought should enter into any man's heart, to communicate his mind unto me in illicit love], she says, revealing her grasp of the nature of his intentions. Through it all, she displays a streak of puckish mischief, audacity, and knowledge that points to concealed immodesty, to disguised desire and gaps in the feminine facade of repression.

If we remember that *Celestina* was probably read aloud to an audience as well as silently by individual readers, it is not unreasonable to think that in its public presentations a reader might have performed the dialogue of the characters with dramatic inflection, bestowing individualized voices to each of them. The work's diffusion might have been implemented through *viva voce* readings in which several readers, in a kind of reader's theatre, played out individual parts of this closet drama. The range of interpretations for the characters' voices would have permitted the type of modulations that Melibea's rhetorical questioning appears to indicate, providing a broad domain for the possibility of inflecting and interpreting both masculine and feminine speech, thus allowing the acquisition of distance from their more stereotypical, expected formulations.[2]

Melibea's ability to desire and her capacity for rationalizing it are further discovered in her next appearance in the text, during her first interview with Celestina in act 6. Having come to Pleberio's house to do Calisto's bidding on the pretext of selling thread, Celestina is received by Melibea and her mother, Alisa, as Melibea stands quietly between them. There, however, upon her mother's incongruent departure, Melibea emerges again as far more vocal and less innocent than she first seems. Left alone in the company of Celestina, it is Melibea who opens the conversation between them, yet again posing a leading question. Hearing Celestina's calculated characterization of old age as a 'mesón de enfermedades, posada de pensamientos, amiga de renzillas, congoja continua, llaga incurable' [an inn full of infirmities, a storehouse of sad and melancholy thoughts, a friend to brawling, a continual grief, and incurable plague] and a 'cayado de mimbre que con poca carga se doblega' [a staff of weak osiers, which is doubled with any least stress you put on it], Melibea perspicaciously intuits the opening offered by the old bawd and asks with feigned simplicity '¿Por qué dizes, madre, tanto mal de lo que todo el mundo con tanta efficacia gozar y ver dessea?' (114) [Tell me, mother, why do you speak so ill of that which the whole world so earnestly desireth to enjoy and see?], a remark that can solely give rise to the desire for an answer. Melibea's question can only constitute an invitation to dialogue, opening the way for Celestina to elaborate upon the ravages of age, implicitly urging Melibea to seize the day and make the most of current opportunities because she, Celestina, stands as the living example that life is short and time is fleeting.

When Celestina finishes expatiating on the brevity of time and her waning beauty, Melibea knowingly responds with the obligatory topical expression of horror ('Espantada me tienes con lo que me has hablado' [Thou hast scared me with thy words]), but immediately presses on with yet one more leading query, now coloured by feigned sympathy: 'Dime madre, ¿eres tu Celestina, la que solía morar a las tenerías, cabe el río?' (118) [Tell me, mother, art not thou Celestina, that dwelt in Tanner's Row near the river?]. In her question, Melibea lets on to her interlocutor that she knows exactly who she is, disclosing just enough through the reference to the location of Celestina's house to demonstrate that she also knows exactly what Celestina does.

Although she seeks to deny it, Melibea knows full well the reason for Celestina's visit, and through the verbal parrying that ensues both she and Celestina steer the conversation to obtain the results that both desire without compromising their well-crafted facades of innocence and decorum. As the conversation advances, Celestina perceives Melibea's tacit receptivity and guides it in a more specific direction, taking licence by stressing familiar forms of address and seeking permission to explain the reason for her visit to Melibea's house ('Pues si tu me das licencia, diréte la necessitada causa de mi venida, que es otra que la que hasta agora as oýdo, y tal que todo perderíamos en me tornar en balde sin que la sepas' [Well, if you will give me leave, I will tell you the necessitated cause of my coming, which is another matter than any you have yet heard; and such as we were all undone, if I should return in vain and you not know it]). Melibea, perhaps even with a wink and a nod, invites the old go-between to declare 'todas tus necessidades' (120) [Acquaint me, mother, with all your necessities and wants], assuring her with an air of hollow *noblesse oblige* that her duty to do good compels her to listen and do everything she can to satisfy her former neighbour's need. Celestina, of course, seizes the opportunity to press on, but not without first invoking poverty due to the lack of a man in her life, just to conclude with a suggestive metaphor that moves her one more graphic step toward achieving the object of her embassy: 'Assi que donde no ay varón, todo bien fallece. *Con mal está el huso quando la barva no anda de suso*' (122, emphasis added) [Where the good man is missing, all other good is wanting. For ill doth the spindle move, when the beard does not wag above it]. Doubtless apprehending the visual image in the trope of Celestina's proverbial response (on spinning and sewing as symbols of sexual congress, see Alzieu, Lissorgues, and Jammes 1975, 45, 76, 77, 81; 89, 130; and Fontes 1984, 1985), Melibea tersely bids her 'Pide lo que querrás, sea para quien fuere' (122) [Ask what thou wilt, be it for thyself or anybody else]. Celestina, catching Melibea's reference to her own obligations to status and position as a cover for her to proceed, prods Melibea to look to sympathy and to mercy now, and fills her in on the young man who, ailing, 'con una sola palabra de tu noble boca salida, que le lleve metida en mi seno, tiene por fe sanará, según la mucha devoción tiene en tu gentileza' (122) [with one word, which should come from your noble mouth, and entrusted in this my bosom, I verily assure you that it will save his life, so great is the devotion which he bears to your gentle disposition].

Feigning ignorance, Melibea urges the bawd for clarification and to provide the details of the case, finally ordering her 'Por Dios, que sin más dilatar me digas quién es ese doliente' (124) [For God's love, without any more dilating tell me who is this sick man], provoking Celestina to pronounce Calisto's name. Hearing the name Calisto, Melibea reproaches the old whore for her audacity in an tone reminiscent of her earlier ambivalent censure of Calisto in the garden: '¡Ya, ya, ya buena vieja, no me digas más! No pases adelante' (124) [Enough, enough! No more, good old woman! Not a word more], with just enough false emphasis in the appositive reference to Celestina as a good old woman to leave an opening for more. In the end, both Celestina and Melibea negotiate covertly the secret surrender of her girdle through a mutually understood simulacrum of an act of charity, propelling the plot forward through the impetus of necessarily repressed but ineluctably present feminine desire. Throughout Celestina and Melibea's first meeting, it is clear, as in her dialogue with Calisto in the garden, that under ostensible verbal veneers of resistance, propriety, and negation, 'no' is often 'yes' for Melibea, and that Celestina grasps this and fully understands the need for it. Experts in the circumlocutious, neologistic idiom of the socially suppressed feminine capacity for passion, both Celestina and Melibea appreciate the need for posturing and mediating desire through verbal parrying that leads ultimately to its discovery, admission, and open proclamation in their next encounter.

At the beginning of act 10, after Celestina's delivery of Melibea's girdle to Calisto, Melibea, alone, albeit aware that Lucrecia is eavesdropping, awaits the old bawd's return to her house. There, in a soliloquy redolent with self-pity, guilt, doubt, even jealousy for an imagined rival, plus concern for what others might think, she gives voice to her emotions, admitting to loving Calisto from the start as she seeks strength to continue to conceal her passion:

¡O lastimada de mí, o mal proveída donzella! ¿Y no me fuera mejor conceder su petición y demanda ayer a Celestina quando de parte de aquel señor cuya vista me cativó me fue rogado, y contentarle a él, y sanar a mí, que no venir por fuerça a descobrir mi llaga quando me sea agradescido, quando ya desconfiando de mi buena respuesta aya puesto sus ojos en amor de otra? ... ¡O mi fiel criada Lucrecia! ¿Qué dirás de mí; qué pensarás de mi seso quando me veas publicar lo que a ti jamás he querido descobrir? ... O soberano Dios, a ti todos los atribulados llaman ... humildemente suplico: des a mi herido coraçón sofrimiento y paciencia, con que mi terrible passión pueda dissimular. (246)

[O wretch that I am! O unfortunate damsel! Had I not been better yesterday to have yielded to Celestina's petition and request, when in the behalf of that gentleman, whose sight had made me his prisoner, I was so earnestly sued unto, and so have contented him and cured myself, than to be thus forcibly driven to discover my heart, when haply he will not accept of it, whenas, already disaffianced in his hope for want of a good and fair answer, he hath set both his eyes and heart upon the love and person of another? ... O my faithful servant, Lucrecia, what wilt thou say of me, what wilt thou think of my judgment and understanding, when thou shalt see me publish that, which I would never discover unto thee? ... O thou high and supreme power! Thou unto whom all that are in misery and affliction call ... I humbly beseech thee, that thou wilt give sufferance and patience to my wounded heart, whereby I may be able to dissemble my terrible passion.]

As Celestina enters, Melibea turns to her in agony and describes her pain: 'Madre mía, que me comen este coraçón serpientes dentro de mi cuerpo' (248) [Truly, mother, I think there be some serpents within my body, that are gnawing upon my heart]. The reference to the serpents eating her body cannot be fortuitous: the serpent is her animalistic emblem, just as the hawk is the icon for Calisto. Calling forth images of the serpent in the Garden of Eden, the textual primal scene for all human desire, Melibea becomes another Eve in the throes of temptation and desire for carnal knowledge. The phallic Freudian connotations of her remark can also not be missed (see Deyermond 1977). More importantly, however, is the evocation of the ravenous serpents that devour her heart, snakes akin to the reptilian lovers of the prologue, who forge the link between Eros and Thanatos as they consume their mates in a struggle of passionate desire, turning the mortal metaphors of love into the deadly reality of nature.

Melibea's body cannot contain her desire as she confesses her suffering and yearning for Calisto through the symptoms that seize her flesh. When Celestina asks what ails her, she responds:

> Mi mal es de coraçón, la ysquierda teta es su aposentamiento; tiende sus rayos a todas partes ... es nuevamente nascido en mi cuerpo, que no pensé jamás que podía dolor privar el seso como éste haze; túrbame la cara; quítame el comer; no puedo dormir; ningún género de risa querría ver ... La causa o pensamiento ... de mi mal, ésta no sabré dezirte ... salvo la alteración que tu me causaste con la demanda que sospeché de parte de aquel cavallero Calisto quando me pidiste la oración. (250)

> [My pain is about my heart, its residence near unto my left pap, but disperth itself over every part of my body. Secondly, it hath been so but of late; nor did I ever think that any pain whatsoever could have so deprived me of my understanding, as this doth; it changes my countenance, takes away my stomach, I cannot sleep for it, nor will it suffer me to enjoy any kind of pleasure ... nothing I can conjecture to be the cause of it, save only a kind of alteration caused by yourself upon request, which I suspected, in the behalf of that gentleman Calisto, when you entreated me for my charm.]

In this way, Melibea's own body speaks in response to her unfulfilled desire, which, like Calisto's, manifests itself with the physical symptoms of melancholia and the *aegritudo amoris*, or love sickness. She has internalized Calisto's absence and the loss transforms itself into the pain produced by the serpents that bore into her heart. Her body utters a language by analogy, the symptoms of desire. The objectifying portraits of highly fetishized courtly ladies are overturned when we listen to Melibea's body talk because, in speaking, she moves tenuously into the position of subject to tell a different story from the one that her otherwise stereotyped body underwrites (see Burns 1993, 109–13).

As with Calisto, Celestina protracts Melibea's suffering until she can stand it no longer. Casting all scruples aside, Melibea begs the bawd to do something – to ravage her flesh and cut out her heart, if needed – to provide relief whatever the cost:

> ¡O cómo me muero con tu dilatar! Di, por Dios, lo que quisieres, haz lo que supieres, que no podrá ser tu remedio tan áspero que yguale con mi pena y tormento. Agora toque en mi honrra, agora dañe mi fama, agora lastime mi cuerpo, aunque sea romper mis carnes para sacar mi dolorido coraçón, te doy mi fe segura, y siento alivio, bien galardonada. (252)

> [O how thou killest me with delays! For god's love, speak what thou wilt, do what thou wilt, for there is not a remedy so sharp as can equal the bitterness of my pain and torment. No, though it touch upon mine honour, though it wrong my reputation, though it afflict my body, though it rip my flesh, for to pull out my grieved heart! I give thee my faith, to do what thou wilt securely; and if I may find ease of my pain, I shall liberally reward thee.]

Although Melibea complains of the physical symptoms that wrack her passionate body – the stabs and pricks of love that strike at her to cleave it open – Melibea's actual wounding, the genuine breach and the opening of the unsuturable *foramen magnum,* will be inflicted on her psyche as her deflowering is carried out through language, through metaphor and speech. It is with words and tropes that Celestina conquers Melibea and ensures that she has capitulated to desire, long before Calisto ever touches her.

In response to Melibea's suffering and anxieties, Celestina counsels endurance and patience: 'Sufre, señora, con paciencia, que es el primer punto y principal. No se quiebre, si no todo nuestro trabajo es perdido. Tu llaga es grande' (254) [Madame, I pray be patient. That which is the chief and principal stitch must not be broken; for all our labour is lost. Your wound is large] she urges while feigning solidarity, surreptitiously attempting to protract Melibea's longing. Punctuated by continuous references to Melibea's wound and to the connotative use of the word *punto* (point, stitch, or loop, as in sewing, knitting, or tying), the ensuing dialogue suggestively tropes the opening and closing of Melibea's wounds, the breaching and stitching of her body, leading to the climactic recognition of her love for Calisto and to her final surrender to desire. Celestina's wooing of Melibea in Calisto's name develops figuratively not from a lure dangled from a rope for a hungry falcon but from a needle and thread, and like a distorted version of Penelope's tapestry, it is woven into a prolonged exercise in waiting and anticipation. Aware of the penetrating nature of Calisto's name, which she has just uttered, Celestina now carefully makes her second point, calling for Melibea to withstand the pain in order to stitch tight her wound:

> Señora, este es otro y segundo punto, el qual si tu con tu mal sufrimiento no consientes, poco aprovechará mi venida, y si como prometiste lo sufres, tu quedarás sana y sin debda, y Calisto sin quexa y pagado. Primero te avisé de mi cura y desta invisible aguja que sin llegar a ti sientes en solo mentarla en mi boca. (254)

> [Madame, this is that other and main point which if you by your impatience will not consent unto, my coming can little profit you. But if you will, as you promised, be patient, you shall remain sound and out of doubt, and Calisto will be well apaid and have no cause to complain. I did before acquaint you with my cures, and with this invisible needle, which before it come at you, you feel it, only but having it in my mouth.]

Directly and indirectly, Celestina continues to weave in references to Calisto until Melibea can stand it no longer, and she begs Celestina to get to the point and tell her what Calisto seeks: '¿De qué ha de quedar pagado? ... ¿Qué necessario es él aquí para el propósito de mi mal? Más agadable sería que rasgasses mis carnes y sacasses mi coraçón, que no traer essas palabras aquí' (254) [Wherein should he be well apaid? ... What necessity is there that we must be driven to use him as the instrument of my recovery? More pleasing would it be unto me, that you would tear my flesh asunder and tear out my heart, than utter such words as these]. Celestina immediately makes the desired point: 'Sin te romper las vistiduras se lançó en tu pecho el amor; no rasgaré yo tus carnes para le curar' (254) [without any rupture or rending of your garments love did lance your breast; and therefore I will not sunder your flesh to cure your sore] and diagnoses the affliction. Melibea suffers from 'Amor dulce' (254) [Sweet love].

Overcome with emotion, Melibea nearly faints – just nearly – when she hears Celestina's diagnosis and Calisto's name yet again, only to recover her composure out of concern for alerting the household to Celestina's presence in the parlour. 'Passo, passo, que yo me esforçaré; no escandalizes la casa' (256) [Softly, speak softly; I'll see if I can rise; in no case do not trouble the house], she whispers to Celestina, urging her to silence while seeking to chasten the bawd's concern for her swoon. Celestina, however, still agitated by Melibea's syncope, fears the unravelling of her work and mumbles 'Creo que se van quebrando mis puntos' (256) [I believe my points are broken], to which Melibea graphically rejoins 'Quebróse mi honestidad, quebróse mi empacho, afloxó mi mucha vergüença' (256) [No, it is my honesty that is broken, it is my modesty that is broken; my too much shamefastness], marking her conclusive surrender to desire by extending Celestina's metaphor to the breaking of the fragile threads of her resistance – the ones that until now held her virginity intact – and to the ones that bound tight her sense of dignity.

Following this climax of recognition by Melibea, the tropes of sewing, tying, and linking all come together in a coda of imagery that underscores the striking intellectual consistency of Fernando de Rojas's creation. In her dialogue with Melibea, Celestina transforms the images of binding and loosing into an erotic rhetoric that fetishizes her words and enkindles Melibea's desire, while at the same time providing linguistic camouflage for her passion for Calisto. Melibea concedes that after her capitulation, symbolized in the broken threads that bound her wound of shame, Celestina has now figuratively provided a means for both her surrender to Calisto and the continued appearance of her propriety: 'Cerrado han tus puntos mi llaga, venida soy en tu querer … Pospuesto todo temor, as sacado de mi pecho lo que jamás a ti ni a otro pensé descobrir' (256–8) [With thy needles thou hast stitched up my wound; I am come to thy bent … By laying aside all fear thou hast gotten that out of my bosom, which I never thought to have discovered unto thee or to any other]. Celestina, renowned for expertise in restoring virgins, persuades Melibea with the suggestive imagery of her 'invisible needle,' conveying how 'los ásperos puntos que lastiman lo llagado, doblan la pasión … si tú quieres ser sana que te descubra la punta de mi sotil aguja sin temor, haz para tus manos y pies una ligadura … rige sin orden la aguja … esta invisible aguja, que sin llegar a ti, sientes en solo mentarla en mi boca' (252) [the sharp incisions (stitches of my needle) which double the pain … if you be willing to be cured … without any fear, frame for your hands and feet a bond … and then shall you see what effects this old mistress will work upon thy wounds]. The wounds of her guilt, shame, and ambivalence sewn tight by Celestina's masterful verbal (and possibly even physical) manipulation, Melibea can now openly declare her yearning as she surrenders to Calisto before he even lays a hand on her.[3]

Melibea has spoken. She has crossed over the barriers set by repression and articulated her capitulation to desire in her own words. Her speech suggests a kind of epiphany that leads to a conscious admission of feminine yearning. Under the veneer of courtly love and the impediments it sets for the representation of women as subjects, *Celestina* disrupts the boundaries that traditionally mark the expectations of masculine and feminine behaviour in it and challenges the configuration of gendered speech that typically structures medieval stories of romantic passion.

Melibea's desire develops as a manifestation of the evolution of her character and the forward movement of the plot. It is a force she feels and then learns to discover in dialogue with Celestina. Although at first she confesses to being unable to explain exactly what she feels and never to have felt it before, when queried by Celestina Melibea describes and locates the exact place of her emotions ('Mi mal es de coraçón, la ysquierda teta es su aposentamiento' [250] [My pain is about my heart, its residence near unto my left pap]), linking her body to her yearning and to carnal hunger through the image of the serpents that devour her heart. Despite her initial resistance and the protestations of her innocence, Melibea quickly learns to understand the sensory experiences offered by her body, deciding to transform her pain into delectation while challenging the patriarchal prohibitions that traditionally police the articulation of feminine desire in privileged society. The gratification she achieves in her trysts with Calisto compel her to forsake all measure of propriety and lead her to admit to the pleasure she derives from them: 'Señor, yo soy la que gozo, yo la que gano' (378) [Sir, it is I that enjoy this; if anybody gain by it, it is I], she says to Calisto, describing herself as the one who achieves the greatest contentment from their liaison. Melibea pronounces the delight of her desire and takes possession of the pleasure traditionally apportioned by courtly love only to its masculine subjects.

As she sets free the pleasures of her body from repression, Melibea detects and begins to understand other forms of feminine desire. The discovery of her sexuality leads to further discoveries of the possibilities inherent in the self. She finds a sense of autonomy and resistance that gives her the courage to speak back, even to restrain and seek to control the forceful compulsions of masculine desire. In this way, she displays her wish to tame Calisto's brutal ardour, reproving him for his rough manhandling of her: 'Cata ... que assí como me es agradable tu visita sossegada, me es enojoso tu riguroso trato; tus honestas burlas me dan plazer, tus deshonestas manos me fatigan cuando passan de la razón' (378) [Thy honest sporting pleaseth me , but thy dishonest hands offend me, especially when they are too far out of reason]. As she gives rise to her own impulses and desires, Melibea discovers the authority to prescribe the terms of physical intimacy with Calisto, at the same time increasing her willingness to take other positions of resistance against the patriarchal world. When she overhears her parents commenting on the possibility of arranging a marriage for her, for example, she rejects their plan, insisting to her confidante Lucrecia on the primacy of her desire for Calisto and the wish to enjoy fully her youth: 'déxenme mis padres gozar dél si ellos quieren gozar de mí. No piensen en estas vanidades ni en estos casamientos, que más vale ser buena amiga que mala casada, déxenme gozar mi mocedad alegre si quieren gozar su vejez cansada; si no, presto podrán aparejar mi perdición y su sepultura' (342–4) [Let my parents let me enjoy him, if they mean to enjoy me. Let them not settle their thoughts upon these vanities, nor think more upon those their marriages. For it is better to be well beloved than ill married. Let them suffer me to enjoy the pleasure of my youth, if they mind to enjoy any quietness in their age; if not they will but prepare destruction for me, and for themselves a sepulchre]. In Melibea's refusal to comply with parental authority, of course, we perceive the menacing shadow that obscures the entire enterprise – death, the price that will be paid by all for the pursuit of their desires. The ineluctable link between Eros and Thanatos is inevitably emphasized again. Yet, Melibea's refusal to marry, and her preference for taking pleasure with Calisto, stand as an indelible mark of her desire for independence, the expression of a feminine voice that insists upon the autonomy to choose the type of life she wants.[4] To be sure, the speech she pronounces just prior to her suicide constitutes the final articulation of her desire to be the full master of her life and body. It is there she has her final word and exercises her full freedom to choose, even if it means leaping desperately into the abyss.

It is surely not a coincidence that Melibea's last words to her father echo those of another recent literary heroine's decision to follow her lover in death. Like Mirabella, who hurls herself to her death in Juan de Flores's *Grisel y Mirabella*, a romance that centres on the theme of the debate on women, or the *querelle de femmes* (on the complaint against women, or *querelle* in fifteenth-century Spain, see Weiss 2002), Melibea declares her determination to die after witnessing her lover expire (von der Walde Moheno 2000, 253). In the penultimate act of the *Tragicomedia*, Rojas doubtless recalled Mirabella's impassioned yet reasoned explanation of her suicide and the affirmation of the pre-eminence of natural over civil law in the debate on gender and the role of women in love as played out in Flores' work (see Roffé 1996). With this in mind he placed Melibea's decision to take her own life squarely into the same polemical context. To be sure, Melibea's suicide, like Mirabella's before her, is a deliberate, conclusive, discursively well-developed act. Like Mirabella, Melibea expresses her desire to follow her lover in death, and in her parting speech she emphasizes that his death implies more an end to her personal pleasure than an expression of grief for the death of Calisto. As María Embeita confirms, Melibea 'llora más la privación del deleite voluptuoso, que el fin del amado' (1977, 130) [laments more the loss of her voluptuous delight, than the death of her lover]. Melibea's suicide is the final expression of her newly discovered will, and it is portrayed by her as a welcome gesture taken to relieve the pain caused by the absence of pleasure and Calisto's death. Positioned in the parapet of the tower from where she intends to leap, Melibea looks down at her father below, and in a speech ironically designed to invert gender roles, begs him to be strong, not to weep or to be sentimental, or to intervene so that she might speak and have her say. Posed physically as well as morally above Pleberio, she acquires the distance that allows her the freedom to speak authoritatively and to explain her motivation and intention to jump to her death. Her words are shaped by chilling logic and are embellished with calculated chiasmus and anaphora:

> Padre mío, no pugnes ni trabajes por venir donde yo estó, que estorvarás la presente habla que te quiero hazer. Lastimado serás brevemente con la muerte de tu única hija. Mi fin es llegado; llegado es mi descanso y tu passión; llegado es mi alivio y tu pena; llegada es mi acompañada hora y tu tiempo de soledad ... sy me escuchas sin lágrimas, oyrás la causa desesperada de mi forçada y alegre partida. No la interrumpas con lloro ni palabras, si no quedarás más quexoso en no saber por qué me mato, que doloroso por verme muerta. (388–90)

> [No, good father, trouble not yourself, nor strive to come to me; you shall but disturb that speech which I am now to make unto you. Now, by and by shalt thou suddenly be wounded to see the death of thy only daughter. My end draws near; at hand is my rest and thy passion, my ease and thy pain, my hour of keeping company and thy time of solitariness ... And, if thou canst hearken unto me for tears, if thine eyes will give thine ears leave to hear, thou shalt hear the desperate cause of this my forced yet joyful departure; see thou neither speak nor weep; interrupt me not, either with tears or words, unless thou mean'st more hereafter to be tormented, in not knowing why I do kill myself, than thou art now sorrowful to see my death.]

Rejecting the possibility of finding any words of consolation in 'aquellos antigos libros que tú, por más aclarar mi ingenio, me mandavas leer' (392) [those ancient books, which for the bettering of my wit you willed me to read], Melibea then enjoins her father to console her mother, spurns the thought of an unmerciful God as she commends her soul to Him, and commits the ultimate act of the human will by hurling herself from the tower.

Among the women in *Celestina*, however, it is not just Melibea who emerges and exhibits a determination to seize the word and fix the course of her desires, to grasp control over her life and even the circumstances of her death. All the women in *Celestina* exceed the expectations that denote their initial characterization to come forth as singular persons conscious of their autonomy who dare to speak their want. In *Celestina*, women's agency bursts on the scene from profoundly reconfigured literary scenarios of courtliness and misogyny to establish a relational dynamic between all the female protagonists and the social formations that surround them. The complex social positioning of the women in *Celestina* allows us to understand them as desiring, empowered, active speakers. They are never subservient, impotent, silent, or passive players as required by the textual traditions from which they spring. Rather, they may be understood better in accordance with Joan Wallach Scott's reading of historical women as discursive sites where numerous competing forces produce political (in *Celestina*'s case, 'literary') subjects (1996, 14–15). In *Celestina*, the effects of oppression and misogyny are perceived as structures that, however monolithic they may seem or claim to be, are fragile, permeable, and always open to resistance. It is clear that female agency in *Celestina* no longer resides solely in acknowledging a male lover's entreaties of unattainable desire, or in a patriarch's delimitations of it. Agency in *Celestina* is not seen as something wielded exclusively by empowered and dominant male protagonists. To the contrary, *Celestina* sets into motion various forms of resistance to the amorous and patriarchal status quo that point toward the presence of more complex subject positions than previously imagined in literary texts at the close of the fifteenth century.

To be sure, *Celestina* not only represents a variety of forms of opposition to the silencing of feminine speech, but a variety of communicative women located across the social spectrum, each of whom wavers vis-à-vis the possibility of being stereotyped. Resistant to the imposition of predetermined roles, each stands out for the heterogeneity of their personalities and the complexity of the responses to their desires. While they appear in the stereotypical roles of mothers, daughters, wives, servants, and prostitutes, the women in *Celestina* nevertheless break with every expectation of their representation as they transcend the limitations imposed by literary convention to offer a unique perspective on their femininity, sexuality, and social ambitions. Although Areúsa and Elicia are both whores, for example – figurative libertine sisters, daughters of their 'mother' Celestina – and each is portrayed in opposition to Melibea, each is fundamentally different, one from the other. While each may serve as a referent to the historical moral scruples and sanctions enacted against clandestine prostitution at the time Rojas was writing his work (see Lacarra 1993), they nevertheless come forth as distinct individuals with their own personalities who seek to claim their heart's desire. Elicia, out of necessity and personal allegiance to Celestina, lives openly as a prostitute with her, while Areúsa practises her profession in the more exclusive, covert environment of her home. Yet both receive the clients Celestina offers, and each distinguishes herself by maintaining a unique relationship with a man. On the one hand, Elicia, despite her notorious availability as a public woman, demands an incongruent fidelity from Sempronio, even displaying jealousy when he praises Melibea's beauty and shows an interest in his master's lady in act 9. On the other hand, Areúsa's mastery of the allusive language of love demonstrates a clear intelligence and perspicacity in the exploitation of one of the most important resources for her work, while her comeliness, seductive personality, and self-confidence make her exceed all of Elicia's claims to charm. Sosia's distinctive description of both to the young Tristán cleaves the difference. For Sosia, Elicia is simply the 'criada de Celestina y amiga de Sempronio, una muy bonita moça' [Celestina's servant and Sempronio's friend: she is a good, pretty handsome, well-favoured wench], while Areúsa incites only encomia. Areúsa is 'una hermosa mujer, muy graciosa y fresca, enamorada, medio ramera, pero no se tiene por poco dichoso quien la alcança a tener por amiga sin grande escote' (326) [a very fair woman, she is exceeding well-favoured, very fresh and lovely: she is half courtesan; yet happy he is, and counts himself so to be, that can purchase her favour for any rate, and win her to be his friend]. Yet it is doubtless out of the desire to emerge on her own and achieve a degree of independence that Elicia later rejects Areúsa's invitation to form a partnership to continue Celestina's business after the old bawd's death.

Despite their differences, both Areúsa and Elicia agree upon one thing: their contempt for Melibea. Yet each holds her in contempt for different reasons: Elicia out of jealousy rooted in Sempronio's admiration for the

from one-dimensional. In Pleberio's conversation with her about his intentions to have their daughter marry, Alisa dutifully submits to patriarchal authority and concedes that the decision is Pleberio's to make, 'como esto sea officio de los padres y muy ajeno a las mujeres' [since this be the duty of fathers and one alien to women], assuring him that 'como tú lo ordenares, seré yo alegre' (342) [as you shall dispose of it, so shall I rest contented] while appearing to validate the established norms of gender. Yet Alisa, as we saw in the previous chapter, only superficially complies with Pleberio's wishes and bends to patriarchal power, leaving Melibea alone to converse with Celestina, whose occupation she fully knows and understands from the moment she again lays eyes on the old bawd, her former neighbour. Whether out of imprudence or deliberate design, when closely examined, Alisa, far from a being a vigilant mother, seems to seek to live her own bygone or unattended desire vicariously through the amorous adventures of her daughter.

Lucrecia, Melibea's maidservant and yet another minor character in *Celestina*, as we have also seen, offers up a complex, multidimensional personality that expresses her freedom to desire. Although Celestina notes that Lucrecia's 'mucho encerramiento' [being shut up so close at home] has kept her from 'el gozo de su juventud' (234) [enjoy(ing) her youth], implying that she is sexually repressed as well as socially oppressed, Lucrecia spies on her mistress and Calisto, listening attentively to their ardent coupling in the garden, as Rojas registers the increase of her desire with each of Calisto's and Melibea's encounters. Unlike her cousin Elicia and her friend Areúsa, Lucrecia has not yet realized her desire to know the full delight of the pleasures of the body, yet that does not restrain her from expressing her yearning for them, as she declares herself to be 'deshaziéndo[se] de dentera' (378) [melt(ing) within, like snow against the sun] as she listens to her privileged mistress half-heartedly shun Calisto's impassioned entreaties. We have seen how, overcome with desire, Lucrecia throws herself physically upon Calisto when he enters Melibea's garden; however, castigated by her mistress, who claims Calisto as her exclusive object of pleasure, Lucrecia is kept by social difference from actualizing her sexual ambitions. Even though Lucrecia is capable of recognizing and acting upon her desire, she is prevented from obtaining the object of it not by her femininity but by the class barriers that delimit her reach.

The women in *Celestina* represent a broad spectrum of feminine agency, yet they are all portrayed as desiring subjects. Far from being stereotypes, they are distinguished by the variety of their experiences and reactions to the social structures intended to contain the realization of their wants. As such, they offer new, and appropriately contradictory, insight into the changing nature of the representation of women at the end of the fifteenth century. If, on the one hand, a maudlin Melibea may rue her suffering by taking mawkish pity on herself by blaming her feminine condition ('¡O género femíneo, encogido y frágile! ¿por qué no fue también a las hembras concedido poder descobrir su congoxoso y ardiente amor, como a los varones?' [246] [O sex of womankind, feeble and frail! Why was it not granted as well unto women to discover their tormentful and fervent flames, as unto men?]), Areúsa, on the other, is constant and meets every adversity with determined strength, going so far as to reproach Celestina when the latter, filled with her own self-pity, bemoans her diminished state and the splendour of bygone times. Urging Celestina not to dwell on the earlier days of her prosperity, at the banquet in Celestina's house, taking a page from Celestina's own book, Areúsa exhorts her to seize the moment, 'pues somos venidas a haver plazer' (236) [since we are come to have pleasure]. More than prudish courtly ladies or bawdy strumpets, women in *Celestina* reveal themselves to be complex desiring subjects who, in addition to seeking to fulfil their carnal yearning, aspire to achieve social agency and express their desire for immediate empowerment.

The presence of a definite sexuality in each of the women characters of *Celestina* has been interpreted by some critics as an early expression of advocacy for women's rights. Diane Hartunian (1992), for example, links the portrayal of feminine desire in the work to the theme of the *carpe diem*, contrasting the latter's manifestation in the *Tragicomedia* with its use in contemporary lyric poetry. Hartunian rightly sees early modern *carpe diem* poetry as an extension of the masculine courtly ideal that, while it exhorts a woman to realize desire, remains a manifestation of the masculine voice and actually impedes it (1992, 76–7). The exaltation of an ideal feminine beauty in the lyric not only serves to vouchsafe the preeminence and authority of the masculine speaking voice in *carpe diem* verse but to transform the feminine into a decorative object that serves only to exhibit the poet's mastery and virtuosity. Although on the surface the poet's exhortation to a lady to seize the day counsels her to delight in the plenitude of beauty and youth, the youth and beauty described in it are stereotypical, never individualized, and thus fail to represent feminine desire and the real possibility of its enjoyment. Rather, *carpe diem* poetry turns in upon itself and becomes an exercise in narcissism in which masculine poets exploit an imagined feminine ideal as a mirror in which to reflect their own desire and profile their verbal proficiency in seduction.

In *Celestina*, however, the presence of the *carpe diem* is introduced by the feminine characters themselves, as in Celestina's first encounter with Melibea or Areúsa's exhortation to Celestina to forget the past and take pleasure in the instant. Through this discursive displacement, it opens the way for the articulation of feminine desire and the urgency of the moment. In this way, there is a definite break – a reconceptualization of the *carpe diem* – that locates the immediate desire for pleasure believably in the feminine. It becomes an appeal by one woman to another to accept and act upon the stirrings of desire before it is too late and the latter are extinguished.

Women in *Celestina* are conscious of their bodies; they are aware of their wants; and they seek to direct and to control both. They are portrayed as individuals who have managed to escape the passivity imposed upon them by literary convention to achieve an autonomy that allows them to express, if not to achieve fully, their personal yearning for pleasure and for something other than what they have. Areúsa and Elicia stand out as paradigmatic female subjects who have full knowledge and take full possession of their sexuality. Although one could argue that as prostitutes they are compelled to confront the realities of their bodies to function as objects of exchange in an oppressive patriarchal economy of desire – Areúsa as the property of Centurio and Elicia as that of Celestina, who ministers to the demands of patriarchy – it is nevertheless possible to agree with Catherine Swietlicki that 'these women are not conscious of their subservience,' that they see themselves as autonomous, and that they 'feel extremely free' (1985, 5).

Elicia and Areúsa take pride in their work and in seeing themselves as Celestina's successors after the latter's death. An expression of this sense of confidence and independence can be located in Areúsa's wish for Pármeno not to leave her company after their heated night of love, even after her initial reluctance to receive him. Feigning continued distress from *mal de madre* (wandering womb), Areúsa provokes Pármeno to enquire into what she needs to relive her discomfort, to which she coyly responds 'Que hablemos en mi mal' (206) [that we talk a little on the matter of my indisposition]. Elicia, on the other hand, while exacting fidelity from Sempronio, does not hesitate to continue sexual congress with Crito, her best and most frequent client. By means of characters like Areúsa and Elicia, Rojas confronts the possibility that prostitution may not just be a kind of feminine perversion, portraying it as something that arises from economic necessity and that, in addition to being a means to an end for women, may even offer personal pleasure to the women who practise it. This is certainly so with Celestina.

While both Areúsa and Elicia revel in the present pleasures of their bodies, Celestina ruefully recalls her own amidst evocations of the ardent sensuality of her youth. As she responds to Areúsa's and Pármeno's reluctance to her presence when she watches them couple from the shadows of Areúsa's room, Celestina longingly evokes her own bygone encounters in which she, like the young Areúsa, revelled in the pleasures of the flesh. Time is Celestina's real oppressor; its effects upon her body prevent her now from finding a mate who can rekindle the pleasures for which she so ardently longs. It is for this reason that Celestina now seeks them vicariously, substituting sight for touch in the pursuit of a desire whose fulfilment still eludes her reach. Celestina's peremptory wish to be transformed into a man, spoken as she inspects Areúsa's body below the sheets ('¡O quién fuera hombre y tanta parte alcançara de ti para gozar tal vista!' [192] [O that I were a man and might gain so great a part of thee as this to glad my sight]), bespeaks of her high-voltage, if obstructed, sensuality; so high, in fact, that it exceeds heterosexual satisfaction, compelling her to seek gratification with another woman. Similarly, her repeated fantasies of nocturnal male assailants constitute, in addition to an evocation of the real threats of the streets Celestina transits, vivid evidence of her yet sexually energized imagination, vestiges of an insatiable desire that yearns still to explore the darker side of passion.

In their exploration of femininity, Hélène Cixous and Catherine Clément have described the obstacles that culture places in the way of the expression of feminine desire and the inhibitions that accompany them. They note that 'Every woman has known the torture of beginning to speak aloud, heart beating as if to break, occasionally falling into loss of language, ground and language slipping out from under her, because for women speaking – even just opening her mouth – in public is something rash, a transgression ... A double anguish, for even if she transgresses, her word almost always falls on the deaf, masculine ear ... it is not where we find our pleasure: indeed, one pays a certain price for the use of discourse' (92). In the fictional universe of *Celestina*, however, the women that populate it overcome fear and inhibition to display an array of voices that speak publicly of feminine ambition and desire. Celestina employs speech as the means to attain what she seeks; Areúsa seizes the word to express her envy and fulminate against the privilege of some that marks the subjection of others; and Melibea discovers her ability to speak of her desire for Calisto and to will her own death without him. In full possession of the word, Melibea confesses her love for Calisto to her father, and calls attention to the loss of her virginity ('perdí mi virginidad' [392] [I lost my virginity] she tells Pleberio factually, without any intimations of regret). Melibea's candour about the loss of her virginity is a projection of her newly discovered ability to speak. In her admission, the freedom to dispose of her body is linked to the freedom to speak candidly about it, marking a victory of sorts – even if at the expense of death – over repression, patriarchy, and misogyny. However, her words are late in coming – too late – and the one dialogue she sustains with her father remains a monologue to which Pleberio, struck dumb by the words of his daughter, can offer no response. With the terrible foretelling of her own death, Melibea closes the circle of the events that have led her to discover self-awareness and find her individuality. Her suicide is as much an expression of her wish to be with Calisto as it is a challenge to the patriarchal world that constrains all feminine desire.

Resisting the inhibition and mystery that Freud ascribed to women when he asked 'What does a Woman Want?'[5] the women of *Celestina* assume their individual identities and their bodies to become protagonists of consciousness, defining themselves as speaking subjects of desire. They are able to say, in one way or another, what they want, even if their freedom to speak comes at a dreadful price and they fail to achieve what they desire. Each one heeds Celestina's call to seek pleasure and to define herself – 'gozad vuestras frescas mocedades' (230) [enjoy thy youth] – and so offer a new perspective on the representation of feminine desire at the threshold of modernity. The revulsion and fear to speak that, according to Cixous and Clément (1986), have always constituted the legacy of women pose no obstacles in *Celestina* to have its women speak. Each from the unique perspective of her femininity, though she may utter truths or lies and never achieve what they seek, takes possession of the word and of herself to exercise a voice that gives her presence in a discursive universe traditionally reserved for masculinity; and one in which both speech and individuality were traditionally denied to all of them.

Yet, while all this is so, none of the women in *Celestina* actually ever attain what they say they need or want. Their yearnings are never fulfilled. Their speech rises from a sense of opposition, resistance, and struggle not just to enunciate but also to realize the desires inscribed by their words. Although Rojas challenges the boundaries of gender that traditionally excluded the feminine voice and made feminine desire invisible in medieval and early modern literature, in the discourse of the women who populate his universe the manifestation of their voices and the articulation of their yearnings, though they may be heard, are never triumphant. Their desires are never grasped, never achieved; they are never fulfilled. Quite the opposite: all their desires fail and are transformed into chimeras. If their speech marks determination, it lacks all celebratory purpose and sense of liberation. From the point of its articulation it is devoid of the possibility of the consummation of their want.

While Rojas acknowledges feminine social and sexual yearning, and while the female characters of *Celestina* also articulate oppositional discourses to patriarchy and traditional feminine gender roles on various levels as they speak their manifold needs and ambitions, all the women characters in the work, including even the puissant, loquacious, and articulate Celestina, never really reach any definitive form of empowerment, any form of satisfaction, or any kind of governance over themselves or the world they inhabit. Beyond their desires and the ability to speak about them, tied to a heightened awareness of newly emerging yet frustrated forms of subjectivity, what *Celestina*'s women underscore more than anything else is Rojas's unprecedented ability to construct three-dimensional characters and to plumb the depths of new subjectivities. There is a devastating irony in all this, as Rojas creates believable human characters ultimately just to turn on all of them, male and female, young and old, low-born and high-born alike, to destroy them and their ambitions in the crucible of desire. Despite the fact that Elicia and Areúsa proclaim their control over their sexuality and say they have chosen their line of work, the climate of violence in which prostitutes lived and died in late fifteenth-century Spain, exemplified in Celestina's brutal murder, gives the lie to the possibility of options and every promise of consummation for them both in fiction and the real world. Melibea's awakening to her sexuality likewise leads only to defeat, delivering her into the manipulative hands of Celestina, exposing her to Calisto's brutish treatment, and finally to dishonour, despair, and self-destruction. While on the surface the women of *Celestina* may indicate resistance to patriarchy and misogyny, the text is intent on accentuating the failure of everyone's individual resistance to an inhospitable world driven by a yearning for the impossible. The economic, social, and existential imperatives that rule everyone's lives make all the assertions of independence and self-reliance impossible, if not at the very best always contingent. As we saw in chapter 1, Celestina helps unleash the forces of desire – in women, in servants, in everyone in the book – but the work does not lionize the ability to express desire as a form of freedom. Rather, it pays heed to, and dramatizes, the anxieties that result from it and the release of social and sexual inhibitions, most often portraying their unleashing as lethal forms of want. The anxieties expressed by Rojas in the truculent images of the prologue and the aggressive discourse of the rest of the prefatory material of *Celestina* belong not just to him. They are projected also onto and through – they are instilled in – all the characters of the work. Love, ambition, and desire all harbour the inevitable reality of disenchantment. While both male and female characters actualize impulses for feeling and enjoyment in *Celestina*, pleasure and enjoyment, manifested chiefly as sexual desire whose stated or implicit end is *jousissance*, always comes at a cost and bears an edge of desperation. Even after consummation, enjoyment carries with it dark intimations of unresolved, continuing frustration, of finality, and of death. All the characters in *Celestina*, regardless of their gender, long for something: for human congress, solidarity, friendship, the attainment of a sense of personal purpose and fulfilment, economic well-being, status or stability – all of which the old whore Celestina seems to promise. Yet they all ineluctably come to realize, in usually terrible, vividly violent ways leading to their material destruction, that the objects of their desire, be they male or female, things, ranks, privileges, or social stations, remain always out of reach. They are perpetually fleeting, unobtainable objects bound up with disappointment, betrayal, predation, chaos, and despair. In *Celestina* everyone, male and female alike, enunciates desire, yet, in the end, no one ever achieves its end. Desire remains inscribed in a language of impossibilities; it is a process whose only end is disillusionment or, finally, death.

7 The Desire to Belong and the Body Politic

Por la filosomía es conoscida la virtud interior.

Calisto (Act 1, 116)

According to Karl Marx, the body, like the world, God, and commodity, 'abounds in metaphysical subtleties and theological niceties' (Marx 1976,163). At the threshold of modernity, the body began to be conceived as something that could be autonomous, self-moving, and conscious of itself, and as a new medium for experiencing the world. An awareness of human corporality began to be imagined as a given reality that could be offered or witheld in every action. It began to be seen explicitly as a vehicle of volition and pleasure, and therefore as an instrument of desire. In this way, the body became a recognized agent of identity and an object of social understanding. Its specific somatic reality could thus be understood symbolically in terms of fashion, health, sexuality, leisure, economics, art, or anything that could confer figurative value upon it. Somatic structures and their sensory faculties were perceived as capable of articulating a dense system of metaphorical relationships that linked them with social understanding.

Although *Celestina* quite conspicuously treats sex, love, the human body, prostitution, and morality, with the exception of Eukene Lacarra few scholars have explored how these topics, in both their orthodox and 'deviant' manifestations, also affect the polity of persons depicted in the text, and how these ideas may be linked to larger cultural and ideological forces shaping the discourses of legitimacy in late fifteenth-century Spain. The sexual underworld defined by the perimeters of Celestina's house in act 9, for example, is – more than a space for promiscuity – a precinct for the articulation of desire that manifests itself in heated partisan debate, as well as sexual commerce, centred on the privileges and freedoms of the person as designated by caste, political economy, blood, and social position. It is there that, in consonance with their passionate corporality, open sexuality, and the consumption of food and other material goods, characters like Elicia, Areúsa, and Lucrecia express their radical social and civic non-conformity as they undermine their masters' authority through the exposure of what they perceive to lie behind the painted masks of their entitled lives.

The descriptions of Melibea's body in act 9 provide the iconic centrepiece for this debate and figure prominently in the scene as the concrete images around which all the apprehensions delimiting the relationship of the servants to their masters revolve. Melibea's portrait, placed there in the mouths of the two whores, Elicia and Areúsa, functions as a figural nexus that subsumes a series of symbolic connections linking sexuality, corporality, nutrition, and desire to questions of social authority, privilege, agency, money, and power. As it does this, Melibea's likeness constitutes a site for cultural negotiation, a representational structure that expresses, more than petty jealousy (Fraker 1939, 138–9; Gariano 1975, 4), deep changes affecting the social and sexual fabric of the world in which all the characters in *Celestina* live.

Pierre Bourdieu has argued persuasively that the body harbours profound cultural significance and that it embraces a form of compressed cultural symbolism that encodes 'in abbreviated and practical, i.e., mnemonic, form the fundamental principles of the arbitrary content of the culture' in which it appears (1977, 94). Bodies, according to Bourdieu, may thus be understood as domains of signification encompassing broad figurative sense and may be interpreted as illustrations of social position, cultural identity, and patterns of belief and authority.

The Middle Ages was a period profoundly preoccupied with bodily representations and both defined and constituted the human body as a crucial element of the symbolic order. The body was an acknowledged medieval site for social figurations. To be sure, echoing Aristotle's *Politics* the medieval and early modern mind viewed the human body as a microcosm (Rico 1986), but especially as a trope capable of depicting political and social systems (Hale 1971). Medievals read bodies explicitly as transparent cultural signs that pointed to things greater than themselves. Indeed, in the Middle Ages all manner of abstractions through the devices of allegory were given corporal form and played a prominent role in defining, mediating, and depicting society's institutions and conventions. The body and its portrayal were thus conceived as a means of knowledge of other things and were understood as iconic devices apt to provoke thought. Looking at, reading about, talking, or writing about human bodies and their functions always implied the presence of a larger interpretive vision at work.

Personality and civic values were reified both in the medieval somatic body as well as in the marks of status and insignia used to embellish it. In the pseudo-Aristotelian *Secreta Secretorum*, one of the most widely disseminated texts of the Middle Ages, for example, Aristotle in the context of the political education of Alexander the Great invokes the science of physiognomy as key to understanding the temperament and inclinations of humankind in questions of statecraft. Similarly, the body, suitably attired and presented, came to overtly symbolize the gender, status, and nature of the person, and that individual's place in the larger sphere of the state and human polity. In the Middle Ages dignity and class came to knights from their shields and armour as well as from their genealogical person, and heraldic signs and sartorial adornment signified a means of both personal and social identification (Fox-Davies 1969, 108). The body's physical constitution and the way it was enhanced, then, were recognized forms of social textuality.

In addition to the Church, which was imagined as the *corpus verum*, chief among medieval embodiments were the specifically political and civic metaphors that portrayed the state and community in concrete terms of human corpora. Ernst Kantorowicz, for example, has shown how the notion of the king's two bodies expounded the dual nature of sovereignty – both human and divine – while the depiction of the monarch as the head of society was used to account for the hierarchy of political and social differences in the order of things (Kantorowicz 1957, Le Goff 1989). The socialized human body often encompassed, then, the central symbolic object around which metaphorical civic definitions, as well as the struggle for power, dominance, and spirituality, were played out (see Hale 1971, Patterson 1991, Dinshaw 1989, Brown 1988, and Bynum 1991).

More than for the simple transcoding of political ideals, however, the body – but primarily the sexually disordered or infirm body – could be used to portray and invoke social upheaval and threats to political and moral stability, as well as to challenge the boundaries that defined and maintained order. The medieval imagination, for example, failed to distinguish between leprosy and venereal disease, and specifically associated leprosy with promiscuity and sexual depravation, reading the leper's outward signs of bodily decomposition as evidence of inner profanity, moral degeneracy, and social undesirability. In this way, the leper incarnated an ethical, physical, and social menace to the citizenry and was isolated in the Middle Ages by rituals, quarantines, and even legal sanctions (Brody 1974). Corporality was thus, in addition to a means for representing order, a vehicle that could personify disorder and convey intangible ethical, political, and civic anxieties. To the medieval imagination a disarranged, profane body signalled a potentially dangerous relationship to everyone in the community.

To be sure, the corporal comparison of the disordered, ailing body was invoked with particular urgency during the wrenching debates on monarchical succession in Castile during the reign of Enrique IV, known to history as *el impotente*. The magnate Pedro González de Mendoza explicitly summoned it at Avila in 1465 to allude to the king, as he cautioned the supporters of Prince Alfonso's rival claim to the throne:

> Notorio es señores, que todo el regno es avido por cuerpo, del qual tenemos el Rey ser cabeza; la qual si por alguna inhabilidad es enferma, pareceria mejor consejo poner las melecinas, que la razon que cree que quitar la cabeza, que la nacion defiende. (Memorias de Don Enrique IV de Castilla, II, 489)[1]

> [Gentlemen, it is well known that every realm may be taken for a body, of which the king is the head; and if that head should, through some indisposition, suffer infirmity, the application of remedies would seem better council than following the advice of those who would remove the head, which defends the nation.]

Indeed, as the struggle for succession and political hegemony between Enrique IV and the partisans of his half-sister, Isabel of Castile, intensified after the death of the young Alfonso in the generation before Fernando de Rojas, the dynastic clash was played out upon the reigning monarch's very body. Rumoured to be sexually impotent, and hence incapable of producing an heir, the right of Enrique's putative daughter, Princess Juana, to succeed to the throne of Castile was openly contested by the opposing Isabeline faction as it asserted Juana's illegitimacy. As a result, in his attempt to salvage his designated heir's claim to the crown, Enrique was compelled to submit to medical enquiries as well as cite evidence from prostitutes that refuted his alleged sexual dysfunction.

It is clear, therefore, that bodily references and descriptions – but especially those linked to forms of sexuality – were something more than simply themselves, and that in fifteenth-century Iberia, as elsewhere in Europe, ordered and disordered bodies often functioned as concrete representations of social entities and ideas – conscious symbols of human polity. In effect, the human body at all levels of society was charged with political significance as it was perceived to personify communal beliefs and contain civic significance. In this larger sense, then, human bodies were envisaged as material representational spaces of community, agency, and power possessing a clear figurative economy, as their substance constituted a parable of the social condition and an image of civic stability or turmoil.

The conspicuous interest accorded to Celestina's facial scar, the sign that truly distinguishes her body, points from the outset to the deep implications of the human body in the events that unfold in Rojas's work. The indelible mark on her face is a clue to the central meanings that reside in the representations of bodies in *Celestina*; it calls attention to corporality as a signifier and as a place where meaning may be etched or inscribed. Put simply, in *Celestina*, the body itself, predominantly through the scenarios of desire, is called upon to embody significance.

Though Melibea's body in *Celestina* has been the object of some critical interest (notably Boullosa 1973, Fraker 1993, Hathaway 1993, and Hartunian 1992), its function as a domain of social as well as sexual signification has been virtually neglected. In the impassioned discussion that her physical attributes incite at Celestina's banquet table (act 9), the description of Melibea's image is subtly transformed into something other than merely itself – it is amplified into a metonymy of the disordered civic body, as class tensions are articulated in terms of competing forms of sexuality and are suddenly projected upon and through it. Melibea's monstrous corporal representation in *Celestina* is contrived as an unequivocal image that equates corrupt social practices – privilege, plutocracy, artifice, and guile – with aristocratic sexual ideals – norms that, according to Elicia and Areúsa (the two sluts who describe her), personify the social abuse heaped upon the humble by Melibea's empowered class. In Melibea's physical depiction as composed by the two whores, affluence and its advantages become the vehicles for the expression not only of sexual but also of social desire and for the portrayal of wealth's human displacements. Melibea's body thus assumes the function of a master trope for challenging and dissolving the boundaries of social and reproductive authority at the centre of blood, class, caste, and legitimacy in late fifteenth-century Castile.

Melibea's portrait as sketched by Elicia and Areúsa at the banquet stands in stark iconographic contrast and rhetorical apposition to the one offered earlier by her aristocratic lover Calisto in act 1, whose description is also inlaid with social messages and ideological significance. Asking first that his servant Sempronio hear him out and 'Mira la nobleza y antigüedad de su linaje, el grandísimo patrimonio, el excelentísimo ingenio ... e la soberana hermosura' (38–40) [consider the nobleness of her blood, the ancientness of her house, the great estate she is born unto ... and lastly her divine beauty'], Calisto launches into the following physical characterization of Melibea:

> Los ojos verdes, rasgados, las pestañas luengas, las cejas delgadas y alçadas, la nariz mediana, la boca pequeña, los dientes menudos y blancos, los labios colorados y grossezuelos, el torno del rostro poco más luengo que redondo, el pecho alto, la redondeza y forma de la pequeñas tetas, ¿quién te la podría figurar? ... la tez lisa, lustrosa, el cuero suyo escurece la nieve ... Las manos pequeñas en mediana manera, de dulce carne acompañadas, los dedos luengos, las uñas en ellos largas y coloradas, que parecen rubíes entre perlas. Aquella proporción que veer yo no pude, no sin dubda por el bulto de fuera juzgo incomparablemente ser mejor que la que Paris juzgó entre las tres diesas. (40)

> [Her eyes are quick, clear and full; the hairs to those lids rather long than short; her eyebrows thinnish, not thick of hair, and so prettily arched, that by their bent they are much the more beautiful; her nose of such a middling size, as may not be mended; her mouth little; her teeth small and white; her lips red and plumb; the form of her face rather long than round; her breasts placed in a fitting height; but their rising roundness, and the pretty pleasing fashion of her little tender nipples, who is able to figure forth unto thee? So distracted is the eye of man when he does behold them; her skin as smooth, soft and sleek as satin, and her whole body so white, that snow seems darkness unto it ... Her hands little, and in measurable manner and fit proportion accompanied by her sweet flesh; her fingers long; her nails large and well coloured, seeming rubies intermixed with pearls. The proportion of those other parts which I could not eye, undoubtedly (judging things unseen by the seen must of force be incomparably far better than that which Paris gave his judgment of, in the difference between the three goddesses).]

Privilege and entitlement are the concealed messages of Calisto's expression of desire for Melibea. Her measured physical attributes illustrate class power and identity and belong to a long tradition of learned descriptive conventions and 'high' aristocratic discourses linked to the world of medieval romance and classical rhetoric (Colby 1965, 25–72; Curtius 1963, 180–2). Melibea's delicate, proportioned form signals the presence of caste and position embedded in a sexual ideal; she is a chosen person, an inhabitant of elevated society – the personification of cleanliness, order, and authority, as well as fertility and physical beauty. Moreover, her bodily make-up is rendered in an idiom that evokes a courtly genealogy of legible texts inscribing visions of perfection, command, and exalted passion. It commemorates the myths of heroic nobility, prerogative, and idealized desire that lie at the centre of the great deeds, venerated beauties, and sentimental legends of the Trojan War, which are its literate subtext. In brief, Calisto's verbal portrait, more than a record of a particular sexual fantasy or a passionate desire, teems with emblems of cultural authority and aristocratic empowerment as it stands as an icon of lofty sensibilities, power, and courtly propriety.

On the contrary, Elicia and Areúsa's later likeness of Melibea constitutes a premeditated, dialectical deformation of those patrician principles – an attempt to cross and contest the physical boundaries that designate Melibea's lordly class, sexual desirability, and cultural command as deployed by Calisto in his earlier semblance. Artificially adorned, deformed, polluted, and spent – yet plutocratically empowered – Melibea's form, as described in act 9 by the whores, invokes an anomalous body in chaotic disarray and constitutes itself as a symbolic inversion of Calisto's socio-sexual reverie – it becomes a site for the expression of conflicting prerogatives and aspirations centred on the differences of wealth, lineage, and blood.

In the midst of their repast, Elicia fires the first descriptive salvo aimed at Pleberio's daughter after she hears Sempronio refer to 'aquella graçiosa y gentil Melibea.' Focusing on the twin themes of artifice and affluence, Elicia looses the following broadside:

> ¡Mal provecho te haga lo que comes, tal comida me has dado! por mi alma, revessar quiero quanto tengo en el cuerpo de asco de oýrte llamar a aquélla gentil ... ¡O quién stoviesse de gana para disputar contigo su hermosura y gentileza! ¿Gentil, gentil es Melibea? Entonces lo es, entonces acertarán quando andan a pares los diez mandamientos. Aquella hermosura por una moneda se compra de la tienda ... que si algo tiene de hermosura es por buenos atavíos que trae. Ponedlos a un palo, tanbién dirés que es gentil ... creo que soy tan hermosa como vuestra Melibea. (226–8)

[The devil choke thee with that thou hast eaten! Thou hast given me my dinner for today; now as I live, I am ready to rid my stomach, and to cast up all that I have in my body, to hear that thou shouldst call her fair and courteous, lovely and gentle ... I will cross myself in pity of thy great ignorance and want of judgment; who I pray had any mind to dispute with you touching her beauty and her gentleness? Gentle Melibea! Fair Melibea! Then shall both these hit right in her when two Sundays come together, or when the ten commandments shall go hand in hand by couple ... All the beauty she hath may be bought at every pedlar's, or painter's shop ... and if she have any jot of handsomeness in her, she may thank her good clothes, her neat dressings, and costly jewels, which if they were hung upon a post, thou wouldst as well say by that too, that it were fair and gentle ... I am every way as fair as your Melibea.]

As Elicia proclaims her own sovereignty in physical perfection and sexual allure, Melibea is reduced to an inventory of capital, a list of talismans that signify affluence over essence. Her sexual and human values are depicted only in terms of the worth of the objects she consumes and arrays in her quest to camouflage her disagreeableness. To be sure, Elicia's portrayal of Melibea's purchased charm alleges that Calisto's lover is a greater whore than she – guiltier of meretricious guile – since the acquired embellishments of her body speak of trickery, deceit, and extraneous merit rather than essential value. Melibea's sex appeal, Elicia claims, has no depth: it is a fabricated illusion – a gesture more illicit than any the low-life characters of *Celestina* could possibly contrive in their pursuit of wealth and in their efforts to make their way in the world. The fraudulence of Melibea's crafted images of desire, Elicia alleges, are the certain measures of both her moral and social worth. As a counterfeit of nature, Calisto's embodiment of aristocratic longing has been transformed into her opposite in Elicia's imagination.

The cosmetic illusion Elicia indicts Melibea of crafting conveys greater depravity than any of the wiles Celestina's whores can fashion, since Melibea fails to seduce without recourse to the ultimate deception: bodily lies. The classic misogynistic metaphor of the courtesan – the exorbitant use of make-up, cosmetics, and other physical adornments – is ironically inverted, turned back upon Melibea by the whore in order to denounce the legitimacy of Melibea's pleasures. She, more than Celestina's sluts, Elicia suggests, is the proven woman of easy virtue, and the ultimate deceiver. The purchased ointments, salves, and unguents, plus the rich clothes she wears, constitute an artificial investment of value, as Melibea is denounced as a sexual charlatan who traffics in misbegotten sensuality. It is at this point that Elicia's indignation suddenly turns to insurgent social ideology and unites with the venerable motifs of medieval misogyny. The result is a subversion of wealth culminating in a likeness of meretricious plutocracy, as Melibea's portrait vacillates between the images of traditional medieval antifeminism and the social coordinates of Elicia's grievances. The idiom of medieval love and sexuality now unexpectedly mediates thoughts of social and political estrangement.

The attack on Melibea's sexuality is escalated when Areúsa enthusiastically amplifies Elicia's sketch, looking deeper as she magnifies the body beneath the cosmetic covering. Claiming physical nausea like her friend at the sight of Melibea, Areúsa presents Calisto's lover as a dishevelled, filthy profligate:

> Pues no la has visto tú como yo, hermana mía; Dios me lo demande si en ayunas la topasses, si aquel día pudiesses comer de asco. Todo el año se está encerrada con mudas de mil suziedades. Por una vez que haya de salir donde puede ser vista, enviste su cara con hiel y miel, con unas tostadas y higos passados, y con otras cosas que por reverencia de la mesa dexo de dezir. Las riquezas las hazen a éstas hermosas y ser alabadas, que no las gracias de su cuerpo, que assí goze de mí, unas tetas tiene para ser donzella como si tres vezes oviesse parido; no parescen sino dos grandes calabazas. El vientre no se le he visto, pero juzgando por lo otro creo que le tiene tan floxo como vieja de cinquenta años. (228)

> [Oh sister! hadst thou seen her as I have seen her (I tell thee no lie), if thou shouldst have met her fasting, thy stomach would have taken such a loathing, that all that day thou wouldst not have been able to have eaten any meat. All the year long she is mewed up at home, where she is daubed over with a thousand sluttish slibber-slabbers; all which forsooth she must endure, for once perhaps going abroad in a twelvemonth to be seen: she anoints her face with gall and honey, with parched grapes and figs crushed and pressed together, with many other things which, for manner's sake and reverence of the table, I omit to mention. It is their riches, that make such creatures as she to be accounted fair; it is their wealth, that causeth them to be thus commended, and not the graces and goodly features of their bodies: for she hath such breasts, being a maid, as if she had been the mother of three children; and are all for the world, like nothing more than two great pompeans or big bottled gourds. Her belly I have not seen, but

judging it by the rest, I verily believe it to be as slack and as flaggy as a woman of fifty year old.]

Melibea's gross portrait, whose ugliness is now specifically contextualized in the realm of the edible, bodily regulation, and corporal exuviae (Elicia, Areúsa's and Melibea's) – as well as sex and capital – does more than simply disavow Melibea's physical attraction: it propels her image into the contemptible sphere of lower bodies, whose iconic function is both to subvert and define structures of social authority (Bakhtin 1968, 19; Stallybrass and White 1986, 8–26). The invocation of Melibea's flaccid midriff and falling breasts, the latter doubly transformed into pendulous pumpkins (*pompeans*) by Elicia's imagination, visually denies, denounces, and converts Calisto's portrait of patrician sexuality and power into one of pollution, ingestion, and vanished desire.

Melibea's grotesque bulk is now constructed of mixed categories connoting filth, exorbitance, concealment, disproportion, protuberance, laxity, and the physical functions of the body. She constitutes a multiple self composed of what Mary Douglas terms 'matter out of place' (1966, 121). As such, Elicia's description reconstitutes Melibea's physical representation into a moral and social image of contamination – one that thwarts the bodily boundaries that defined the iconography of aristocratic desire symbolizing blood, class, gravity, and propriety in Calisto's portrait. The conventional metaphors of misogyny and courtly love, though present in the description, extend beyond their usual sexual, sentimental, and moral connotations as they are elusively conjoined to the metaphor of the body politic and the discourses of social legitimacy in the work, enacting a partisan drama of civic discord. The language and images of medieval sex and ethics are recast and compelled to articulate a clash of class and political economy.

Elicia's and Areúsa's insistence upon Melibea's deformity, profanity, and sexual impurity symbolically despoils her of the insignias of prerogative and position affiliated with social elites. In fact, as Douglas has shown, physical representations like this are often crafted in order to translate questions of social authority, position, and legitimacy into terms of bodily purity an impurity, where a despised class is generally conceived as grotesquely slovenly and unclean just as the preferred one is imagined as free from pollution (1966, 123). In order to express the social disjunctures Melibea personifies to the marginalized women who sketch her portrait, the signifiers that make up her foul countenance are deliberately detached from their conventional semantic fields as they pose a challenge to a dominant group through displacement and disfigurement of those elements that earlier were invoked by Calisto as corporal icons of exalted status.

The vile bodily imagery employed by Elicia and Areúsa subverts Melibea's sexuality and constitutes, then, a semiological code that belongs less to the tradition of misogyny, which portrays women as covetous deceivers, than to a counter-discourse of bourgeois authority and political legitimacy. To be sure, Elicia's indictment of Melibea, as it incorporates familiar terms and images from medieval antifeminism, dissociates itself from the latter since her sketch separates the problem of ornament from the inherent aberrations of the female sex. Melibea is described as something degenerate, enervated, and sexually spent, something that no lotion or colouring or salve can restore or purify – infertile, impotent, and incapable of plenitude – but not because she is a woman. She is a simulacrum of strangeness, disintegration, and exhausted wantonness because she belongs to a plutocratic world of licence and ease denied Elicia and Areúsa. More than carnal impotence, Melibea is meant to personify a dangerous body that has lost mastery over itself and threatens others – a devitalized social standard whose meretricious essence is now revealed as she is verbally stripped of the characteristic marks of entitled beauty and exposed as a fraud by a competing class.

To Elicia and Areúsa, the ornamented, wanton, and disfigured Melibea constitutes an embodiment of the gentry's distortion of truth and nature, and her disfigurement marks the measure of their social disaffection. Their representation of Melibea's perverted and precarious female body is a proclamation of their profound civic alienation – a deformation and disfigurement of Pleberio's economic and social status as vested in his daughter, as much as it is a unique attack upon Calisto's lover.

Melibea's loathsome sexuality brutally proclaims the decomposition of authority in the civic body and signals the aristocracy's estrangement from the forces of production. More than a sign of feminine guile, the allegations of Melibea's purchased allure become figures of consumption and the power of money to transform the infamous and monstrous in nature through lies. They cast the dialogue into the realm of political economy, female commodification, and consumable goods, while linking the political, the economic, and the erotic orders (see Rubin 1975). The revulsion provoked by Melibea's physically grotesque portrait – circumscribed by themes of barter, commerce, and exchange – registers an abhorrence not just of the person but of all she represents.

Calisto, Areúsa, and Elicia all construct verbal portraits of Melibea that offer, more than objective images of the latter's sexual charms, a likeness of the speaker's own erotic and social cravings. They construct Melibea as Other from their positions as subjects, and speak her form in the fashion they wish her to materialize. They thus implicate the portrait they draw in a clear ideological economy. The mimetic aspects of Melibea's images are mediated by two forms of yearning – carnal and social – and her body's conflicting representations may be read as explicit evidence of tension in the human polity depicted in the work. The whores' caricatures of Melibea encapsulate contradiction and irreconcilability as they give vent to a broad critique of social patterns, practices, and ideologies.

From the contrast of the two portraits, it is clear that neither Calisto's nor the servants' likeness of Melibea can be seen as gestures to picture a real-life character. The physical conventions invoked by each of the speakers constitute signs of status and moral disposition, and belong to a greater web of signification pointing toward the realm of community and to a clash of sexual norms with political convictions. To Calisto, Melibea incarnates a sexuality unrelated to labour, the functions of the lower body, and other non-patrician marks. As he sees it, Melibea's body is imaginatively grounded in a learned legacy of texts and a genteel, courtly discourse rather than in nature; it constitutes for him a site of vicarious visual and sexual pleasure. Melibea personifies the notions of order, measure, and harmonic composition that lie at the heart of her and Calisto's pretensions to gentility and their claim to noble sensibilities and the rights of authority. Her sexual charms, though clearly infused with physical desire, are encoded in legendary terms that refer us to myth and to heroic times, as the most alluring parts of her body are tactfully elided, euphemised, and compared to the golden apple Paris gave to Aphrodite. Yet, simultaneously that fleeting reference to Aphrodite's apple couples Melibea's somatic body to the later banquet scene at Celestina's house, where the wider links between desire, nutrition and the edible, sexuality, and the power of wealth are made explicit.[2]

At Celestina's banquet table, sex and somatic desire, as they are connected to food and prostitution, are explicitly linked to wealth and economic exchange. They are translated into a larger discourse alleging social and political guile as they point to conflict and contradiction in the social order and to the bonds between corporal regimen and regime. Norbert Elias has shown just how such seemingly trivial acts as eating and other conduct implicated in bodily regulation conceal figurative interconnections to the larger domain of ideology and subjectivity, and may be read as evidence of social class and hierarchy (1978, 150). To be sure, images and themes of material well-being, sexuality, and social power intersect at Celestina's table in a moment that underscores the servants' inner quest to be free of the regulations imposed by class, blood, and social convention. Put simply, somatic and social appetites converge there and are shown to be contingent imperatives in the servants' imaginations.

In the newly delineated space furnished by Celestina's house and table (a utopian parenthesis opened to express the servants' sense of the insufficiency of the outer world around them, as well to proclaim their forthright sensuality), we see the confluence of the discourses of sex and bodily regimen with notions of social place. New forms of speech aimed at contesting the structures of the old civic order begin to emerge. Celestina's house thus materializes as an underground precinct for both sex and politics: a site where the questions of nutrition, procreation, and bodily control suddenly reveal their social underpinning and their connection to the struggles for power, class, privilege, and domination. Celestina's home serves as the battleground for the clash of two mutually exclusive ideologies: the economic liberalism of an emerging working class and traditional pre-capitalist patriarchal oligarchy.

It is not by coincidence that act 9, which exhibits Melibea's deformed countenance as the centrepiece of Celestina's table, begins by invoking hunger, poverty, and want as the forces that stir the imagination and embolden speech. Turning to Sempronio, Pármeno summons the lesson and sets the thematic preamble for the table talk and sketch to follow:

> La necessidad y pobreza, la hambre, que no ay mejor maestra en el mundo, no ay mejor despertadora y abivadora de ingenios. ¿Quién mostró a las picaças y papagayos ymitar nuestra propia habla con sus harpadas lenguas, nuestro órgano y boz, sino ésta? (224)

> [Necessity, poverty and hunger, than which there are no better tutors in the world, no better quickeners and revivers of the wit. Who taught your pies and parrots to imitate our proper language and tone with their slit tongues, save only necessity?]

Arriving late to the feast, Sempronio aphoristically excuses his delay by noting that 'quien a otro sirve no es libre, assí que sojeción me relieva de culpa' (224) [he that serves another is not his own man. He that is bound must obey. So that my subjection frees me from blame] and pleads that

they all move to the table, where they celebrate sexuality, social fellowship, and the comforts of an abundance of food underwritten by
Celestina's traffic in the flesh.

Focusing on carnal pleasures, the enjoyment afforded by the surfeit of
victuals, and a place to share them – as well as incessantly objecting to
the misery of servitude – the dialogue at the banquet signals a ritual of
social solidarity, sexual companionship, and an extended yearning for
material comfort. In fact, it is as he holds forth on the pleasures of love
and the camaraderie of the table, that Sempronio appeals to them all to
seize the moment and speak about Calisto and 'aquella graçiosa y gentil
Melibea' (226) [that fair, handsome and courteous Melibea], uttering
the words that kindle Elicia's and Areúsa's inflammatory ripostes and
provoke their grotesque verbal portrait of her. As the latter draw their
loathsome sketch, the conversation becomes tangled in exchanges that
persistently refer to the social issues and tensions subtending Melibea's
sexuality. The interchange culminates in a dispute between Sempronio
and Areúsa that shifts the focus away from Melibea's sexual body to her
social one – specifically to questions of caste and lineage.

Conceding that even if Areúsa's freakish countenance of Melibea were
true, Sempronio states that Calisto's passion for the patrician lady is inexorably animated by a cry of the blood, as he pinpoints the social sym-
metry of the lovers' desire:

Y aunque lo que dizes concediesse, Calisto es cavallero, Melibea hijadalgo;
assí que los nascidos por linaje escogidos búscanse unos a otros. Por ende
nos es de maravillar que ame antes a ésta que a otra. (230)

[And howbeit I should admit all you have spoken to be true, yet pardon me,
if I press you with this particular. Calisto is a noble gentleman, Melibea the
daughter of honourable parents; so that it is usual with those that are de-
scended of such high lineage, to seek and inquire after each other; and
therefore it is no marvel, if he rather love her than another.]

Indignant at the thought, Areúsa vehemently rejects Sempronio's views
and underscores the primacy of the person in defining sexual allure and
social merit, while emphasizing her own value:

Ruyn sea quien por ruyn se tiene; las obras hazen el linaje, que al fin todos
somo hijos de Adán y Eva. Procure de ser cada uno bueno por sí, y no vaya
a buscar en la nobleza de sus passados la virtud. (230)

[Let him be base, that holds himself base; they are the noble actions of men, that make men noble. For in conclusion, we are all of one making, flesh and blood all. For it is known that we are sons of Adam and Eve. Let every man strive to be good of himself, and not go searching for his virtue in the nobleness of his ancestors.]

From nutrition, to the repulsive denunciation of patrician power embodied in Melibea's sexual body, to a rejection of the categories of lineage, capital, and privilege, the conversation now twists back and forth until Lucrecia, Elicia's cousin and Melibea's maidservant, knocks at the door. Prefaced by Celestina's comment that Lucrecia will doubtless advance the current debate, Lucrecia's arrival stirs Areúsa's memory with the plight of domestic servitude. With this, she unleashes the full force of her social disaffection:

> éstas que sirven a señoras ni gozan deleyte ni conocen los dulces premios de amor. Nunca tratan con parientas, con yguales a quien pueden hablar tú por tú, con quien digan: '¿qué cenaste?; ¿estás preñada?; ¿quántas gallinas crías?; llévame a merendar a tu casa; muéstrame tu enamorado; ¿quánto ha que no te vido? ... ' y otras cosas de ygualdad semejantes. ¡O tía, y qué duro nombre y qué grave y sobervio es 'señora' contino en la boca. Por esto me bivo sobre mí, desde que me sé conoscer, que jamás me precié de llamar de otrie sino mía. Mayormente de estas señoras que agora se usan. (236)

[these same chamber-maids, these forsooth that wait upon ladies, enjoy not a jot of delight, nor are acquainted with the sweet rewards of love. They never converse with their kindred, nor with their equals, with whom they may say thou for thou; or so hail fellow well met, as to ask in familiar language; 'Wench, what hast thou to supper? Art thou with child yet? How many hens dost thou keep at home? Shall we go make our bever at thy house? Come, let us go laugh and be merry there. Sirrah, show me thy sweetheart, which is he? Oh wonderful! How long is it since I saw thee last? ...' And a thousand other the like unto these. Oh aunt! how hard a name it is, how troublesome, and how proud a thing to carry the name of a lady up and down continually in one's mouth! And this makes me to live of myself ever since I came to years of understanding and discretion. For I could never endure to be called by any other name than my own, especially by these ladies we have nowadays.]

Centring first on expressions of inequality and the use of honorifics in language that mark social difference, Areúsa goes on to detail the lack of personal freedom, the humiliations, abuses, and deceptions inflicted upon all those who by social circumstance and lack of means are compelled to serve. Areúsa concludes her diatribe against the wives of the gentry by declaring that she would rather earn a living as a whore, and be her sovereign self, than earn her living as a domestic: 'Por esto, madre, he querido más vivir en mi pequeña casa, exenta y señora, que no en sus ricos palacios sojuzgada y cativa' (238)[3] [And this, mother, is the reason, why I have rather desired to live free from controlment, and to be mistress in a poor little house of my own, than to live as a slave and at command in the richest palace of the proudest lady of them all].

The invocation of Melibea's vile body, followed by the servants' condemnations of the privileges of class and the anathema of servitude, prevent us from seeing Elicia's and Areúsa's gruesome portrait of her sexual allure as a momentary truancy expressing feminine envy, or less, as a crude affront directed at a specific person. It is, rather, a decisive instance of what Hayden White in his investigation of wildness calls 'ostensive self-definition by negation,' or a type of reflex that often appears in conflicts between social classes and political institutions seeking to authenticate their pre-eminence vis-à-vis one another (1986, 151–2). The traditional tropes and monstrous images of medieval misogyny are appropriated and employed here by Areúsa and her cohorts in a political way, and are hurled at Melibea in order to expound the as-yet-unpublicized anxieties of their own subjective values, fears, and aspirations. From their perspective, Melibea's sickening body incarnates their social alienation, subjugation, and exploitation – it stands as monument to their frustrated desires. Melibea's contemptible form serves to codify Elicia and Areúsa's alternative sexual and social identity through emphatic contradiction, and by means of its unnatural deformity provides a unique perspective on the ruptured civic and psychological landscape portrayed in *Celestina*.[4]

Confirmation of the iconic and socially transgressive function of Melibea's portrait follows fast, then, upon its appearance in act 9 when the conversation unexpectedly veers toward the abuses and deceptions that domestics suffer at the hands of their masters. As it unfolds, the dialogue guides us to the point where the images of Melibea's disordered sexuality intersect with grievances defined by class burdens and identity. The encounter at Celestina's table, with its denunciation of social hierarchies, prodigal wealth, abusive privilege, and ostentatious consumption, culminates symbolically in a comparison of corporalities – Elicia's, Areúsa's, and Melibea's – and, as the discourses of sex and nutrition are transformed into the discourses not simply of sexual but also of social desire, we are left with the impression that there is little distinction to be made between the edible, the female body, sexual allure, and social worth. To be sure, the body, sex, and other appetites and desires, far from effecting a displacement of class conflict, become the very centre of the controversy, the heart of the matter where a contest of opposing ideologies materializes in *Celestina*. The combination of diet and the images constituting other corporal necessities depicts the effective commingling of the essential forces driving the characters – desire at work, both social and somatic. Female bodies, as symbols of power, privilege, and subjective domination, are assimilated to a discourse of dietary pleasure, sexual freedom, individual fulfilment, and somatic well-being as they appropriate and sublimate constitutional political ideals and desires: social equality, agency, and personal sovereignty.

Melibea is portrayed by Elicia and Areúsa as the wanton and grotesque excluded Other in a conversation ostensibly centring only on sexual desirability. Yet, as this happens, the whores blur and shift the iconographic boundaries of class and propriety. Clouding and confuting the borders that traditionally define the alluring aristocratic body, Areúsa and Elicia destabilize the notion of high-born station, blood, and agency in the world they inhabit as they betray an ideology troubled by difference and beset with anxieties about sex, caste, and identity. As they interrogate, and invert, the patrician physiognomy assigned earlier to Melibea by Calisto, Melibea's sexual body becomes the distinguishing point of tension where the integrity and position of the subject is both defined and placed into question. Elicia and Areúsa repulsively rewrite Melibea's patrician sexuality in order to dispute and encroach upon the social perimeters that customarily define her kind and exclude them from her empowered world.

Melibea's body in *Celestina* conceals, then, more than carnivalesque inversion, sexual covetousness, or expressions of shallow envy and conceit. It constitutes an ideological crux that harbours contradictory images of contending socio-economic convictions and imperatives expressed through conflicting ideals of sexuality as it tropes class rivalries steeped in resentment. Areúsa's comments on the toil and humiliation of servitude, which follow fast upon Melibea's description, confirm that there is something much more afoot in the portrait than an extravagant, topsy-turvy moment of Bakhtinian excess. The impulses of the body emerge in *Celestina* as explicit threats to the extant system of social order and control and are inscribed in a clearly articulated discourse of social rancour and competition. The desire for food, money, and sex become integral components of a larger discourse of political and ideological hegemony. The potential anarchy posed by an imperative of bodily appetites linked to social aspirations is loosed and fails to be subordinated or contained by institutional controls – by wealth and patriarchy – just as personal and group interactions crack, rupture, and finally collapse.

Celestina in this way portrays an emerging dialectical opposition between competing forms of somatic and social desire and their confrontation with civic order. The body's needs are represented first as a consumable good, and then as a threat to orderly succession and the authority of patriarchy and the family. The open expression of material, social, and sexual volition voiced by Elicia and Areúsa defiantly repudiates, as Mary Gossy states, 'the legitimizing and controlling power of the church and the economic influence of the patriarchal family' (1989, 38). Women at this juncture in the work appear as both the subjects and objects of exchange, symbolically determining commerce as feminine. Areúsa is aware that in prostitution women can sell themselves, thus implying she lives in a world where everything and everybody is for sale. She makes evident what remains unspoken and repressed throughout society: that everybody and everything can be bought or sold.

In *Celestina*'s discrepant portraits of Melibea we discover nothing less than an early modern confrontation of the aristocratic and plebeian subject – a portrayal of competing forms of being and concepts of legitimacy. Clearly, the metaphoric nature of the aristocratic body – and by extension the body politic – was undergoing profound changes and transformation. It was being subverted and displaced by new forms of sexual and social corporalities that emphasized pleasure and natural imperatives as sources of empowerment and a sense of self. However, *Celestina* superficially camouflages the discourses of subjective difference by sublimating, transcribing, and displacing them only toward the realm of sexuality. Yet, as the characters speak of pleasure, desire, and love's fulfilment we see strategies of social domination and resistance spring forth from the plot at the very point where sex is most openly commodified and defined in terms of social mobility and consumable goods. Under the guise of the traditional medieval denunciation of sexual sin, boundaries marking the frontiers of caste and class are crossed to pose stark challenges to the rights of well-born privilege.

Sex, the body, and its desires in *Celestina* thus function as a means of access for an underlying sense of civic disorder in the work; they become primary sites of ideology and serve as registers of apprehension. We see that, more than a locus of carnal pleasure or prohibition, the libidinous, desiring body is conceived as a symbolic vehicle for incarnating social conflict as well as for upending human hierarchies. Through its representation of transgressive sexualities and corporalities, *Celestina* portrays an aggregate of associated communal perils in the late fifteenth-century Spanish imaginary and seeks to provoke, by extension, a rethinking and redefinition of the notion of political power, order, and legitimacy. Prostitution, passion, nutrition, and social stratification all intersect in the symbolic economy of sex and the body in late medieval Castile as if they were each different facets of one subversive prism.

The representations of the sexualized body in an author like Fernando de Rojas (not to mention others like Fernando del Pulgar, Alfonso Martínez de Toledo, and Fernán Pérez de Guzmán) capture prevailing political anxieties as they register apprehension and suggest that human corpora stand as models for social structures and behaviour. As Mary Douglas confirms, the body can never be rendered as a neutral or disinterested object – its valences are always predicated on ideological considerations – as cultures persistently turn to 'the symbolism of the body's boundaries ... to express danger to community boundaries' (1966, 122).

In brief, the discourses of the body, sexual and somatic desire, prostitution, and social trespass converge in *Celestina* to form a microcosm of a conflictive body politic perilously close to dismemberment. These discourses make visible the progressive dismantling of traditional structures just as they define emerging types of subjectivity radically at odds with the governing ideology of a patriarchal culture. By the closing decades of the fifteenth century in Castile there was underway a reconfiguration of social roles just as class distinctions were being designated in and through clashing sexual and corporal representations. Figurations of alternative and competing forms of the subject like the ones depicted in *Celestina* were not contrived for idle entertainment or for insipid moralizing, but constitute testimonials of a crisis centred on the notion of the prerogatives of the individual. They were produced by fundamental shifts in ethical, cultural, and socio-economic conditions at the close of the Middle Ages.

In *Celestina*, as in many other contemporary Iberian texts, political and civic anxieties were grounded in sex and subsumed by the body; they linked inexorably the physical constitution of the person to questions of moral worth, social legitimacy, and agency in an ongoing struggle for power, validity, and prestige. Far from innocent embodiments of nature, human bodies in late fifteenth-century Castile could be ideologically charged vehicles for thought that directed attention beyond themselves toward community tensions – toward the body politic. As elsewhere in Europe, in early modern Iberia crossing the boundaries of sex, the body, and desire implied crossing ideological and doctrinal frontiers. Positioned at the threshold of modernity, *Celestina* provides, then, a notable illustration of both the semiotics of the body and the somatics of fiction.

8 Precincts of Contention: Locating Desire and Ideology in *Celestina*

Subjectivity is a category of thought that is accountable for the way people define themselves, are perceived by others, and are affected by the things around them. Within the notion of subjectivity, people are conceived as thinking beings who disclose a presence through continuous action and change. Their emotions, feelings, and intentions, as well as their perceptions and ideas, undergo continuous transformation. Although tied to a body but distinct from it, human subjectivity always locates itself in physical space. The world is divided between subject and object, body and mind, and space is conceived of as a location where body and place are located and inextricably bound. The distinction between object and subject gains importance because space is regarded as something that is everywhere the same, an extension that becomes significant only through the manner in which it is acted upon, occupied, thought, or talked about.

When thought of within the context of subjectivity, space is thus much more than a geometrical category. It becomes a term that denotes not only isotropic physical regions but metaphorical mental and social ones as well. With the appearance of Henri Lefebvre's *The Production of Space* (1991; originally published in French in 1974) the idea that space could be imaginatively constructed to meet epsitemological needs changed our understanding of how the geometrical world was perceived and imagined by humans, allowing us to see the metaphorical interplay in culture between mental categories and physical areas. Before Lefebvre, Walter Benjamin, Pierre Bourdieu, and Michel De Certeau all, in one way or another, also taught us to be mindful of the way space was represented. But Lefebvre remains the most influential theorist and historian of space in modern times. He has demonstrated that spatial conceptions

are central to the constitution, representation, and reproduction of social and ideological categories that are symbolically implicated in the
notion of order, power, knowledge, desire, and domination. The portrayal of any space is thus unfailingly engaged in economic, political,
ideological, and existential issues as it combines mental, or abstract,
space with spatial practice and defines the relationship between thought
and defined locations.

Frances Barker in *The Tremulous Private Body* (1984) discusses the creation of new social spaces from the point of view of texts and discovers a
progressively ramified division of social space from a predominantly
public space to a proliferation of increasingly privatized spaces in the
history of culture. Barker uses the physicality of this new privatized space
as a metaphorical link to the emergence of psychological and socially
symbolic private space that is elicited by its physical complement. In this
regard, the attention paid to the development and representation of
separate interior spaces is crucial to the appearance of the concept of
the self-conscious individual, which modernity calls the sovereign subject. Similarly, in his *Segmented Worlds and Self,* Yi-Fu Tuan (1982) notes
the relationship between architectural space and human subjectivity.
Over time, Tuan notes, it is possible to trace the advent of an increasing
social and epistemic privatization, a parsing of space, that leads to the
idea of the individual as we understand it today. The development of a
palpable awareness of self can be followed beginning in the late Middle
Ages and seems to be accompanied by a withdrawal of portions of a person's attention and energy from the public sphere toward an interiority,
a self-awareness, that is symbolized in the creation and occupation of
private physical spaces. When closely examined, *Celestina* is a work profoundly preoccupied with the representation of of just this sort of space,
especially private space, in relation to the characters it portrays.

To be sure, *Celestina* is the first work of early Iberian literature to depict
space, especially urban spaces, in any in-depth, detailed, concerted fashion (on the variety of urban spaces *Celestina* records, see Botta 1994;
Maravall 1968, and Samoná 1972). Through the complex manipulation
of dialogue, descriptions of locations and settings are almost impercepti-
bly embedded in the characters' speeches and become integral parts of
the narrative fabric of the work, complements of what the characters do,
say, and believe (on narrative inlaying see Lida de Malkiel 1970, 81–107).
As Stephen Gilman notes in his masterful study of the art of *Celestina*, the
representation of material space is a decisive component of the work's
verbal art. The dialogue takes the reader

a través de una estructura de acaeceres radicalmente espacial, sucediéndose en constante progresión cinematográfica: dentro, fuera, adelante, abajo, arriba, hacia atrás, a través de iglesias, escaleras arriba, al interior de los jardines ... del comienzo al fin de la obra. Y cuando surgen obstáculos (muros, puertas, etc.) lo son en efecto para los deseos de los personajes y no simple decordao o mero juego de detalle escénico. Esta libertad espacial es la que, mejor que ningún otro rasgo, produce en nosotros esa ilusión engañosa de realidad identificable en la ficticia ciudad de *La Celestina*. (1974, 368)

[through a structure that is radically spatial, occurring in a constant cinematographic progression: inside, outside, in front of, below, above, behind, through churches, up stairs, inside gardens ... from the beginning to the end of the work. And when obstacles emerge (walls, doors, etc.), they do so in reference to the characters' desires and not simply as decoration or details of scenic adornment. It is this spatial freedom, more than any other characteristic, that produces the deceptive illusion of an identifiable reality in the fictitious city portrayed in *La Celestina*.]

Several critics have pursued Gilman's acute observations. George Shipley, for one, has explored an essential irony of place in *Celestina*, showing how the spatial imagery that constitutes Melibea's garden mimics the *locus amoenus* of the medieval amatory tradition and how it is verbally and situationally undermined to produce in the reader 'complex and tense reactions which can properly be called disconcerting' (1973–4, 287). This is accomplished through the violation of the artistic protocols of the garden motif and the decentring of its commonplaces, resulting in a sense of incongruity and dislocation toward the unknown. Similarly, expanding upon Gilman's commentary concerning the figurative role played by locations in *Celestina*, Deborah Ellis has focused on the symbolic value of the home and finds in the work's conflictive portrayal of domestic sites a meta-representational likeness of a psychic alienation that pervades the text – a portrayal of 'a world whose limits are disappearing and whose order is overturned,' a depiction whose imagery bespeaks 'insecurity and destruction' (1981, 15). Finally, Erna Berndt Kelley (1993) and Isidro Rivera (1995) have examined the way in which the work's verbal evocation of place was visualized by the artists who composed the woodcuts in the oldest known printing of *Celestina*.

That there is space in *Celestina*, that there are visualized places, is not a disinterested fact or a routine convention, but a significant occurrence that points to the presence of ideas and convictions in the text. As linguistic constructs, imagined sites in *Celestina* are much more than straightforward renderings of place. Rather, they constitute representations: verbally constructed interpretations of the physical world implicated in a broad network of concepts, sense, and connotation. The visualization of space, as Gaston Bachelard observes, always carries with it an implicit ideological and phenomenological significance: when we imagine spaces and scan locations, places, and rooms we generally 'read' those sites for the values vested in them, seeking the relevance they embrace for us and for the individuals who inhabit them (1994, 14; see also Tuan 1974 and Lutwack 1984). Similarly, Peter Stallybrass and Allon White note that 'space is never completely independent of social place' and that 'the formation of new kinds of speech can be traced through the emergence of new sites of discourse and the transformation of the old ones.' Each real or imagined site, they say, 'constitutes a nucleus of material and cultural conditions which regulate what may and may not be said, who may speak, how people may communicate and what importance must be given to what is said' (1986, 80). Utterances may thus be legitimized or dismissed according to the place where they are produced, while the history of social and political struggle can be seen as the chronicle of attempts to command significant sites and spaces of communication. In short, locations may prompt, sanction, and promote, as well as inhibit, certain kinds of actions, thoughts, and speech, and they may be approached as correlatives of ideology, which can be revealed by examining 'the relation between an utterance and its material conditions of possibility' (Eagleton 1991, 223).[1] In this way, the representation of physical space contains a significant extension of the domains of discourse and signification. The verbal portrayal of location fits into a larger scheme that forms part of an organized semiotic system that conveys sense upon both language and its material whereabouts.

Celestina is filled with dialogues that unfold in specific, verbally constructed, three-dimensional spaces, just as it is fraught with oblique descriptions of the city in which it transpires, and the money-making activities that occur there. Quite in passing, for example, an exchange between minor characters (Sosia and Tristán in act 14) may inform us that tradesmen of every sort eager to work awaken at dawn to go to their shops along the narrow streets to the centre of town: merchants, carpenters, blacksmiths, farriers, gardeners, and weavers alike all set forth, 'cobdiciosos de temporales bienes' (318) [covetous of temporal goods], evoking the bustling economic life of the city. Similarly, all manner of professionals (doctors, lawyers, judges, and bailiffs) practise their craft near the urban sites through which the characters pass. In the early morning on the outskirts of the town, too, 'suelen levantarse ... los trabajadores de los campos y labranças, y los pastores ... [y] en este tiempo traen las ovejas a estos apriscos a ordeñar' (318) [your day-labourers, your ploughmen and your shepherds rise, who about this time unpen their sheep, and bring them to their sheep-cotes to be milked]. Everywhere the characters turn, beyond their immediate conversation there is a sense of inhabited room teeming with purposeful activity. More than a barren stage for the drama of love and death that unfolds in the work, the imagined city in which *Celestina* transpires is a thriving urban locale resonating with noises, voices, and every kind of enterprise – a flourishing centre of both legitimate and illicit talk and commerce.

Celestina and her confederates, for example, are identified as creatures of the street. On more than one occasion we follow them in their dialogue as they walk to and from Calisto's, Celestina's, and Melibea's houses. However, the streets they traverse are described less for their value as empirical points on a map than as scenarios of conspiracy and perilous precincts of violent social and economic plunder. As they perambulate through them, Sempronio and Celestina plan Calisto's despoilment; and Celestina when ambling alone pleads for the Devil's intercession in her plan. At night, she tells us, those same streets become civic battlegrounds lurking with danger, where the anonymous citizens who pass through them are both victims and perpetrators of violent crimes. Obliged by prudence to walk at night down the middle of the lane, Celestina informs Elicia 'que jamás me subo por poyo ni calçada sino por medio de la calle. Porque como dizen, no da passo seguro quien corre por el muro, y que aquel va más sano que anda por el llano. Más quiero ensuziar mis çapatos con el lodo que ensangrentar las tocas y los cantos' (272) [for I never go near any bridge, bench, pit or causeway, but rather down the centre of the lane. For, as it is in the proverb, he goes not safe, nor never shall, who goes too close unto the wall; and he goes still most safe and sound, whose steps are placed on plainest ground; and I had rather foul my shoes with dirt, than bebloody my kerchief at every wall's corner]. The potential of robbery, rape, and plunder lurks around every corner and every dark doorway in this imagined city. During her nocturnal wanderings, Celestina can only find solace in the fact that her advanced age and worn condition will save her from becoming a target of urban aggression. In this way, *Celestina* opened up the possibility of imaginatively recreating a certain urban topography and demography, of crime and social deviance, finding and exploiting in it a new area of interest.

The creation of spaces and locations in *Celestina* is, then, both substantial and complex. In addition to the psychological and ironical manifestations outlined by Gilman (1974), Ellis (1981), and Shipley (1973) it often involves a series of presuppositions concerning the nature of human social, political, and economic activity. Issues of class and authority are linked to wealth, ownership, and the control of property, reflecting the cultural and historical developments taking place at the end of the fifteenth century. As Maravall (1968) has shown, the economic transformations of the period led to the disintegration of the traditional paternalistic organizational structures of society and to the creation of a radical sense of acquisitive individualism, to the free expression of desire regardless of caste or class. The equation of space and property with power and personal identity in· *Celestina* – the image of affluence and place as the visible domains of agency – provides the nucleus for the work's social and ethical confrontations. Landscape and architecture in it contribute to the mapping of ideological realms that give form and value to human attitudes about class status and society not yet articulated in a consciously systematic fashion. In a time when Spain had embarked on an extended conquest and colonization of the world, the visualization of the relationship between human subjects and physical spaces, property, and wealth emerges explicitly in *Celestina* and may be seen in terms of a politics of domination – the control of the inhabitants of one locale by those of another.

The representations of certain types of sites in *Celestina* are enmeshed in the contest for power, the desire and justification of the ownership of property, and the construction of the human subject. This is clear, for example, in the depiction of Celestina's and Areúsa's houses. The latter, shunning the humiliation of domestic servitude in the dwellings of the rich, prefers to be a prostitute and 'bivir en mi pequeña casa esenta y señora, que no en sus ricos palacios sojuzgada y cativa' (238) [desired to live free from controlment, and to be mistress in a poor little house of my own, than to live as a slave and at command in the richest palace of the proudest lady of them all]. In this way, prostitution in *Celestina* becomes a means not so much for wealth itself but for the recovery of a place of sanctuary and repose for the plebeian subject, an activity whose end affords the acquisition of a sense of autonomy, privacy, and personal dominion.

Ironically, then, Celestina's and Areúsa's houses are also imagined as their homes, places of shelter, respite, and comfort as well as emporiums of sexual commerce, witchcraft, and carnal industry. Their abodes form an integral part of a larger system that endows property and wealth with animating attributes – with individual meaning – and accounts for their roles as personal motivators in the text. Yet despite the yearnings of the inhabitants of these houses, privacy and abundance in the domestic economy of their homes may only be had at the expense of transgression – of harlotry, theft, and peculation since, as we learn, the money that pays the rent, and the food that fills the table at Celestina's banquet, must be filched from the likes of Calisto and Pleberio (218). The complex image of Celestina's house, invoked first with the concision of a proverb, is used to express a sense of ownership, group solidarity, and a radical insouciance at the thought of ill-gotten wealth. Her house (or 'our house,' as she invokes it to overcome Pármeno's initial resistance) stands as an arresting image of both group identity and unprincipled ambition. To Pármeno's objection that 'no querría bienes mal ganados' [I would no for thrive by ill-gotten gain] she retorts, 'Yo sí. A tuerto o a derecho, nuestra casa hasta el techo' (70) [but so would I: right or wrong, so as my house may be raised high enough, I care not].

The verbal description of Celestina's house itself invites the reader not merely to imagine the physical structure, but to formulate it as an expression of an idea: a desire suffused with both personal and political significance. In addition to a brothel, it is, as Alison Weber remarks, envisioned by the servants as a 'utopian alternative to the master's house/prison': as a 'place of peace and rest, rather than enforced labor; a *hospital* of maternal care rather than emotional neglect; a *purse* of plenty rather than deprivation; a *strongbox* of financial security rather than economic instability. It is a place where homosocial bonds complement heterosexual fulfillment' (1997, 133). Celestina's abode stands as a monument to the craving for personal empowerment through the ownership and dominion of possessions – as a fantasy of stability and legitimacy that lies at the centre of proletarian illusions. Its dining room, a figurative extension of these ideas, must be read as a spatial image of the hunger for personal gratification and the resolution of social and historical contradictions. To be sure, it is in Celestina's egalitarian refectory that, in the heat of partisan debate concerning the value of the rich, characters like Areúsa loudly reject the notion of a privileged class defined by genealogy: 'Ruyn sea quien por ruyn se tiene,' she exclaims, 'las obras hazen linaje, que al fin todos somos hijos de Adam y Eva. Procure de ser cada uno bueno por sí, y no vaya a buscar en la nobleza de sus passados la virtud' (230) [Let him be base, that holds himself base; they are the noble actions of men, that make men noble. For in conclusion, we are all of one making, flesh and blood all. For it is known that we are sons of Adam and Eve. Let every man strive to be good of himself, and not go searching for his virtue in the nobleness of his ancestors]. It is there, too, that as a former domestic servant she boisterously illustrates how servitude in patrician dwellings thwarts privacy, pleasure, friendship, and ultimately a sense of self:

éstas que sirven a señoras ni gozan deleyte ni conocen los dulces premios del amor. Nunca tratan con parientas, con yguales a qien pueden hablar tú por tú, con quien digan '¿qué cenaste?; estás preñada?; quántas gallinas crías?; llévame a merendar a tu casa; muéstrame tu enamorado; ¿quánto ha que no te vido?; ¿cómo te va con él?; quién son tus vezinas?' y otras cosas de ygualdad semejantes. ¡O tía, y qué duro nombre y qué grave y sobervio es 'señora' contino en la boca. Por esto me bivo sobre mí, desde que me sé conoscer, que jamás me precié de llamar de otrie sino mía. (234)

[these forsooth that wait upon ladies, enjoy not, nor are acquainted with the sweet rewards of love. They never converse with their kindred nor with their equals, with whom they may say thou for thou, as to ask in familiar language; 'Wench, what hast thou to supper? Art thou with child yet? How many hens dost thou keep ? Shall we go make our bever at thy house? Show me thy sweetheart, which is he? How long is it since I saw thee last? How is it with thee, wench? Tell me I pray thee who are thy neighbours now?' And a thousand other the like unto these. O aunt! How hard a name it is, how troublesome, and how proud a thing to carry the name of a lady continually in one's mouth! And this makes me to live of myself ever since I came to years of understanding and discretion, especially by these ladies we have nowadays.]

Celestina's abode becomes a site which reminds us that, although the servants who congregate there may be economically reliant on Calisto's and Pleberio's households, they refuse to view themselves as socially and psychologically dependent on them. Although Areúsa's words reveal an acute awareness of her place in the social economy, it is clear that as a person she refuses to submit to it. Within the safety of its walls, Areúsa's prostitution is represented not as a form of damnable deviance but as a lived circumstance arising from her social vulnerability. In the politically transgressive speech all the characters give vent to at Celestina's house, they strive to challenge and dispute the system of exchange that governs them and imposes limits on their place in the world. Celestina's residence exists, then, as a spot that, in addition to offering rest and reassurance, provides a provisionally controlled space that sanctions the freedom to express their desires and imagine, as well as publicly utter, dissident thoughts. At the same time, too, it becomes the explicit scenario for the expression of what Fredric Jameson has termed 'commodity lust' (1981, 159), or the articulation of longings for wealth, property, and prosperity through the evocation of material things.

The bounteous description of the victuals that fill Celestina's dining room represents them not simply as food but as social signifiers – as a reverie of plenty imagined from a position of lack, as an expression of desire. More than a simple inventory, the edible objects that spill over onto Celestina's table fill out a symbolic space and constitute an image of coveted opulence that reflects the condition of those who do not regularly enjoy it. The 'pollos, y gallinas, anserones, anadones, perdizes, tórtolas, perniles de toçino, tortas de trigo, lechones' (242) [chickens and hens, geese, ducks, partridges, turtle-doves, gammons of bacon, tarts made of wheat flour, good suckling pigs] and the fine wines of Monviedro, Luque, Toro, Madrigal, and San Martín, plus many other choice vineyards, overwhelm the regions of the social imagination just as the real objects they signify at the height of her prosperity once engulfed the old bawd's dining room. The praise of plenty that reverberates at Celestina's table marks a sense of constitutional deficiency, a deprivation of empowerment that energizes all the characters motor of transgression.

Although always open to the street (224), Celestina's house is portrayed as a secure, enclosed space, a setting for three types of concealed activities: bartered sex, the consumption of pilfered food, and, most meaningfully, underground partisan debate centring on the perquisites of wealth and status. It is the latter enterprise, of course, that gives symbolic meaning to the two former activities, providing the basic rationale for their existence in the work. More than the sexual friction under the table, the social friction expounded at table places into perspective the contentious and civically transgressive nature of the servants' hunger and sexuality. Motivated by appetites of the social imagination rather than of the body, it is made clear in the intimacy of Celestina's house that caste difference and a sense of constitutional lack stand at the centre of the servants' drives.

The old bawd's house is the central place where all the 'marginal' characters in the work converge, a collective expression of their desire for sanctuary as well as of the social alienation and disorder around which all the events in the work turn. The craftsmen who created the woodcuts for the earliest edition of *Celestina* clearly understood this and represented its space as an expression of the yearning for material comfort, freedom

Figure 8.1 Celestina's House. Woodcut from the Burgos, 1499? edition of the *Comedia de Calisto y Melibea.* Hispanic Society of America, New York. With permission.

of movement, and sociability. The neatly draped banquet table they portray appears with food plates in the background of their substantial interpretation of the dwelling, whose populated doorway is open to the comings and goings of the street.

Linguistic and visual images converge in the woodcuts of the earliest *Celestina* to reveal an awareness of the subtle significance of the spatial matrices evoked in the characters' dialogue and embedded in the oblique descriptions of their environment.

To be sure, even the physical location of Celestina's house constitutes a complement to a larger figurative significance. Two studies (Russell 1989, Lacarra 1990) have dwelled on the fact that the text pointedly situates Celestina's house in separate locations: prior to the action it had been in Pleberio's neighbourhood; but now, as events transpire, it is located near the Tanner's Row, by the river on the outskirts of town according to Pármeno (52). While this may reflect an actual historical occurrence, as Lacarra and Russell assert, the peripheral location of Celestina's house may also be viewed in terms of the social stratification expressed through the spatial segregation of classes that began to appear in cities at the end of the fifteenth century. As municipalities began to grow, urban development was characterized by the dispersal and distribution of the population into neighbourhoods defined strictly along socio-economic lines. The lower classes were gradually moved out from the centre to the fringes of town (Ackerman and Rosenfeld 1989). Viewed from the perspective of early modern urban transformations, Celestina's move doubtless harbours more than historical detail: it is charged with symbolic value, expressive of the fact that the old mixed community of the medieval city has been economically and socially segregated and now remains spatially divided. Indeed, Celestina did not just move house: she was compelled to do so by community forces that sought to isolate not just prostitutes and beggars but all members of the lower classes. Separate and marginalized, conspicuously obliged to relocate to the geographical as well as social perimeter of power, her new abode at the edge of town accentuates her increasingly peripheral civic position as well as her desire for wealth as a means of enfranchisement.

In stark contrast to Celestina's plebeian dwelling, Pleberio's *domus* stands at the centre of the town and incorporates the traditional symbolic elements of aristocratic discourse, architectural components we associate with power and the patriarchal world of courtly texts: a tower, a beautiful maiden, an enclosed garden, and walls that isolate it from an encroaching world. A secure, almost fortified structure with multiple doors (entrances with 'antepuertas' [239] [double doors]), its imagery is vertical and constitutes a closed place above, as well as apart, from the fray – a space that keeps its back to society. Yet it is a space with other than aristocratic intimations: it is expressive of unease, suffused with apprehension, a house filled with vigilant, anxious inhabitants who startle at the slightest sound as they stand watch over its human capital, Melibea ('¿No oyes bullicio en el retraymiento de tu hija?' [290] [Do not you hear some noise in your daughter's withdrawing chamber?]). The wariness of its inhabitants contradicts the images of consummate power and control we traditionally associate with privileged settings. The interiors of Pleberio's mansion remain cloistered from the world around it, yet they are vulnerable to desire. Entry there is tightly regulated and is both difficult and protected; those who live in it remain ever watchful of trespass. Defended from intrusion by physical barriers that stand as metaphors of social as well as sexual segregation, the space encompassing Pleberio's house can only be accessed by furtive means – literally breaching its walls – even by those who claim to be its master's equals, like Calisto.

Resting at the centre of Pleberio's mansion is his most guarded possession, Melibea, who is repeatedly characterized as an extension of the contained universe she inhabits. She is, as she says, an 'encerrada doncella' (246) [a recluse shut up from all company], an image that more than describes her condition valorizes Pleberio's concern for his family's high status and unblemished genealogy. The house that impounds Melibea is constituted as a symbolic representation of Pleberio's exclusionary social and familial practices, as the concrete correlative of his claim to a patrician identity.

Yet that identity is challenged by Calisto, Celestina, and the servants, broken down through the literal breaching of the walls that symbolize it, culminating, as remains to be seen, in the spatial images of the final scene. It is for this reason that Theresa Ann Sears remarks that 'In perhaps no other literary work are more walls – real and figurative – leveled than in Fernando de Rojas' *Celestina*' (1992, 95). The incursion into Pleberio's physical space negotiated by Celestina and her confederates constitutes the disintegration of the illusory walls of class and identity erected by Pleberio to keep two worlds apart.

The final scenes depicting physical spaces in *Celestina* function as ironic counterpoints to the social contest depicted in the work. The proverbial enclosed garden, rather than the setting for life, love, and exuberance, is rapidly transformed into a place of rupture, grief, and death. To be sure, even Melibea's suicide is symbolically portrayed as a final gesture of enclosure: 'Quiero cerrar la puerta, por que ninguno suba a me estorvar mi muerte' (386) [I will shut fast the door, that nobody may come up to hinder my death] she says as she secures the door to the tower from which she leaps to her extinction. Moreover, although the tower in Pleberio's garden opens up onto the horizon, the landscape before it symbolizes mourning, called forth to be observed only after Melibea hurtles to her death. Pleberio's verbal circumscription of the land beyond the confines of his garden is a gesture that seeks to claim the outside world: the inventory of ships, trees, and towers he invokes in his valedictory (396) are objects on the landscape that are simultaneously his – desired – but are now devoid of purpose. And still, in his most calamitous moment, the description of place and setting carries with it the freight of class interest in controlled property. The broad vista incorporates the horizon as a metaphor of affluence and power – an image suggestive of a mercantile, colonial ideology. Yet it is now distant, inaccessible and unmoving. 'The real estate endures, for reasons Pleberio cannot understand,' remarks Shipley (1973–4, 299). It remains as a bitter reminder of his personal helplessness despite his earlier ability to acquire and control the physical, spatial universe. Pleberio's urge to create and command space, the aspiration to encompass and master the visible world, is macabrely foreshortened in Melibea's steep drop from the tower. The landscape that the eye captures, cluttered with the owned objects Pleberio invokes, is suddenly and dramatically compressed. Our eye falls down into the abyss below from the horizon: the notion that ownership and power are interchangeable topples to his feet symbolically along with the body of his only daughter. The exchange values of property and the desire of mastery are, in the end, denied. The fixed system of meaning assigned to dominion and wealth shatters as it is spatially represented as something that, though belonging to Pleberio, is radically disconnected from him at the moment of his greatest vulnerability. It is as if at the close of *Celestina*, power and the space it affords remain inscribed in a new domain: a realm of impotence. Melibea's self-inflicted end guarantees an end to her father's line and an end to his authority: in its headlong trajectory to the ground it quite literally signifies the Fall of the House of Pleberio. To be sure, in an ironic prolepsis, Melibea invokes the forthcoming fall of her father's house. Upon receiving the news of Calisto's fall into oblivion, she announces her own intention to fall and bring down her father's house. She calls for Lucrecia to help her to the top of the tower and prefigures the larger outcome of the measures she will take: 'ayúdame a subir, Lucrecia, por estas paredes, veré mi dolor; si no, hundiré con mis alaridos la casa de mi padre' (382) [Help me, Lucrecia, to get up this wall, that I may see my sorrow, unless you will have me bring down my father's house with cries].

In ironic contrast to the fate of Pleberio's *domus* after the death of Melibea, Celestina's house, inherited by Elicia ('jamás perderá aquella casa el nombre de Celestina' [338] [that house will never lose the name of Celestina]), encompasses continuity and constitutes an assurance that the old bawd's world, though she is dead and gone, is guaranteed succession (Deyermond 1993, 17–18). There is a sensation of vitality and progression in this image that contrasts dramatically with the feeling of both spatial and existential enclosure developed in the final scene at the foot of Pleberio's tower.

***

The representation of space and architecture in *Celestina* signifies something more than mere passive description or an interest in observing the material world. It constitutes a medium for codifying human action and principle that projects both values and desires, and a specific knowledge of their function in human affairs. Both Pleberio's and Celestina's houses constitute crucial signs that help define the world in which the characters move. They operate as indispensable parts of the total system of representation in *Celestina*, a pattern of spatial imagery designed to convey messages to the readers outside the text about the ambitions of the inhabitants in it. Through the production of space in the characterss' speech, we see a communal imagination at work in the movement of the characters through a landscape that fuses the world inside the work with the world outside it. The analogical progression from the spaces described inside the *Tragicomedia* to the world outside it, the everyday space occupied by the historical reader, provides a mesmerizing confirmation of the actual existence of a single community that embraces both the fictive characters of the text and their historical readers. Pleberio's and Celestina's houses conjure up historical spaces that, though not in themselves of unique importance, are full of comparable social circumstances, points of comparison for individuals familiar with comparable people living comparable lives. As such, these domains possess a metonymic relation to the central ideological themes that make up the work. The depiction of space in *Celestina* marks a decisive development in the representation of the human subject in late fifteenth-century texts: it becomes the depository of desires, the material field that stands as an emblem of the characters' identities and ambitions. A fetishizing of the material world is now clearly connected to the process of socially defining the individual.

Celestina offers a prime example of how the appropriation of the physical world serves as a cornerstone of early modern ideology: sites in it acquire constitutive power for the subjects who occupy them; and the latter are constructed and reconstructed not only by how but where they live and the property they own. Put simply, inhabiting owned property becomes a significant gesture of personal and social identity in the work. Location in it is thus infused with significance and often functions, more than as mere setting, as the battleground for depicting a larger social drama. The places that pretend to be embodiments of the real are in fact encampments of conviction and desires, nothing less than correlatives of the work's social anxieties and thematic contentions.

While it is a truism that as readers and critics we tend often to fall into the historicist fallacy that locations in literary works correspond to actual topography, the Salamanca of Fernando de Rojas (*pace* Russell 1989;

9 Pleberio and the Ends of Desire

Omnia in idem profundum cadunt.

Seneca, *Epistulae Morales* (I.323)

The aim of all life is death.

Freud, *Beyond the Pleasure Principle*

Celestina is a work that taught Spaniards how to live without ideals.

Ramiro Maeztu

Behold abandoned man, the abandonment of man. Behold man, the abandoned being. The destiny of *amor* is bound up with this abandonment.

Jean-Luc Nancy, *The Birth to Presence* (41)

The final act of *Celestina* is one of the most disquieting and controversial scenes in all of Spanish, indeed all of early modern European, literature. It is Pleberio's soliloquy spoken before the lifeless bodies of his wife, Alisa, and his suicide daughter Melibea. Superficially, the scene rehearses a long-established tradition of medieval sacred and profane texts, but especially texts from the dramatic and elegiac traditions. Yet in its poignant intensity and the intellectual postulates that sustain it, act 21 of *Celestina* represents both the culmination and the dissolution of these traditional elements since in it the consolatory oration, or *planctus,* and the figure of the expositor, or *interpres,* of the medieval drama (see Curtius 1963, 80–2; Chambers 1945, 10–11, 26, 30, 48) become vehicles for the expression of a whole new set of values and ideas that challenge the history and meaning of the very forms from which Pleberio's lament emerges. English medieval literature affords abundant examples of the expositor figure. In the mystery *Abraham and Isaac*, in the morality known as *Everyman*, and in the interlude of *The Four PP*, for instance, the audience at the end of these theatrical works is confronted with masculine characters that offer a synopsis of the action and intone the moral message of the piece, much as Pleberio does in *Celestina*. However, the moralizing and recapitulatory figure that appears in almost all the dramas of the late Middle Ages merges in Rojas's work with another well-established literary topos – that of the funeral elegy – whose object was to provide comfort and reassurance of the righteousness of a departed soul. Although Pleberio's lament is not a *planctus* in the strict rhetorical sense of the word, it nevertheless can be associated with the medieval elegiac tradition since it coincides thematically with many elements of the funerary valedictory. Bruce Wardropper, for example, demonstrated how the motif of the unmitigated grief of a patriarchal figure is found in vernacular texts as early as the Spanish epic *Roncesvalles* fragment and the legend of the Infantes de Lara (Wardroppper 1964, 140–52). However, our purpose here, like Pleberio's in his closing speech, will be to discover meaning rather than textual precedent in the last act of *Celestina*, and seek to understand how that meaning is expressed in the broad context of the literary motifs of the expositor and planctus tradition; to discover the unorthodox and profound originality of the ideas in Pleberio's lament.

Rojas prepares his readers for Pleberio's lament in act 20, where Melibea, disconsolate over Calisto's death, confides in her servant Lucrecia and says:

De todos soy dexada; bien se ha adereçado la manera de mi morir ... no me impidan la partida, no me atajen el camino por el cual en breve tiempo podré visitar en este día al que me visitó la pasada noche. Todo se ha hecho a mi voluntad; buen tiempo terné para contar a Pleberio mi señor la causa de mi ya acordado fin. Gran sinrazón hago a sus canas; gran ofensa a su vejez; gran fatiga le acarreo con mi falta; en gran soledad le dexo. (386)

[They have all left me. The manner of my death falls fit and pat to my mind ... that nobody may come up to hinder my death, nor disturb my departure, nor to stop me in my journey, wherein I purpose to post unto him, not doubting but to visit him as well as this very day as he did me this last night. All things have fallen out as luckily as I could wish; I shall now have time and leisure enough to recount to my father Pleberio the cause of this my end. I

confess, I shall much wrong his silver hairs, and offer much injury to his
elder years; I shall work great woe unto him with this my absence ; I shall
leave him in great desolation.]

Melibea prophesies her father's pain and loneliness and the suffering he
will feel as a result of her demise; she foresees the grief that subsequently
plays the central role in Pleberio's closing speech. But more importantly,
Melibea intuits and anticipates the extraordinary vision of the world –
one of incomprehension, total solitude, and abandonment – offered by
Rojas later through the mouth of Melibea's despondent father.

Pleberio's recapitulatory and moralizing function was initially recognized by María Rosa Lida de Malkiel (1970, 473), and is easily discernible
in any reading of the text itself. After long, anguished condemnations of
the World, Love, and Fortune, Pleberio synthesizes the action of everything that has preceded the suicide of Melibea. Addressing the world, he
summarizes the key events of Celestina:

> La falsa alcahueta Celestina murió a manos de los más fieles compañeros
> que ella para tu servicio emponçoñado jamás halló; ellos murieron degolla-
> dos, Calisto despeñado. Mi triste hija quiso tomar la misma muerte por
> seguirle. Esto todo causas. (400)

> [That false bawd, Celestina, who died by the hands of the faithfullest com-
> panions that ever she lighted upon in her life, for their true performance
> in this thy venomous and impoisoned service, they lost their heads; Calisto
> he brake his neck; and my daughter to follow him submitted herself to the
> selfsame death. And all of this thou was the cause.]

This brief digest of the plot comes at the close of his lengthy vituperation
of the World, and hence represents his judgment upon its effects in the
course of the lives whose trajectory he has just traced in his summation.
As is customary in the didactic literature of the late Middle Ages, there is
a conscious attempt to structure and recapitulate occurrences ranging
first from their underlying abstractions to their reification in an individual thing. Ideas are abruptly embodied, since we are told by the interpres
how they affected the outcome of the action and the destiny of the characters themselves.

Pleberio constitutes far more than a didactic mouthpiece, however.
Lida de Malkiel also noted nearly fifty years ago that, although 'Rojas
mantiene dentro de la *Tragicomedia* la máscara docente que recita la

moraleja ... esa máscara es al mismo tiempo un personaje, un concreto caso humano, y su lamento, atestado de aforismos y ejemplos generalizadores, acaba en una desgarradora pena individual' (1970, 473) [Rojas in the *Tragicomedia* maintains the didactic mask that recites the moral ... that mask is at once a personage, a concrete human being, and his lament, shot through with aphorisms and generalizing examples, ends in wrenching individual pain]. Rojas's originality lies precisely in the fact that Pleberio is individualized through his suffering. 'Characters, incidents [in *Celestina*]', as Charles Fraker notes, 'are invented so as to illustrate certain laws of life ... [However,] the events, the characters, do not signify anything: they are themselves, but as themselves they illustrate, they embody principles' (1966, 527). Pleberio's role in *Celestina* is thus indeed one of recapitulation and exemplification, but the examples he draws from the events that have befallen him are transformed into an anguished expression of deep personal sorrow. He is the recognizable figure of the expositor, but one that is now endowed with a profound sense of consciousness and self-awareness. It is through this unanticipated ability to feel and introspect by means of the questioning provoked by suffering that Pleberio surpasses the identifiable textual tradition from which his character springs.

In his capacity of *interpres* in act 21, Pleberio pronounces an elegy that points to a moral. Unlike the traditional elegy, however, the moral Pleberio extracts from the events he narrates is far from consolatory. To be sure, Pleberio's words constitute an aggressive and irreverent judgment upon the World and, by extension, all of Creation. Pleberio describes a hopeless universe in which humankind's existence consists of perpetual self-deception and false security – a topsy-turvy world ruled by confusion, devoid and despairing of transcendental answers to his questions and empty of all consolation and solutions. The topical figure of the expositor and the well-known consolatory themes of the elegy are ironically overturned in Pleberio's speech to convey a cruel vision of what Stephen Gilman calls the 'arbitrary aggression' of Creation (1972, 375). They are, in fact, debased, turned inside out in relation to their traditional reassuring function.

The consecrated forms of the medieval didactic and consolatory tradition undermined in Pleberio's speech become decoys that mask a radical nihilism in his message. Inverted, hackneyed figures of moral rhetoric are broken down to convey a sense of human isolation and vulnerability in a universe created by a distant God ruling over a detached, impassive nature, materialized in the meaningless trees Pleberio has planted, and the ships and edifices he has built, which he invokes as he stands by the side of the lifeless body of his daughter (337). The scene's emotive force, its striking poignancy, emerges from the negation of an expected reciprocity between literary form and content. As Américo Castro has argued in regard to *Celestina*,

Esta obra, para tantos lectores admirable, surgió como una ruptura de la tradición literaria de la Europa medieval y de la grecorromana. No puede, por consiguiente, ser calificada ni de medieval ni de renacentista. El intento de sus autores no fue continuar o desenvolver temas y formas anteriores, sino embestir contra ellos, derrocarlos y trastrocar su sentido ... Fernando de Rojas precedió a Cervantes en la aventura de trastornar el sentido de la materia literaria anterior a ellos, de servirse de ella para fines imprevisibles, como un pretexto más bien que como un texto ... En *La Celestina* encontramos negados los signos positivos de lo literariamente admitido, no con miras a destruir por destruir, sino a fin de poner a desnudo la escueta voluntad de existir, demostrar la posibilidad de que una obra literaria continue subsistiendo privada de su marco típico, como una negación de su forma previa, como un rebelde que compensa con su desatada violencia la pérdida de lo que había sido serena e indiscutida perfección. (1965, 95–6)

[This work, admirable for so many readers, arose as a break from the Graeco-Roman and medieval European literary traditions. It cannot, therefore, be classified as either medieval or Renaissance. The intention of its authors was not to continue or develop prior themes and forms, but rather attack them, overthrow them and change the nature of their meaning ... Fernando de Rojas preceded Cervantes in the adventure of upsetting the meaning of prior literary matter, of exploiting it for unimagined purposes, as a pretext rather than a text ... In *Celestina* we encounter the negation of the positive signs of what was literarily admissible, not with the purpose of destruction for its own sake, but to lay bare the simple will to live, and to demonstrate the possibility that a literary work could exist deprived of its typical frame, as a negation of its previous form, as a rebel who compensates with unfettered violence the loss of what before had been deemed serene and undisputed perfection.]

With this in mind, it is possible to examine how the outer form of Pleberio's lament traces the general order of medieval elegiac texts, and how that order is subsequently interrogated through strikingly new content.

In his well-known study of Jorge Manrique's *Coplas por la muerte de su padre* [Couplets upon his father's death], Pedro Salinas describes the topical elements that appear in the medieval lament for the dead. According to Salinas, the emphasis upon death's equalizing power is of paramount importance: it is what gives both moral authority and urgency to the discourse (1962, 56). In Pleberio's threnody there is a similar thought. However, the original design is altered: rather than invoke death's egalitarian, levelling effect, as for example in the *Danza general de la muerte* [Dance of death] or in the *Coplas* themselves, Pleberio conjures the universally destructive powers of life, the 'dance of life' as Gilman calls it (1972, 377). It is a collective, senseless, circular game – a part-song round of pain – that encompasses all humankind in the dance step of worldly torment:

> me pareçes un laberinto de errores [Mundo], un desierto spantable, una morada de fieras, juego de hombres que andan en corro ... hazes mal a todos, porque ningún triste se halle solo en ninguna adversidad, diziendo que es alivio a los míseros, como yo, tener compañeros en la pena. Pues desconsolado viejo, ¡qué solo estoy! (396–8)

> [Thou seemest unto me [World] to be a labyrinth of errors; a fearful wilderness; an habitation of wild beasts; a dance full of changes ... Thou dost hurt unto all that no man may boast that others have not their crosses as well as we; telling them that it is some ease to the miserable to have companions in their misery. But I alas, disconsolate old man, stand all alone.]

The leveller in Pleberio's speech is the World, whose common legacy to humankind comprises deception, misery, and solitude. Spiritual pain and loneliness are the only shared experiences of the human species. All its members join hands in a circle to dance to a chorus of grief, to the painful cries of the living. Adding irony to injury, despite the universality of the experience, no comfort or fellowship may be found in common misery, only solitude and silence. Suffering is apportioned only to life in Pleberio's speech – not to death – and marks incongruously the unique fellowship of the living.

Although Pleberio's grief is personal, he stresses the need to proclaim it in order to share it and grieve with others, to mourn and to assuage his anguish: 'Ayúdame a llorar nuestra llagada postrimería. !O gentes, que venís a mi dolor! ¡O amigos e señores, ayúdame a sentir mi pena!' (394) [O ye good people who come to behold my sorrows, and you gentlemen, my loving friends, assist me to bewail my misery]. However, no one answers Pleberio's call for comfort and companionship in his sorrow. The compulsion to convey and share the suffering, to grieve and expiate his pain through communal mourning, is precluded by a basic isolation. Pleberio stands alone in the presence of the dead, in absence of any living being. In this way, the ubiquity, and at the same time paradoxical silent loneliness, of the tomb is cast upon the landscape. Pleberio finds only solitude where the consolatory tradition offered remedies through the possibility of the shared experience of collective grief. Put simply, the last act of *Celestina* portrays a world of the living dead. Pleberio's soliloquy is a lament upon the purposelessness and solitude of life. It constitutes a dirge directed at the World and underscores the final irony of a bleak and lonesome end.

Yet another important element in medieval elegiac texts is the invocation of death's implacable cruelty. Captured in the *Libro de buen amor* when the narrator apostrophizes death ('Non ay en ty mesura, amor nin piadad' [There is neither moderation, lover nor mercy in thee]), it emphasizes death's ruthless brutality. Veering in an opposite direction, however, Pleberio's speech applies the ravages of annihilation to existence itself. Apostrophizing the World, he describes his life in it as if it were a type of brutal torture:

¡O vida de congoxas llena, de miserias acompañada, o mundo , mundo! ... Yo pensaua en mi más tierna edad que eras y eran tus hechos regidos por alguna orden. Agora, visto el pro y la contra de tus bienandanças, me pareces vn laberinto de errores, un desierto spantable ... verdadero dolor. (396)

[O life fulfilled with grief and accompanied with nought but misery! O world, world! ... I thought in my more tender years that both thou and thy actions were governed by order, but now I see thou art pro and con; there is no certainty in thy calms. Thou seemest now unto me a labyrinth of errors, a fearful wilderness ... true sorrow.]

The World and life – not death – offer insufferable pain. The suicide of Pleberio's only daughter constitutes an unmatched loss, greater than death itself. He does not, however, lament Melibea's demise but the 'causa desastrada de su morir' (338) [The disastrous cause of her death] – the World, Love, Desire – the driving forces of existence itself. Melibea's self-destruction offers Pleberio a welcome lesson: it brings disabuse and allows him to put life and its cruelty into perspective. Melibea's suicide – the loss and self-destruction of everything he has lived for – provides ironical clarity: the freedom to see clearly the meaningless of existence. Invoking Melibea, he confesses that 'Agora perderé contigo, mi desdichada hija, los miedos e temores que cada día me espavorecían. Sola tu muerte es la que a mí me haze seguro de sospecha' (398–400) [Now shall I lose together with thee, most unhappy daughter, those fears which were daily wont to affright me. Only thy death is that which makes me secure of all suspicions]. Melibea's leap from the tower conveys a sudden realization; it permits Pleberio to see life as a process whose only end and purpose is death. He incongruously expresses relief with that insight, since he says that by means of it he now understands that there is no purpose or reason to the World other than suffering and pain; and that to believe the opposite is an illusion. At the crossroads of Pleberio's encounter with the finality and the ultimate reality of material death – the spectre of the Real in Freudian and Lacanian terms – it is no longer necessary to fear Fortune or contingency, whose ultimate ends always prove adverse. Life is in time ultimately defined only by extinction; living becomes a process of self-destruction marked by blindness and unforeseen grief. The human will to achieve is a fraud: all aspiration, all desire, is condemned to failure from inception. Hope is futile, and life is merely a slow progress toward an end that culminates in corporal death. The world to Pleberio is an non-transcendental 'prado lleno de serpientes, huerto florido y sin fruto, fuente de cuydados, río de lágrimas, mar de miserias, trabajo sin prouecho, dulce ponçona, vana esperança, falsa alegría, verdadero dolor' (396) [a meadow full of snakes; a pleasant garden without fruit; a fountain of cares, a river of tears, a sea of miseries; trouble without profit; a sweet poison, a vain hope, a false joy, and a true sorrow]. Presided over by love and desire, Pleberio stresses life's constitutional emptiness, its spiritual misery and horror, whose end is an inevitable encounter with nothing.

If Manrique's *Coplas* stands as the great consolatory text at the close of the Castilian fifteenth century, Pleberio's lament at the end of *Celestina* constitutes the single most intense expression of grim pessimism of the period. Surrounded by the lifeless, physically broken bodies of his family, there is no solace for the lone survivor; no reassurance beyond the unendurable pain of the moment. To be sure, Pleberio sees Melibea's and Alisa's insensibility in death as an enviable alternative to his own existence in a universe spilling over with unmitigated anguish, and guided by blind desire and deceit. Addressing Alisa's lifeless body, Pleberio covets her repose:

si ya has dexado esta vida de dolor, ¿por qué quesiste que lo passe yo todo? En esto tenés ventaja las hembras a los varones, que puede un gran dolor sacaros del mundo sin lo sentir o a lo menos perdéys el sentido, que es parte de descanso. (396)

[if thou hast left this life, why let me remain here alone? In this ye women have a great advantage of us that are men; for some violent grief can make you go out of the world without any pain; or at least cast you into a swoon, which is some ease to your sorrows.]

Pleberio's lament offers up an anagnorosis, or a sort of tragic self-recognition and sudden awakening that is brutally expressed through a breakdown of language, a kind of enjambment in Pleberio's speaking register. Taken totally unawares by his realization, his disabuse transforms all rational thought into the pained, colloquial exclamation he directs at Alisa when she initially comes upon the scene: 'Ay, ay, noble mujer, nuestro gozo en el pozo; nuestro bien todo es perdido; no queramos más bivir!' (394) [Ay me, my most noble wife! Our solace is in the suds; all our happiness is quite overthrown; let us now no longer desire to live]. Wishing to die, for the decorous Pleberio everything is suddenly 'down the tube,' 'in the suds'; continued existence offers greater pain than death itself.

The illocutionary force of Pleberio's summation rests on the fact that it is composed not so much of affirmations of suffering but exclamations of bewilderment and questions that search for an explanation. The larger part of his lament consists of a torrent of interrogations and interjections, a deluge of probing anaphora that, for lack of an interlocutor and the absence of a response, remains just that, a flood of cries and questions that are never answered. In the strictest sense, Pleberio's questioning and expostulation become rhetorical, and in their very formulation and lack of reply his one-sided inquisition of the World provides its own response: silence. His are empty questions devoid of meaning, exclamations that receive no answer, iterations that are met with stillness.

Life for Pleberio is now devoid of solutions and empty of sense; even God exterminates those he creates. Rather than affirm the consolation of a providential salvation, Pleberio underscores the absurdity, futility, and anguish of the individual at war with temporality, in blind pursuit of things that ultimately signify nothing. He points to a loss of hope, confirmed by what he sees around him. Yet, he clamours for a sense of order, for a telos, and for a yearned but patently absent providence.

Seeking a point of reference, Pleberio invokes textual authorities from the classical past, only to have them fail to give reassurance. He rejects the examples of stoical fortitude of fathers like Aemilius Paulus, Pericles, and Xenophon, none of whom can offer comparison to Pleberio's own personal and immediate loss. Contrary to these epitomes of classical forbearance, Pleberio, fails to find a way to share his pain and discover strength to resist the shock of his ill fortune.

Although it might be tempting to see irony or even comedy in Pleberio's rejection of these authorities and comparisons, it is a mistake to judge him as a vain, irresponsible father more concerned with himself than the well-being of his daughter, or to fault him for not having married her in a timely fashion (O.H. Green 1965; Dunn 1975, 124–5). There is nothing in the text that instructs us to read his words in this way, just as there is nothing that points to the presence of some moral principle whose understanding could have led to an avoidance of the events Pleberio has just witnessed and retold. His words must be taken at face value, rather than as an expression of a set of ethical or transcendental references. Love guides the World, it is inescapable; its ends are destructive. To be sure, some studies have even attempted to interpret Pleberio from a Carnavalesque perspective, finding comedy in his speech and concluding that his 'lament brings all that is abstract and spiritual ... down to the concrete and corporal level' (Fothergill-Payne 1993, 47). However, scenarios of death form the privileged places of gravity and meaning in literary tradition. Moreover, Rojas tells us that his first audience had understood his conclusion to be sombre. In the prologue to the revised twenty-one-act version of his work, added between 1499 and 1502, Rojas attests to his contemporaries' serious understanding of its end, and notes that since his readers had felt that it 'acabava en tristeza' [ended in sadness] they clamoured for him to change the original title from *comedia* to *tragicomedia*. Bending partially to his readers' desires, he settled on *tragicomedia*, acknowledging the presence of black irony (81).[1]

Tracing the stark limits of human existence, mortality is that against which most literary discourse defines itself. Standing before the shattered body of his only daughter, apprised of all the events that have led to this catastrophe, Pleberio endures as the lone witness to the final coalescence of human desire and death, denying all possibility of consolation. The confrontation with the real of Melibea's demise ruptures the symbolic order of his longing and opens it out into its beyond, to what Freud calls the realm of *das Ding*, the realm of the unspeakable, and to the breakdown of language itself. At the ends of desire, Pleberio cannot hold to anything; he finds only the material finality of existence. All the vitality, all the energies of desire that drive the characters in the *Tragicomedia* are reduced to a brutal, corporal, substantive, material death. It is at this moment that Pleberio realizes love and desire cease to entice and demonstrates only how they mutilate and profane their objects and their subjects alike. Human aspiration embodies the pursuit of an impossible and absolute union that can culminate only in destruction. Love and death are inextricably bound because desire only achieves its ultimate and final goal in the transgression and separation of death. For Pleberio, love provides the allegory for this self-destruction, its quest leads to a total loss of self, to annihilation, in the pursuit of the desire of living.

Georges Bataille notes that sexual climax, equated with *jouissance*, is often characterized as *la petite mort*, the place where the human subject transgresses the discontinuities of life to dissolve into continuity with the rest of the universe. He observes that its ultimate consequence can lead to placing the very existence of human consciousness into question (1957, 34). Witness to the wages of love, Pleberio is led to carry out a similar interrogation of the illusion of the possibility of unity through love and the human aspirations for ecstasy and fulfilment, and to underscore the impossibility of any transcendental consummation. The true object of desire, its end and final resting place, is nothing, only death. It is this intimate coalescence of desire and death, Eros and Thanatos, without transcendence that shapes Pleberio's world and understanding; it marks the absence of any metaphysical perception and a feeling of radical estrangement from anything beyond existence. It is for this reason that we can broaden J.A. Maravall's fundamentally Marxist observation that *Celestina* 'encierra el primer episodio en la lucha contra la enajenación, que constituye el más hondo drama desde el Renacimiento a nuestros días' (1968, 165) [makes up the first episode of the struggle against alienation, which constitutes the most profound drama from the Renaissance to the present day] to include something well beyond class struggle.

In her study of *Celestina*, Dorothy Severin concludes that 'all the literary models fail at the end of the work; courtly love, classical antiquity, neo-stoicism, scholastic lore, aphorisms, and even estates satire' (1989, 117; see also Haywood 2001). After examining the sources and rhetorical structure of Pleberio's lament Severin agrees with our conclusion that the latter 'fails in its primary function. It does not lead to acceptance and resignation but to the desolation or isolation of the survivor who is sad and alone in the vale of tears' (1989, 115).

To be sure, although Peter Dunn finds that the final words of Pleberio's lament, 'in hac lachrymarum valle' [in this valley of tears], do offer a hopeful allusion to the closing words of the hymn 'Salve Regina' (Dunn 1975, 417), and that they constitute an affirmation of that prior textual authority, the reference must be placed, like the gloss of the beatitudes immediately preceding it, within the context of all the other evocations of scripture and pious moral and religious texts in *Celestina*; that is, within a discourse of irony, denial, and contradiction. The textual and scriptural points of reference in Pleberio's threnody point to empty pieties and to the sterility of textual authorities expected to admonish and guard against human desire. Pleberio's grieving in every way exceeds its own textual genealogy just as he fails to find authority for consolation in the very consolatory texts he invokes and searches in his desperation.

Although taken at face value the opening passages of *Celestina* place it in the medieval *reprobatio amoris* [reprobation of love] tradition, its stark end clearly contradicts the lessons taught by the latter. In all their formulations, the texts of *reprobatio amoris* ultimately call for the redirection of desire toward God, the sublimation of passion and its transformation into a metaphysically directed force of spiritual redemption. The Arcipreste de Talavera's *Corbacho* (1438) [The whip], for example, demands the love of God above all things and condemns as sin any pursuit of worldly love. *Celestina* clearly fails to invoke such an ending and fails to enact the redirection and transformation of desire in any metaphysical way, into a force of spiritual salvation.

However, it is not only literary and textual models that collapse at the conclusion of *Celestina*: the ideals that sustain and animate them also break down. The redemptive quality of love, desire's saving grace, meets a dead end, but not to be greeted by compassion or to be condemned in a pious *reprobatio amoris,* but to show instead that the aristocratic and religious versions of earthly and divine love of the late Middle Ages are both fictions. At the end of *Celestina,* Rojas confirms that it is just as impossible to live life like a Christian as it is to live it like a courtly lover.

Celestina systematically forecloses every expectation of redemptive desire as expressed in textual authority and tradition. Rather, we are left with doubt and the painful vital process of separation from all the ennobling myths, the master narratives of transcendence. Pleberio discovers that he has lived in an unknown, desacralized universe. Although *Celestina* at the outset seeks to locate itself within the textual tradition of the dialectic of earthly and divine love, its final assertions about love and human aspiration exceed that possibility and all its righteous underpinnings.

Pleberio stands as a witness to universal indifference. His pain springs from the cruelty and emptiness of life in an unsympathetic world driven by blind passion, ambition, and yearning. Certain that he is trapped by life, the only certainty beyond is annihilation in an indifferent world. As Wardropper rightly observed long ago, Pleberio expresses 'the anguish of man in spite of and beyond the consolations of religion' (1964, 152). However, this is no momentary truancy from orthodoxy, but a final and conclusive statement of fact. In *Celestina*, Pleberio's threnody is not followed by recantation, palinode, or understanding. We are left with a vision of a world that is never reconciled to conform to Christian beliefs. Throughout the last act of the work, there is an undermining of both the expected forms of the medieval drama and the traditional themes and conclusions of the medieval consolatory tradition.

To be sure, Pleberio's summation proved sufficiently disturbing to early modern readers so as to compel momentous changes in it, to add a moral, draw a lesson, and offer a consolatory message through significant rewritings. This is clear from several of the sixteenth-century translations of *Celestina* that have come down to us. In Christoph von Wirsung's 1534 German translation, for example, Pleberio emphasizes how Melibea succumbed to passion, but was punished and paid for her sin by not being permitted to marry the man she loved. In 1577 Lavardin, the French translator of the work, created an entirely new character, Ariston – Alisa's brother – who tempers the radical nature of Pleberio's words. Ariston interrupts Pleberio as he speaks to comfort him and counsel him to accept his fate and heed his duty as a father (Drysdall 1974). But it is the anonymous Dutch translations (1550–80) that point to the broad-based social and doctrinal discomfort that many early modern readers must have perceived in *Celestina*, and how they intentionally sought to foreclose the possibility of a less than Christian understanding of the work. At the very end of act 21 in the Dutch translation, Pleberio's speech is extended beyond his last words in the Castilian original. Between his closing interrogation, in which he dryly invokes the dark valley of tears inscribed in Psalm 84:7 as well as in the 'Salve Regina' ('Por qué me dejaste triste y solo in hac lacrimarum valle?' [402] [Why hast thou left me comfortless, and all alone, *in hac lachrimarum valle*, in this vale of tears]), the Dutch translator makes Pleberio speak the following additional words:

> Oh lamentable death, painful farewell, oh obstinate heart of my daughter! Oh deformed, ghastly, corrosive, disheartening deed! Oh painful death, oh tormenting love! I, poor miserable old man, now find myself alone in the

world. What shall I begin to undertake now? For the life of Adam's children is nothing but hay! Mirror yourselves on this, parents: see to it well how you educate your children. Let your eyes not be deceived; observe with care and see to it that you not enter in the distress in which I, wretched father, find myself on account of my passivity, an example for you all. I must and I wish to offer everything up to the Lord: may He be our help and refuge in this miserable vale of tears. Amen. (Trans. and ed. Behiels and Kish, 43n.104)

Clearly Pleberio's affirmations that the order of things does not hold to human expectations and biblical pieties (in his universe children die before their parents [396]; the sins of children are visited upon their elders [398]; and the blessed are those who never know the world [400]; humankind inhabits a labyrinth of errors [396] where everything deceives and points to something other; and where the possibility of salvation is implicitly denied by remaining unmentioned), compelled a number of early modern responses that sought to detour Pleberio's message in Rojas' original by adding other characters or unambiguous words that underwrote or pointed to a Christian moral.

Act 21 of *Celestina* thus provoked contention among its early modern readers. Couched as a lament on the misery of existence demonstrated through the use of traditional medieval didactic literary devices presented in an unorthodox, topsy-turvy way, elements from the traditional elegy are merged with the figure of the expositor but utilized to articulate the message of humankind's unavoidable impasse with an existence abandoned by God. While the medieval desire to exemplify is very much a part of Rojas's art, the lesson taught by it is, in the end, amoral just as it is extraordinarily in tune with modernity. The lesson taught by *Celestina* remains disquieting and conflictive rather than consolatory, sceptical rather than believing, pessimistic rather than confident. Pleberio, in finding no comfort for his grief and suffering, synthesizes the disillusionment, barrenness, and suspicion of Christian orthodoxy that many Castilians felt – doubtless Rojas among them – at the close of the fifteenth century. As Francisco Márquez Villanueva has argued, there persisted a strong current of Averroistic scepticism in Castile at that time, exacerbated by social crises (civil war, Inquisition, the Expulsion of the Jews, etc.), that adhered to the notion of a universe created by a *Deus otiosus*, a God removed from all concern with the sublunar world inhabited by humankind. Although many intellectuals like Rojas were technically Christian, they were so only in name as they cleaved to the idea of humanity's abandonment to chaos in a contentious world driven by natural imperatives and devoid of providence (1994, 284).

Pleberio's speech does not portray Melibea's death as a punishment for promiscuity or paternal disobedience, or as the wages of sin. Rather, her demise stands as brutal material proof of something intuited but never quite comprehended by Pleberio until the moment he contemplates his daughter's lifeless body, namely, that death inhabits human desire: perversely, lethally, ecstatically. Existence is governed by a ceaseless process of desiring inseparable, in the end, from an inconsolable sense of loss, always in excess of anything in particular. It is Pleberio's experience of the implacability of desire and loss that shapes *Celestina*'s originality; it derives from the tension between the yearning for a transcendent, fixed reality to exist, and thereby redeem loss, and the understanding that, in fact, it does not. The possibility of happiness for Pleberio is irrevocably foreclosed. The result is an unprincipled universe circumscribed by a resolutely materialist outlook that repudiates a belief in providence, immortality, and hope. For Pleberio, it is as if an inscrutable God – if he exists at all – had created a world without His presence; one in which there is no distinguishable moral law, and where eternity is nothing more than the transformation of things into material death. It is a world in which an inanimate nature only punctuates the insubstantiality and futility of human life. Pleberio's insight is the discovery of the void of his subjectivity in a world blind to spiritual essence, a place without a telos.

Pleberio stands as witness that the only telos is the one that belongs to the progress of desire, which moves only toward extinction. Life is represented as a form of being that exists only to perish. Desire, which he calls Love, is the central negative principle that emerges as the constitutive force of finite life; as an axiom of the perpetually altering location of the self within a network of internal relations. In an effort to escape the vulnerability and nihilism of a life that fails to extend itself beyond being, desire animates the body with the negation of life's finitude, seeking to proclaim it as transcendent. Desire seeks to escape the doom of death by pre-empting it with the illusions of power and consummation, only to be jolted by death's material finality. In Melibea's example, Pleberio discovers the reality of life and the body: corporality only as a guarantor of death. The promise of a new life – one beyond death – no longer shapes his moral horizon. He grasps the lie of desire, which endows its illusory end with value, and he understands it as a drive whose object is imaginary.

A suffering desire for what cannot be fulfilled, for what is known now to be radically absent, Pleberio's speech constitutes an expression of mourning whose intensity is sufficient to kill. All his attempts to live beyond human desire, to prolong his life beyond it, are now recognized as futile. The evidence that there is no beyond desiring comes too late. He discovers that the lack of satisfaction as well as the satisfaction of the callings of human yearning end only in material destruction. Pleberio understands the impossibility of his earlier conviction that self-preservation and the preservation of family, honour, and estate could be realized through the renunciation, policing, or suppression of desire. Both the absence and the presence of desire, however, can yield only one meaning: the inexorable finality of death. Caught in the synthesis of the dialectic of desire, Pleberio's speech marks a profound turning point in the history of the portrayal of consciousness in literature.

Pleberio comes to realize that desire destroys meaning and that, in its obscurity, it ends by casting light on what we take to have meaning; that the meaning of meaning is in fact its meaninglessness, whose sense is impossible to discover without the catastrophic breakdown of human aspirations. Desire discovers meaninglessness for Pleberio because he comes to see that it operates beyond the strictures of all law and order, which serve only to defer, displace, or repress it. It also remains beyond the powers of language and signification, which cannot name it. Desire can neither be denied nor controlled. Life is perceived as a constantly unfolding narrative or circular dance driven by hunger and hope that claims truth when it should be questioning it, which endows value where there is none. The metaphysics of presence, which evokes a stable centre of values, a redemptive core, and the possibility of transcendence, fails to materialize in Pleberio's grief. Life's imagined centre neither holds nor exists. The forces of desire, he says, operate beyond every notion of a centre and a metaphysical presence. They point only to absence; to a deep, empty silence at the depths of the valley of tears.

In a perverse leap, Pleberio in his imprecation against Love and the World finds that the material energies of the universe reside not in the generative force of life but in the disintegrative potency of death. The destructive power of death is found at the heart of love, at the very centre of the desire for generation. Through Pleberio's eyes, the world becomes disenchanted: nothing lies beyond the immediate actuality of the forces and events that propel it. There is no longer any mystery in being. The material impermanence and destructibility of things signals the fragility and fragmentation of being itself, rather than, as for an earlier age, their apparent stability and permanence had symbolized coherence and transcendence. Pleberio can no longer imagine himself as a protagonist in life's drama and imagines himself now only as a spectator in a world of objects and events, as if he were watching a baffling play whose plot was initially envisioned as expressive of his own will and purpose but which has now turned unintelligible.

Pleberio's lament constitutes the last thwarted outburst of longing in *Celestina*, a liminal primal scene where the energy to realize human ambition is simultaneously understood as an impulse toward death. Its release of emotional intensity and energy points to human desire as nothing but a struggle against the end, a detour before the abyss. At the close of events, then, seeking to impose control and understanding upon the Symbolic order of his world through the mastery of the word, speech fails him and Pleberio is confronted by the Real: with death. Cut off from everyone, with no response to his pleas, he can only turn to himself in his quest for subjective understanding. Literally and figuratively the incarnation of Lacan's Law of the Father, Pleberio's quest for subjective individuation is thwarted by his inability to impose order on things in the face of annihilation. He both actually and symbolically fails to incarnate the Law, and his words remain inadequate, full of sound and fury but unanswered. Caught between the yearning for a mastery of the Symbolic power of language, which cannot be reinstated, and the finality of death, Pleberio falls headlong into a confrontation with the Real, into annihilation, impelled by a failed craving for the reparation of the loss of Melibea and the realization that death is desire's only cure.

The genius of *Celestina* is based on a process of creative disintegration. Rojas through Pleberio offers an outsider's perspective on conventional literary and religious topics. The *Tragicomedia*, and especially Pleberio's lament, represents a rebellion against the ethos of religious and literary convention. Under the very cloak of conventionality the work mounts an aggressive attack on the established values and norms of conduct of the Spanish Middle Ages, and an undermining of a predictably tendentious consolatory literature, philosophy, and social imaginary that constituted life in Castile at the end of the fifteenth century.

The radical lack of transcendence in Pleberio's final vision of the world, its brutal materialism, can be traced, according to Márquez Villanueva, to a current of Averroist thought in fifteenth-century Spain identified with the *converso* community. Márquez Villanueva discusses 'la relativa frecuencia con que los procesos [del Santo Oficio] acusan a los reos de rechazar toda perspectiva sobrenatural y creer, o afirmar, que "no hay sino nascer e morir"' (1994, 273) [the relative frequency with which the trials (of the Holy Office of the Inquisition) accuse prisoners of rejecting all supernatural perspective and belief, or of affirming 'that there's nothing more than birth and death'] and notes that the available documentation points to a prevalent 'incredulidad radical en la inmortalidad y espiritualidad del alma, así como en toda sanción ultraterrena' (273) [lack of belief in the radical immortality and spirituality of the soul, as well as in every punishment beyond life]. Consolación Baranda confirms this materialistic orientation of the *Tragicomedia*, originaly intuited by Menéndez y Pelayo (131) and subsequently explored by Angel Alcalá (1976), but attributes it to certain neo-Epicurean affinities that, she argues, stem from Rojas's practise of the law, 'una ciencia eminentemente práctica' (206) [an eminently practical science] that made him 'contemplar la realidad en términos de litigio, a poner el punto de mira en los desórdenes sociales y sus responsables y fijarse preferentemente en los comportamientos del hombre en este mundo; se ocupa de la dimensión social, no de una dimensión trascendente' [see reality in terms of litigation, and set his eyes on social disorder and those responsible for it, and look upon human conduct in the world with preference; he occupies himself with a social as opposed to a transcendental dimension] and concludes that 'en eso es la suya una mirada "materialista"' (207) [in this way his perspective is a materialist one]. Regardless of its specific origins, the intricate tragic understanding of life's radical material embodiment produces an irrefutable sense of mourning in Pleberio that goes beyond any simple, eventually remediable grief for his dead daughter. His distress, although rooted in a father's sense of loss for a deceased child, produces a sudden understanding of the non-transcendental nature of human aspirations and human existence, the illusions that abide about the world and about the human place in it.

Although Rebeca Sanmartín Bastida would find a moral lesson in the 'teatro de la violencia física' (2005, 122) [theatre of physical violence] portrayed in the closing pages of *Celestina* – a visual sermon composed of the broken bodies that litter the text (Pármeno's, Sempronio's, Celestina's, Calisto's, Melibea's, and Alisa's) – which warns against the pursuit of pleasure in a retributive society, the very physicality of the material tearing and shattering of bodies in the work speaks to a greater, fundamentally worldly and temporal fragmentation: to a process of the amoral transformation of souls, the putative spiritual essences of human life, into inert, lifeless stuff. Melibea's demise teaches no lesson other than the senselessness of existence and provokes an anguish that defies relief. Through it, Pleberio defines himself and everything against mortality. He understands that life is discontinuous; that life is only intelligible as finite and that we can no longer envisage it as something that passes beyond finitude. Any attempt to recover or preserve the human spirit is set off against the silence of others and the sudden perception of the stark social and biological limits of every human aspiration. Human desire reaches its extremity in Pleberio, transformed into a longing to contract into nothingness. While all the various dialectics of desire that constitute the action of *Celestina* have been played out and find their ironic culmination in Melibea's shattered body, Pleberio reaches an ontological level at which the real destiny of desiring human subjects is finally exposed. Pleberio's final outburst does nothing less that stage the moment where perception breaks through repression to reveal the unmoving essential quality of life, its end in material disintegration.

Celestina in this way exposes Pleberio as the last remaining paradigmatic human subject in the world, left adrift in a fundamentally secular, hopelessly cynical universe moved wholly by insatiable want, which is but a mask for death. Abandoned and alone like Lear before the storm, and cursed with the true understanding of the limitlessness of the valley of tears called forth in his last utterance before falling silent and away from language, Pleberio is left to mourn and contradict all religious doctrine by failing to invoke it. He belies commonplace ideals by being unable to discover any manner of solace in his grief.

Not even Freud's observations on the process of mourning can be applied here. Speaking of loss, Freud invokes the immediate human quest to repair it, noting that 'Each single one of the memories and situations of expectancy which demonstrate the libido's attachment to the lost object is met by the verdict of reality that the object no longer exists; and the ego, confronted as it were with the question whether it shall share this fate, is persuaded by the sum of the narcissistic satisfactions it derives from being alive to sever its attachment to the object that has been abolished' (1953–74, 14: 255). The ego's abolishment of what is lost and the reconciliation that marks the completion of mourning, as described by Freud, is never hinted at, let alone achieved, in *Celestina*. We are left with a shattered Pleberio who is forced to bear witness not just to Melibea's mortality, but to all mortality, and who sees nothing but death in the very generative force of life. Love is but a foreshadowing of human extinction. Nothing exists beyond the material reality of death, nothing can repair or compensate for it. Pleberio's attempt to mourn becomes a moment of self-realization and reflection in which Melibea's suicide constitutes a glimpse into the abyss, the lens that permits him also to see not only her irrevocable absence but the image of himself caught in the snares of worldly desire and mortality. His words declare the incommensurability of loss and reparation to proclaim the final inadequacy and impotence of the human wish for transcendence. The expected conciliatory transaction of grief and mourning with the logic of consolation as defined in the economy of reassurance that structures the medieval Christian telos is ruptured and the promise of all exchange foreclosed. Contrary to religion, which conceals it, Pleberio sees the proximity of life to the void and, in the absence of all reassurance, acknowledges the void as the only final truth.

The medieval Christian religious paradigm constructs an image of desire that, for good or ill, is always transcendent. The pursuit of God affirms desire's consummate goodness, the pursuit of the flesh its infinite evil; eternal salvation or damnation are always figured in it. In one way or another, through affirmation or denial, desire's transcendence is always asserted but never annulled. Yet in *Celestina*, desire is figured always as a sign of absence for which any presence is impossible. The work's genius and modernity lies in the representation of the human subject as something that emerges out of this reconceptualization of desire and from the trauma of the realization that desire's end is desire itself, something non-transcendental and destined always to be obstructed. As a result, it produces only melancholia, the inability to mourn and transform loss into consolation, as it forecloses the promise of redemption or catharsis by means of grief and sorrow. There is no compensation for loss and pain in the blank economy of salvation discovered by Pleberio. The shattered body of his daughter, the ruin of his world, are framed by a deeply nostalgic discourse of unredeemable loss and impossibility. Only grief abides and beyond it, death.

In his questioning Pleberio discovers the amorality of desire, which turns love into annihilation. The work's end looks back to trace the path of unbridled yearning and announce its inevitable encounter with the Real – with death – which, like in Freud's Death Drive formulated in *Beyond the Pleasure Principle*, remains the only genuine cure for the constitutional lack felt by all human beings. In a universe of insatiable lack, only death can silence the discourse of wanting. *Celestina* ends at the only place its ending is possible: at the crossroads of death and desire. At the end of Eros's subjugating chain, Thanatos is acknowledged as the only sovereign master of the human subjects of desire. *Celestina* thus concludes with a bold challenge to literary clichés and their ethical foundations. In it we see the internal haemorrhaging of both literature and spirituality, the death throes of a way of life that once dead rose from its corpse to reveal, in the words of Américo Castro, 'la posibilidad literaria del futuro personaje novelístico, nacido de la expresión de una autognosis conjugada con un acto de voluntad' (1965, 125) [the literary possibility of the future character of the novel, born of the expression of a sense of self-awareness in conjunction with the exercise of the will.]

In an important article on sacrificial desire in courtly love, Simon Gaunt poses a question that is implicitly answered in Pleberio's interrogation of love, want, and mortality. Gaunt asks 'Is courtly literature's appropriation of sacrificial desire what enables the creation of a secular ethics in Christian western Europe?' (2001, 501). Through Pleberio's vision of an non-transcendental human mortality, the final act of *Celestina* casts off metaphysics and creates a space for just such an engagement with the only alternative, secular ethics; one that is removed from the notion of sin, retribution, and the sphere of religion, and one that marks the emergence of a modern epistemology that organizes the representation of a new kind of human experience. By coming to grips with their own temporality and the profound anxieties alluded to in something like Pleberio's lament, human beings at the threshold of modernity were required both to confront and to assume a more earthly sense of responsibility, one inexorably shaped by secular time and civic, rather than religious, duties, priorities, and obligations. In short, the last act of *Celestina*, I believe, signals a decisive turn in the history of the portrayal of desire and in the direction of the emergence of the early modern human subject.

Conclusion

At its close, through the vestigial figure of Pleberio, *Celestina* conjures an unprecedented understanding of the radical non-transcendence of human ambition. Pleberio's self-conscious reflection on the world, everything's place in it, and the failure of human longing to locate meaning only to find death and the void in its search constitutes a decisive rupture between the old and the new order by detaching itself from nature and from its own textual prehistory. Pleberio's revelation identifies the real of human yearning with what he experiences: something inhabited by nothing. His vision displaces the authority of metaphysical illusions with the pre-eminence of experience in understanding, and it portrays consciousness of the world as a self-generated and autonomous realm of knowledge, which makes the idea of experience itself central to its reality. At the same time, this perception points to the insignificance of all metaphysical myths – the love of God and the god of love – that seek to define human life as subordinate to, and dependent upon, a greater spiritual, and therefore hypothetical, reality that it symbolizes. In Pleberio's world, life is presided over by an acute self-awareness saturated with doubt, as meaning ceases to emanate from any external transcendental principle. Only the self remains, immanence as the only medium of knowledge. Whereas the traditional understanding of modernity places its origins at the beginning of the seventeenth century, hand in hand with Descartes and the *cogito*, in which the subject becomes the 'subject of knowledge,' for Pleberio at the end of the fifteenth century a similar human self-consciousness constitutes the centre of his world.

To be sure, for Pleberio the world can now only be understood through the relations among things that belong exclusively to it. In this formulation, which reflects an entirely new ontology, metaphysical doubt generates a persistent self-awareness that postulates a fundamental distinction between subjects and objects – a distinction that in the pre-modern world view had little or no significance – to bring forth a new type of human subjectivity. A completely different set of differences ordered the structure of the pre-modern cosmos where the distinction between subject and object had no fundamental place (see Lovejoy 1960, Gurevich 1985, Haren 1985, and Ginzburg 1986) in a framework of interdependencies, where each thing owed its existence to a greater being. For Pleberio at the ends of desire, the human realm is understood as a self-defining domain that is not limited by or subordinated to a presumed pre-existing cosmological order. Whatever order is revealed is only the result of the human craving for transcendence.[2]

This can be understood as the principle in *Celestina* that allows for imagining the transformation of society from organic feudal forms of relationships toward individualized as well as capitalist modes of life. The relationship of subject and object, of self and other, becomes redolent with doubt and inclined toward a perception of continually shifting boundaries between familiarity and strangeness, order and disorder (Kristeva 1991, Ricoeur 1992). It is for this reason that Columbus's almost exactly contemporary encounter with the New World, originally conceived as a confrontation between the civilized and the primitive, between righteous Christianity and the fallen heathen world, became a dialectic in ensuing years in which doubt undermined any possibility of authentication. The voyage of discovery would become a powerful image for both physical and psychological investigation after 1492 (Pagden 1993), but the process of self-discovery rather than reveal the righteousness of self-certainty trapped thinking subjects in a deepening well of despair.

As Martin L. Pine suggests, 'the immortality of the soul was an important aspect of the Renaissance,' since 'immortality became the mode through which individual achievements were projected into eternity. Should a man's soul perish with his body, the very essence of his achievements would be lost forever. Thus the projection of a life beyond mortal decay became a part of human dignity' (1986, 56–7). At the threshold of modernity, being in the world, however, could also be perceived, as in the case of Pleberio, as an exposure to an unprotected existence, divorced from every possibility of support from a fundamental metaphysical cause or order. In the latter case, existence would become the subject's ontological duty, and precede every form of political, judicial, and moral responsibility. In the absence of God, only a form of secular ethics and temporal distinction could provide both continuity and a refuge from a hostile universe. In Spain, later works in the sixteenth and seventeenth centuries like *Lazarillo de Tormes* (1554) and *Don Quijote* (1605), both profoundly influenced by *Celestina*, would develop just that possibility and confront the existential dilemma portrayed by Fernando de Rojas at the ends of desire as one that could only profitably be approached through the growth, cultivation, and exercise of a secular human conscience.

Notes

1. The Chain of Desire: Linking Language and Longing in Celestina

1 For a listing of the Castilian editions and two extant manuscripts before 1650, see Rojas (2000, 355–60).

2 *Méconnaissance* in Lacanian psychoanalysis designates a 'failure to recognize,' or a 'misconstruction' of what is perceived. The concept is central to Lacan's thinking, since, for him, the acquisition of knowledge (*conaissance*) is inextricably tied to its opposite, *méconnaissance*. The term *méconnaissance* corresponds roughly to the English words 'misunderstanding' and 'mis-recognition.' The French term is usually left untranslated when alluding to Lacan and his theories in English. This is to underscore the fact that it is the obverse of *connaissance*, or 'knowledge.'

3 The chief exponent of the theology of Christian desire is, of course, Bernard of Clairvaux. The best source on Bernard's exposition of the doctrine of the love of God remains Etienne Gilson, whose study of the saint's mystical theology was published in 1940. Gilson's studies are complemented by those by Giles Constable (1979) and Michael Casey (1985). The earliest sustained articulation of Christian desire was that of Saint Augustine in the *Confessions*. Later, in the fifteenth and early sixteenth centuries, its basic tenet of the search for transcendence was adopted by the humanists Marsilio Ficino, Leone Ebreo, and subsequently by Giordano Bruno. See Kristeller (1964), Feldman (2003), and Nelson (1958). James F. Burke (1998) has explored how the expression of Christian desire is disrupted in early medieval Spanish texts by means of the introduction of contrary marginal, often subliminal, images or allusions to an external web of supplementary trangressive meanings.

4   Lacan illustrates the human sublimation of desire into language by recalling the game played by Freud's infant grandson as the latter describes it in *Beyond the Pleasure Principle* (1961, chapter 2). In the game, the child associated the appearance and disappearance of a toy reel tied to a string with the sounds *o-o-o* and *a*, elements of the exclamation *Fort!* (signifying *gone* in German) and *Da!* (*here*). Freud ultimately explained the game as the boy's way of symbolically renouncing complaint in the alternating disappearance and reappearance of his mother. For Lacan, however, the child's symbolic use of signs raised desire to a second degree, since the action effaced the object of desire that it caused to appear and disappear by contemplating its absence and presence. Freud's grandson's action for Lacan thus opposes the forces of desire in order to become its own independent object. Through symbolization the child became engaged in the concrete system of discourse of the environment, by reproducing more or less approximately in *Fort!* and *Da!* the sounds that he acquired from it. The boy's use of language to express desire thus becomes the desire of another, of an alter ego who dominates him and who, as an object of desire, henceforth becomes his burden. (See Lacan 1977, 'The Function of the Field of Language,' 103–4.)

5   Kaspar von Barth in his 1624 neo-Latin translation of *Celestina*, titled *Pornoboscodidascalus Latinus*, agrees and questions the efficacy of the old bawd's incantations and belief in magic, noting that Celestina's rhetorical powers far exceed the need for the application of magic in Melibea's capitulation: 'Minimum sane hic incantationes egerunt, quamquam et huius sceleris crimini anum veneficam illigarunt, quibus etiam demptis, vix quaequam puella caeteris talibus assultibus restiterit' (Barth 2006, 55) [Celestina's incantations did not help much, except in adding one more crime to her long list, because, even without these, no young girl could have resisted such attacks].

2. Celestina, Mistress of Desire

1   The name *Celestina* first appeared as the title of the book in the eighth edition of Alfonso Ordóñez's Italian translation, printed in Venice by Cesare Arrivabene in 1519. In addition to Juan de Valdés, Juan Luis Vives and Antonio de Guevara, both writing in the 1530s, also refer to the book by the old bawd's name. Valdés's reference is unique, however, for the manner in which Marcio conflates the character and the book by means of prosopopoeia.

2   Mark Albert Johnson (2007) confirms that images of bearded women in
    early modernity served to subvert patriarchal ideology by symbolically
    threatening economic and sexual castration by means of their appearance.
    There are several painted portraits of bearded women from sixteenth- and
    seventeenth-century Spain. Lo Spagnoleto's (Juseppe de Ribera's) portrait
    of Magdalena Ventura, her husband, and their infant son (figure 2.1, 1631),
    which presently forms part of the collection of the Palacio de San Andrés, or
    Casa de Pilatos, in Seville, and Juan Sánchez Cotán's *La barbuda de Peñaranda*
    (figure 2.2, ca 1590), now in the Museo del Prado, are notable examples.
    The former is especially disconcerting. It forms a striking visual paradox
    given Magdalena's apparent domesticity. In the picture, featuring her
    vigorous black beard, she stands in the foreground of the frame, breast
    exposed, suckling the child. Her aged, frail husband, with a thinning grey
    beard, is situated to the left in back of her, occupying a clearly submissive,
    secondary position. Early modern witches were also commonly believed to
    have beards (see also Sanz Hermida 1994).
3   Perhaps it is Elicia who, tired of mourning for Sempronio and just prior to
    the appearance of the pimp Centurio, provides the best clue to the possible
    origins of Celestina's scar. She evokes the violent atmosphere of the demi-
    monde in which she lives and the 'cuchilladas' [knife wounds] of the brawls
    between men who have competed violently for her attentions: 'Mal me va
    con este luto; poco se visita mi casa, poco se passea mi calle; ya no veo las
    músicas de la alvorada; ya no las canciones de mis amigos, ya no las
    cuchilladas ni ruidos de noche por mi causa' (348) [I do myself wrong to
    mourn thus. Few do visit my house; few do pass this way. I can hear no music
    nor stirring betimes in the morning; I have no amorous ditties sung by my
    lovers ... there are no frays and quarrels before my door; they do not cut
    and slash one another a-nights for my sake].
4   In act 13, when Calisto hears the news of Celestina's violent death from
    Sosia, his immediate reaction is linked to the visual image of the scar on her
    face. 'Pues si esso es verdad' [If this be true], he tells Sosia, 'mátame tú a mí,
    yo te perdono, que más mal ay que viste ni puedes pensar si Celestina, la de
    la cuchillada, es la muerta' (308) [kill thou me too, and I will forgive thee.
    For sure there is more ill behind, more than was either seen or thought
    upon, if that Celestina be slain, that hath the slash over her face].
5   Gilman comments on the passage, calling it 'The great monologue of
    Act XIV, perhaps the greatest achievement of the additions,' and stresses
    that the soliloquy 'was possible only on the morning after the night of love.
    Both Rojas and Calisto know it; both know that the release from amorous

urgency has exposed an underlying ugliness' (1956, 216). The 'ugliness' that they intuit is, of course, the realization of the unfulfillable nature of desire.

6 *Celestinesca*, the international journal of *Celestina* studies founded by Joseph Snow in 1977, has continued to record and catalogue the prodigious sum of scholarly work and cultural production inspired by *Celestina* throughout the world and through the ages.

3. Calisto's Hunt: The Pursuit of Carnal Knowledge

1 For a comprehensive catalogue of animals in *Celestina*, see Blay Manzanera and Severin (1999).

2 'La bívora, reptilia o serpiente enconada, al tiempo de concebir, por la boca de la hembra metida la cabeça del macho y ella con gran dulçor apriétale tanto que le mata, y quedando preñada, el primer hijo rompe las yjares de la madre, por do todos salen y ella muerte queda; él quasi como vengador de la paterna muerte' (16) [The viper, a crawling creature and venomous serpent, at the time of engendering, the male puts his head into the mouth of the female, and she, through the great delight and sweetness of her pleasure, strains him so hard that she kills him. And conceiving her young, the eldest of the first of her brood breaks the bars of his mother's belly, eats out his way through her bowels, at which place all the rest issue forth; whereof she dies, he doing this as the revenger of his father's death].

3 Calisto describes his eager advances toward Melibea in terms of *de'faire*, or the breaking and dressing of newly hunted game. Responding to Melibea's protestations of modesty, he says: 'Señora, el que quiere comer el ave, quita primero las plumas' (378) [Madame, he that will eat the bird must first pluck the feathers]. He then continues too tear at her clothes to undress her. Metaphorically, Melibea has become the falcon's avian prey, which he now deplumes.

4 Blay Manzanera and Severin conclude that 'birds are the animals which predominate in *Celestina* imagery' (1999, 27).

5 The *De Amore* was known in manuscript in the Iberian Peninsula as early as 1387 and was widely cited by early fifteenth-century authors like Alfonso Martínez de Toledo and Juan Rodríguez del Padrón (see Gerli 1976, 119–22).

6 The *Archivo Iberoamericano de cetrería* defines *señuelo* as an 'armadijo de cuero con forma de pájaro, emplumado y encarnado que sirve para atraer el ave de cetrería' [a device made of leather in the form of a bird, plumed and red-colored used to attract a hunting bird] (http://www.aic.uva.es/

vocabulario/voces.html#seccS). The *señuelo*, or lure, is tied at the end of a long cord that the falconer whirls over his head, always keeping it just out of the bird's reach. The technique requires special skill since the bird must be suspended in a state of hunger and temptation until it submits to the will of the trainer.

7 On the *aegritudo amoris* in late medieval culture, see Wack (1990).

8 Sempronio's thought has Ovidian echoes: 'quod licet, ingratum est; quod non licet acrius urit' [What is licit is unwelcome; what is illicit prods us on] (*Amores* II 19.3). Freud restates the principle: 'The psychical value of erotic needs is required in order to heighten libido; and where natural resistances to satisfaction have not been sufficient men have at all times erected conventional ones so as to be able to enjoy love,' 'On the Universal Tendency to Debasement in the Sphere of Love' (*SE*, vol. 11, 187). Lacan, in 'God and the *Jouissance* of Woman,' agrees (1982, 138).

9 Jean Dangler argues that several discourses, including ancient medical texts, classical literature, Christian sources, and love poetry converge in *Celestina* to pathologize desire. The resulting illness thus becomes a physical ailment that attacks Calisto and Melibea's mental and imaginative faculties (2001, 149). The medieval notion of lovesickness is a precursor of modern theories of melancholia, most notably Freud's, since the two find their roots in a common origin and manifest themselves in similar ways. Whereas studies on Calisto's ailment abound, few if any relate it to Freud's notion of melancholia.

10 Anamorphic representation was a staple of early modern cultural production and did not limit itself solely to pictorial media. David R. Castillo (2001) has traced and studied its presence in texts produced in Spain during the sixteenth and seventeenth centuries and has examined strategies for reading them, especially in the works of Cervantes and the early picaresque.

4. Yearning to Look: Desire and the Pleasure of the Gaze

1 Research into the representation of gender and homoeroticism in medieval Spanish texts has constituted something of a taboo and has remained, with only one or two notable exceptions, off limits to Spanish scholars. An excellent introduction to the subject in a pan-European context, and the importance these types of studies have taken on in cultural studies in general during the last twenty years, may be found in the work by Mérida Jiménez (2000).

2 Noting the similarity of listening and seeing, Roland Barthes has suggested that 'we ought to be able to say *écouteur* as we say *voyeur*' (1974, 132).

3   There are two additional texts from fifteenth-century Iberia that rely upon
the faculties of sight and sound to portray scenes of desire and the extension
of the senses. One of these can be found in chapter 233 of *Tirant lo Blanc,*
where 'Tirant és convidat per Plaerdemavida a contemplar el bany
de la princesa' [Tirant is invited to observe the princess'bath] through a
peephole from his hiding place, and the other is the 'Villancico a tres fijas
suyas,' attributed to the Marqués de Santillana, where the poet eavesdrops
upon and observes his daughters as they complain of the pangs of love.

5. Complicitous Laughter: The Sounds of Desire

1   It is curious that neither Gilman (1974), Lida de Malkiel (1970), Severin
(1989), Fothergill-Payne (1993), nor Lacarra (1990), in their subtle discussions of the devices of dialogue and characterization in *Celestina,* have
touched upon the important role played by laughter in it. While Severin,
Lacarra, and Fothergill-Payne make laughter central to their discussions of
the work, they circumscribe their vision of it to something residing solely in
the reader. Yet laughter in *Celestina* comes forth also from the characters
themselves as they consciously comment upon and expose each other's
foolishness, or unconsciously betray the nature of their deepest thoughts
through involuntary snickering or giggling. It is especially odd that Gilman
in his pathbreaking appraisal of Pármeno (1974, 123–4) should refer to
Bergson's *Le rire* for his notion of 'making one's life by living it,' plus
formulate his explanation of the dynamics of Pármeno's personality upon it,
yet not notice the clear significance of Pármeno's laughter in proclaiming
the genuine nature of his personality and intentions.
2   Evoking their prior dalliance and her excursions into paedophilia,
Celestina asks Pármeno rhetorically '¿Acuérdaste quando dormías a mis
pies, loquito?' [Ah! You little rogue, dost thou remember when you layest
at my bed's feet?]. To which he responds, 'Sí, en buena fe; y algunas vezes
aunque era niño, me subías a la cabecera y me apretavas contigo, y porque
olías a vieja, me huya de ti' (66) [Passing well: and sometimes also, though
I was then but a little boy, how you would take me up to your pillow, and
there lie hugging of me in your arms; and because you savoured somewhat
of old age, I remember how I would fly from you]. There are numerous
other clues to Pármeno's early history as a voluptuary. For example, his
subsequent equivocal allusion to his transient life and to having spent nine
years in the charge of the friars of Guadalupe: 'He andado por casas ajenas
harto tiempo y en lugares de harto trabajo; que nueve años serví a los
frayles de Guadalupe, que mil vezes nos apuñeávamos yo y otros' (288)

[I have gone many a time through other men's houses and places of much travail. Nine years was I servant to the friars of Guadalupe, and a thousand times myself and others were at buffets]. This reference, rather than a sign of principled strength, conceals a further ironic suggestion of his shady youth as it points to the proverbial pederasty of friars in late medieval and Renaissance Spain (for specific examples of Spanish proverbs, see Sbarbi 1943, 411; allegations of friars' special predilection for young boys were widespread in the Middle Ages, see Szittya 1986 and *Decameron* 5: 10). Pármeno's allusion to the friars of Guadalupe also refers to the tendency to associate aberrant sexuality with heresy and apostasy. Following popular belief, the Inquisition lumped heretics and sodomites together, taking special aim at orders and at convents where *conversos*, crypto-Jews, and homosexuals were rumoured to have taken refuge. One of the most well known of these was reported to be the Hieronymite monastery of Guadalupe (see Bennássar 1984, 305–6; García Cárcel 1976, 211–13; and for historical and literary insinuations of sodomy among friars, see Thompson and Walsh 1988; on the suspicions and allegations directed against the friars of Guadalupe in the fifteenth century, see Sicroff 1965; and Castro 1970, 60–97). It is also well to remember that Pármeno is the son of Claudina, Celestina's exemplary colleague, whom she claims was the very epitome of their mutual profession. Alberto, Pármeno's father and Claudina's 'husband,' was also a skilled denizen of the underworld whose mastery of pandering, Celestina implies, established a comfortable legacy for his son (see the two articles by Snow).

3 In his *Traité du Ris*, or *Treatise on Laughter* (completed in 1560), Laurent Joubert discusses the origins of laughter in relation to the sensitive, or appetitive, faculty of the soul and speaks of its links to covetousness and to desire (1980, 30–3). He concludes that 'the principal cause of laughter is contained under desire, which ... follows the imagination and obviously moves the heart, inciting it to various emotions' (36).

4 Lida de Malkiel, in what remains one of the most discerning appreciations of Pármeno, remarks that 'Aparte la sensualidad, Pármeno no exhibe afectos ni pasiones; la codicia, señaladamente, parece en él más cerebral que espontánea' (1970, 608; see also Beltrán 1980, and Snow 1989) [Aside from his sensuality, Pármeno fails to exhibit affects or passions; greed in him, especially, seems to be more cerebral than spontaneous]. Contrary interpretations of Pármeno, which fail to capture the ironic nuances of his speech, the wicked resonances of his laughter, and his self-righteous posturing, are offered by Barón Palma (1976) and Fernández Márquez (1967, 110–24).

5   I use the term 'defamiliarize' as employed by Juri Lotman in his *The Structure of the Artistic Text* (1977), where it conveys the notion of a sign which disrupts the regularity of a communicative act and, through contrast, heightens the awareness of meanings in a text. Another Russian formalist, M.M. Bakhtin, specifically notes laughter's ability to disclose the unofficial side of language and to set off 'a relocation of the levels of language ... the making contiguous of what is normally not associated and the distancing of what normally is, a destruction of the familiar and the creation of new matrices, a destruction of linguistic norms for language and thought' (1981, 237).

6   While a systematic search through Spanish medieval and Renaissance texts reveals that *Celestina* is the earliest work to record the sounds of laughter, its later imitations, like Francisco Delicado's *La lozana andaluza* (1528), follow suit and assign a distinctly bawdy register to high-pitched giggles (see, for example, 52, 58, 166). See also Feliciano de Silva's *Segunda Celestina*, published in 1534 (119, 121, 141, 164–5). Both of the latter, however, fail to capture the full range of the nuances of laughter Rojas and the *antiguo autor* inscribe in their text.

7   For the euphemistic connection between sewing, weaving, and copulation, see the studies by Manuel da Costa Fontes. On the relationship of language and business in *Celestina*, see Gaylord (1991).

8   Rojas may indeed have been thinking of this scene from the *Libro*, whose manuscript had been housed since at least 1440 in the library of the Colegio de San Bartolomé of the University of Salamanca, where he was a student. On the history of the manuscript at Salamanca, see Cátedra 1989, 25.

9   Doubtless aware of the long tradition of the mother as go-between in Mediterranean societies, the *antiguo auctor* and Rojas deliberately captured it in ironic terms by transferring the appellation of *madre* [mother] to Celestina herself. For the historical use of the term *madre* to designate the woman in charge of a brothel, see Galán Sánchez and López Beltrán (1984, 164).

10 Another painting attributed to the School of Murillo portrays a similar pair – a young woman and an older one, scarf in hand perhaps ready to cover up any facial gesture that could betray complicity – who peer out from a barred window at the spectator. Significantly, this one has borne the popular title 'Celestina and Her Daughter' since the late seventeenth century, although it is now listed according to the title of 'Two Women Behind a Grille.' It forms part of the collection of the Hermitage Museum, Saint Petersburg.

11 Twelve of the seventy-seven historical instances of the corruption of young women cited by Rossiaud (1988, 41n.61) refer to a mother, or mother-in-law, as the principal instigator of the affair.

12 The dialogue evoked the following gloss, centring on the legal and moral
ramifications of Pleberio's remarks, from the anonymous author of *Celestina
comentada*: 'Antes pareçe que por leyes esta ordenado que no solamente el
consentimiento de los hijos para se casar es menester que intervenga sino
tambien el consentimiento de los padres como es ley que ansi lo dize la la
1.2.ff., De ritu nuptiarum ... y solo en consentimiento del padre, si no
interviene el del hijo expresso o tacito, no queda el hijo obligado a se
casar ... Pero si [los hijos] se cassasen sin guardar este consentimiento a
los padres, bien valdria, como avemos dicho como cosa espiritual que los
padres no tienen en ello voto ni pareçer de fuerça, como en muchas partes
del derecho se trata' (451–2) [Rather, it seems that by law it is ordained that
not only the consent of the children is needed to marry, but also that the
consent of the parents also be involved, as it is said in the law that stipulates
it, 1.2. ff On the rite of marriage ... and if it is only to comply with the wish
and consent of the father, the child is not obliged to marry without his own
express or tacit consent ... But should [children] marry without this
consent of the parents, it would be better, as we have said, as a spiritual
thing, that the parents not force or have a say in it, as is said in many places
in the law]. See also Corfis (1992, 399–400).

13 Castilian civil law since the *Siete Partidas* confirms that, in cases where a
couple was caught *in flagrante* followed by a charge of seduction, the
remedy was marriage. Indeed, Pleberio and Alisa's dialogue appears to
centre directly on Partida 4.1.11, 'En cuya escogencia deve de dar, o de
tomar alguna de las fijas, que desposasen sus padres' [In regard to whom
daughters who have been promised by their fathers may take or choose to
be given], which deals with both the freedom of a daughter to choose a
mate and the remedy for the offence of the seduction of a daughter. The
remedy in the latter case provides that if a man 'con alguna de las fijas de
algun ome yoguiesse con alguna dellas, ante que gela el padre diesse, o
señalasse, tenudo es de tomar aquella por muger. E si no[n] quisiesse,
develo apremiar que la resciba' [should lie with the daughter of another
man, before the father should give her to him, or indicate that he is to take
her for a wife, and should he not then consent to marry her, then he should
be forced to receive her] (I have regularized the use of u̲ and v̲ in the
citation). See also Stone (1990, 36–7).

6. Melibea Speaks: Language and Feminine Desire

1 To be sure, Slavoj Zikek sees the courtly lady as a total abstraction lacking
any human identity, an object whose substance has been emptied and

substituted by words that deny her any possibility of individuality. He confirms her link to Lacan's *objet à* and Freud's *das Ding*, or the unattainable and the unspeakable, thus rendering the woman a monstrous, contumacious Other impossible to behold and just as impossible to attain (1994a, 89).

2 Lawrance discusses dramatic readings and semi-theatrical representations among the students at the University of Salamanca around the year 1501, (1993a, 84–5). Gilman comments that, just as *Celestina* was written, 'so its author author expected it to be read: out loud to an in-group' (1972, 319).

3 Melibea's capitulation to desire disturbed at least one early sixteenth-century reader. Assessing the different characters in *Celestina*, Valdés, the main character in Juan de Valdés's *Diálogo de la lengua* (1535), observes that 'la persona de Melibea pudiera estar mejor … A donde se deja muy presto vencer, no solamente a amar pero a gozar del deshonesto fruto del amor' (182) [The character of Melibea could be better … where she lets herself be conquered too quickly, not just by love but by the pleasure of the unchaste fruits of love].

4 Mary Elizabeth Perry, in her study of gender in Seville at the beginning of the sixteenth century, remarks that 'families of wealth could exert consider-able pressure on a young woman to marry a particular propertied suitor … they had to consider the marriage of their sons and daughters as a strategy for safeguarding or enriching the family estate' (1990, 67).

5 'Was will das Weib?' in a letter to Marie Bonaparte (Jones 1955, 2:3:16).

7. The Desire to Belong and the Body Politic

1 Angus MacKay (1987, xiv, 9–25) brilliantly uncovers the symbolic signifi-cance of the ritual divestiture of Enrique IV's body in effigy by the rebellious magnates during the so-called Farce of Avila in 1465. Earlier in the century, the royal bureaucrat Juan Alfonso de Baena had poetically portrayed the political ills of the kingdom through the image of an infirm body in the admonitions directed at Juan II in his 'Dezir que envió Juan Alfonso de Baena al señor Rey sobre las discordias por qué manera podían ser remedi-adas' [Declamation that Juan Alfonso de Baena sent to the King concerning the discords and the manner in which they could be remedied]. See Dutton and González Cuenca 1993, 739–79, but especially 747–9.

2 The connection between sexual desire, hunger, and the edible is made brutally explicit by Calisto when, in act 19 as he pulls her clothing off her, he responds to Melibea's protestations against his indelicacy: 'Señora, el que quiere comer el ave, quita primero las plumas' (324) [Madame, he who wishes to eat the bird must first pluck its feathers]. The association of food

and sex in the medieval Iberian imaginary is made explicit in the battle of
Don Carnal and Doña Cuaresma in the fourteenth-century *Libro de buen amor.*

3 Catherine Swietlicki, centring on these remarks and looking at the episode
from a feminist perspective, comments that both Areúsa and Elicia constitute 'outspoken female defenders of their liberty. Areúsa … [embodies] a
voice of class equality;' and that 'Rojas' choice of two prostitutes as spokes-
women for liberty and equality was unprecedented' (1985, 5).

4 Stallybrass and White (1986, 5–6), commenting upon the representation of
low-Others in carnivalesque discourse produced by subjects 'on top,' note
how the images of the low Other actually serve to define the writing subject
in the way that Hegel describes the master-slave relationship in the
Phenomenology. Celestina presents a conspicuous inversion of this dynamic: the
low Others (the whores Elicia and Areúsa), as they claim sexual and social
parity or superiority, appropriate the rhetoric of carnivalesque corporal
distortion and apply it to the subjects 'on top' in their quest to define
themselves subjectively. In *Celestina* the low subject thus symbolically
embraces the top as an inverted eroticized component of its own desire and
fantasy. The result is a psychological reliance on the excluded Other who,
disavowed at the level of social discourse, remains central for the definition
of identity.

8. Precincts of Contention: Locating Desire and Ideology in *Celestina*

1 I use the word 'ideology' in terms of the connection between discourse and
power. Eagleton notes that 'Discourses, sign-systems and signifying practices
of all kinds … produce effects, shape forms of consciousness and uncon-
sciousness, which are closely related to the maintenance or transformation
of our existing systems of power … "ideology" can be taken to indicate no
more than this connection – the link or nexus between discourses and
power' (1980, 210).

9. Pleberio and the Ends of Desire

1 On the nuances and modulations of the titles assigned to Rojas's work, see
Lawrance (1993a).

2 On the crucial question of the representation of immanence, transcendence, and presence in philosophy, literature, and the humanities in general,
see Nancy (1993), Schwartz (2004), and Gumbrecht (2004).

Works Cited

Ackerman, James S., and Myra N. Rosenfeld. 1989. 'Social Stratification in Renaissance Urban Planning.' In *Urban Life in the Renaissance*, ed. Susan Zimmerman and Ronald E. Weissman, 21–49. Newark: University of Delaware Press.

Alcalá, Angel. 1976. 'El neoepicureismo y la intención de *La Celestina*.' *Romanische Forshungen* 88: 224–45.

Alfonso X, el sabio. *Las siete partidas del sabio rey don Alonso el nono, nuevamente glosadas*. 1974. Ed. and commentary by Gregorio López. 3 vols. Salamanca: Andrea de Portonoariis, 1555; repr. Madrid: Edición facsímil. Boletín Oficial del Estado.

Allouha, Malek. 1986. *The Colonial Harem*. Trans. Myrna and Wlad Godzich. Minneapolis: University of Minnesota Press.

Alzieu, Pierre, Yvan Lissorgues, and Robert Jammes. 1975. *Poesía erótica del Siglo de Oro*. Toulouse: Université de Toulouse–Le Mirail.

Andreae Capellani. 1930. *De Amore Libri Tres*. Ed. Amadeu Pagès Castellón de la Plana: Sociedad Castellonense de Cultura.

Archivo Iberoamericano de cetrería http://www.aic.uva.es/~cetreria/.

Arcipreste de Hita. 1988. *Libro de buen amor*. Ed. G.B. Gybbon-Monnypenny. Madrid: Castalia.

Aristotle. *On the Parts of Animals*. Trans. William Ogle. The Internet Classics Archive. http://classics.mit.edu/Aristotle/parts_animals.html.

Armistead, Samuel G., and James T. Monroe. 1989. 'Celestina's Muslim Sisters.' *Celestinesca* 13, no. 2: 3–27.

Armistead, Samuel G., and Joseph H. Silverman. 1979. *Tres calas en el romancero sefardí (Rodas, Jerusalén, Estados Unidos)*. Madrid: Castalia.

Arthurian Women: A Casebook. 1996. Ed. Thelma Fenster. New York: Garland.

Bachelard, Gaston. 1994. *The Poetics of Space*. Trans. Maria Jolas. Boston: Beacon Press.

Bakhtin, M.M. *Rabelais and His World*. 1968. Trans. H. Iswolsky. Cambridge, MA: MIT Press.

– 1981. *The Dialogic Imagination*. Trans. Caryl Emerson and M. Holquist. Austin: University of Texas Press.

Bal, Mieke. 1991. *Reading Rembrandt: Beyond the Word-Image Opposition*. Cambridge: Cambridge University Press.

Baranda, Consolación. 2004. La Celestina *y el mundo como contienda*. Salamanca: Ediciones Universidad de Salamanca.

Barker, Frances. 1984. *The Tremulous Private Body*. London: Methuen.

Barón Palma, Emilio. 1976. 'Pármeno: la liberación del ser auténtico. El antihéroe.' *Cuadernos Hispanoamericanos*, no. 317: 383–400.

Barth, Kaspar von. 2006. *Pornoboscodidascalus Latinus*. Ed. Enrique Fernández. Chapel Hill: University of North Carolina Press.

Barthes, Roland. *S/Z*. 1974. Trans. Richard Miller. New York: Hill and Wang.

– 1975. *The Pleasure of the Text*. Trans. Richard Miller. New York: Hill and Wang.

Bataille, Georges. 1957. *Erotisme*. Paris: Editions Minuit.

Bataillon, Marcel. 1961. La Celestine *selon Fernando de Rojas*. Paris: Didier.

Beltrán, Luis. 1980. 'La envidia de Pármeno y la corrupción de Melibea.' *Insula* 198: 3, 10.

Bennássar, Bartolomé. 1984. *Inquisición Española. Poder político y control social.* Barcelona: Editorial Crítica.

Bennett, Judith M. 1992. 'Medieval Women, Modern Women: Across the Great Divide.' In *Culture and History, 1350–1600: Essays on English Communities, Identities, and Writing*, ed. David Aers, 147–75. New York: Harvester Wheatsheaf.

Benvenuto, Bice, and Roger Kennedy. 1986. *The Works of Jacques Lacan: An Introduction*. London: Free Association.

Berger, John. 1972. *Ways of Seeing*. London: Penguin.

Bergson, Henri. *Laughter: An Essay on the Meaning of the Comic*. 1937. Trans. Cloudesley Brereton and Fred Rothwell. New York: Macmillan.

– 1956. 'Laughter.' In *Comedy*, ed. Wylie Sypher. Garden City, NY: Doubleday.

Berndt Kelley, Erna R. 1993. 'Mute Commentaries on a Text: The Illustrations of the *Comedia de Calisto y Melibea*.' In *Fernando de Rojas and* Celestina: *Approaching the Fifth Century*, ed. Ivy Corfis and Joseph T. Snow, 193–227. Madison, WI: HSMS.

Blanco, Emilio. 1999. 'Ver, oir, y callar en *La Celestina*.' *Actas del VIII Congreso de la Asociación Hispánica de Literatura Medieval* Santander. 365–71.

Blay Manzanera, Vicenta, and Dorothy S. Severin. 1999. *Animals in* Celestina. Papers of the Medieval Hispanic Research Seminar, 18. London: Queen Mary and Westfield College.

Bloch, R. Howard. 1991. *Medieval Misogyny and the Invention of Western Romantic Love.* Chicago: University of Chicago Press.

Boccaccio, Giovanni. 2009. *Decameron.* Translated by J.G. Nichols. New York: Alfred A. Knopf.

Botta, Patrizia. 1994. 'Itinerarios urbanos de *La Celestina* de Fernando e Rojas.' *Celestinesca* 18, no. 2: 113–31.

Boullosa, Virginia H. 1973. 'La concepción del cuerpo en la *Celestina.*' In *La idea del cuerpo en la letras españolas (siglos XIII a XVI) I*, ed. Dinko Cvitanovic, 80–117. Bahia Blanca, Argentina: Instituto de Humanidades, Universidad Nacional de Sur.

Bourdieu, Pierre. 1977. *Outline of a Theory of Practice.* Trans. Richard Nice. Cambridge: Cambridge University Press.

Brooks, Peter. 1992. 'Freud's Masterplot.' In *Reading for the Plot: Design and Intention in Narrative.* Cambridge, MA: Harvard University Press.

Brody, Saul Nathaniel. 1974. *The Disease of the Soul: Leprosy in Medieval Literature.* Ithaca, NY: Cornell University Press.

Brown, Peter. 1988. *The Body and Society: Men, Women, and Sexual Renunciation in Early Christianity.* New York: Columbia University Press.

Brundage, James. 1982. 'Rape and Seduction in Medieval Canon Law.' In *Sexual Practices and the Medieval Church*, 141–8. Buffalo, NY: Prometheus Books.

Burke, James F. 1998. *Desire Against the Law: The Juxtaposition of Contraries in Early Medieval Spanish Literature.* Stanford, CA: Stanford University Press.

– 2002. *Vision, the Gaze, and the Function of the Senses in* Celestina. University Park: Pennsylvania State University Press.

Burns, E. Jane. 1993. *Bodytalk: When Women Speak in Old French Literature.* Philadelphia: University of Pennsylvania Press.

Bynum, Carolyn. 1987. *Holy Feast and Holy Fast: The Religious Significance of Food to Medieval Women.* Berkeley and Los Angeles: University of California Press.

– 1991. *Fragmentation or Redemption: Essays on Gender and the Human Body in Medieval Religion.* New York: Zone.

Casa, Frank P. 1968. 'Pleberio's Lament for Melibea.' *Zeitschrift für romanische Philologie* 84:20–9.

Casey, Michael. 1981. 'Spiritual Desire in the Gospel Homilies of Saint Gregory the Great.' *Cistercian Studies* 16:297–314.

– 1985. 'In Pursuit of Ecstasy: Reflections on Saint Bernard of Clairvaux's *De Diligendo Deo.*' *Monastic Studies* 16:139–56.

Castells, Ricardo. 2000. *Fernando de Rojas and the Renaissance Vision.* University Park: Pennsylvania State University Press.

Castillo, David. R. 2001. *(A)wry Views: Anamorphosis, Cervantes, and the Early Picaresque.* West Lafayette, IN: Purdue University Press.

Castro, Américo. 1965. La Celestina *como contienda literaria.* Madrid: Ediciones de la Revista de Occidente.

– 1970. *Aspectos del vivir hispánico.* Madrid: Alianza Editorial.

Cátedra, Pedro M. 1989. *Amor y pedagogía en la Edad Media: Estudios de doctrina amorosa y práctica literaria.* Salamanca: Secretariado de publicaciones, Universidad de Salamanca.

– 2001. *Tratados de amor en torno de* Celestina. Ed. Pedro M. Cátedra et al. Madrid: Sociedad Estatal España Nuevo Mundo.

2005. Celestina: *An Annotated Edition of the First Dutch Translation (Antwerp, 1550).* Ed. Lieve Behiels and Kathleen Kish. Leuven, Belgium: Leuven University Press.

2002. Celestina *comentada.* Ed. Louise Fothergill-Payne, Enrique Fernández Rivera, and Peter Fothergill-Payne. Salamanca: Ediciones de la Universidad de Salamanca.

Chambers, E.K. 1945. *English Literature at the Close of the Middle Ages.* Oxford and New York: Oxford University Press.

Chrétien de Troyes. 1952. *Les Romans de Chrétien de Troyes:* Erec et Enide. Ed. Mario Roques. Paris: CFMA.

– 1957. *Les Romans de Chrétien de Troyes.* Ed. Alexandre Micha. Paris: CFMA.

Cixous, Hélène, and Catherine Clément. 1986. *The Newly Born Woman.* Trans. Betsy Wang. Foreword by Sandra M. Gilbert. Minneapolis: University of Minnesota Press.

Colby, Alice M. 1986. *The Portrait in Twelfth-Century French Literature.* Geneva: Librairie Droz.

Constable, Giles. 1979. *Religious Life and Thought (11th and 12th Centuries).* London: Variorum Reprints.

Corfis, Ivy A. 1992. 'Laws of Head of Household in *Celestina.*' In *Romance Languages Annual,* ed. Jeanette Beer et al., 397–401. West Lafayette, IN: Purdue Research Foundation.

Curtius, Ernst Robert. 1963. *European Literature and the Latin Middle Ages.* Trans. Willard R. Trask. New York: Harper and Row.

Dangler, Jean. 2001. *Mediating Fictions: Literature, Women Healers, and the Go-between in Medieval and Early Modern Iberia.* Lewisburg, PA: Bucknell University Press.

Davis, Kathleen. 2006. 'Sovereign Subjects, Feudal Law, and the Writing of History.' *Journal of Medieval and Early Modern Studies* 36:223–61.

Delicado, Francisco. 1972. *La lozana andaluza.* Ed. de Bruno Damiani. Madrid: Castalia.

Derrida, Jacques. 1972. 'Freud and the Scene of Writing.' Trans. Jeffrey Mehlman. *Yale French Studies* 48, French Freud: Structural Studies in Psychoanalysis: 74–117.

– 1997. *Of Grammatology.* Trans. Gayatri Chakravorty Spivak. Baltimore: Johns Hopkins University Press.

Deyermond, Alan. 1977. 'Hilado-cordón-cadena: Symbolic Equivalence in *La Celestina.*' *Celestinesca* 1, no. 1:25–30.

Deyermond, Alan. 1961. 'The Text-book Mishandled: Andreas Capellanus and the Opening Scene of *La Celestina.*' *Neophilologus* 45:218–21.

– 1993. 'Female Societies in *Celestina.*' In *Fernando de Rojas and* Celestina, ed. Ivy A. Corfis and Joseph T. Snow, 1–31. Madison, WI: HSMS.

Dinshaw, Carolyn. 1989. *Chaucer's Sexual Poetics.* Madison: University of Wisconsin Press.

Dollimore, Jonathan. 1991. *Sexual Dissidence: Augustine to Wilde, Freud to Foucault.* Oxford: Clarendon Press.

Douglas, Mary. 1966. *Purity and Danger: An Analysis of the Concepts of Pollution and Taboo.* London: Routledge and Kegan Paul.

Drysdall, Denis L., ed. 1974. La Celestina *in the French Translation of 1578 by Jacques Lavardin.* London: Tamesis.

Duby, Georges. 1994. 'Courtly Love.' In *Love and Marriage in the Middle Ages.* Trans. Jane Dunnett. Chicago: University of Chicago Press.

Dunn, Peter. 1975. *Fernando de Rojas.* Boston: Twayne, G.K. Hall.

Dutton, Brian, and Joaquín González Cuenca, eds. 1993. *Cancionero de Juan Alfonso de Baena.* Madrid: Visor Libros.

Eagleton, Terry. *Literary Theory.* 1983. Minneapolis: University of Minnesota Press.

– 1991. *Ideology: An Introduction.* London: Verso.

Elias, Norbert. 1978. *The Civilizing Process.* Vol. 1: *The History of Manners.* Trans. E. Jephcott. New York: Pantheon.

Ellis, Deborah. 1981. '"¡Adiós paredes!": The Image of the Home in *Celestina.*' *Celestinesca* 5, no. 2:1–17.

El Saffar, Ruth, and Diana De Armas Wilson, eds. 1993. *Quixotic Desire.* Ithaca, NY: Cornell University Press.

Embeita, María. 1977. '*La Celestina,* obra del Renacimiento.' In La Celestina *y su contorno social: Actas del I Congreso Internacional sobre La Celestina,*125–34. Under the direction of Manuel Criado de Val. Barcelona: Hispam: Borrás Ediciones.

1994. *Encyclopedia of Psychology.* Ed. Raymond J. Corsini et al. 2nd ed. New York: J. Wiley and Sons.

Eschenbach, Wolfram von. 1961, 1962, 1965.*Parzival.* Ed. Leitzmann. 3 vols. Tübingen.

Evans, Dylan. 1996. *An Introductory Dictionary of Lacanian Psychoanalysis.* London: Routledge.

Faulhaber, Charles. 1977. 'The Hawk in Melibea's Garden.' *Hispanic Review* 45:435–45.

Feldman, Seymour. 2003. *Philosophy in a Time of Crisis: Don Isaac Abravanel: Defender of the Faith.* New York: Routledge-Curzon.

Felman, Shoshana. 1983. *The Literary Speech Act: Don Juan with J.L. Austin, or Seduction in Two Languages.* Ithaca, NY: Cornell University Press.

Fenster, Thelma. See *Arthurian Women: A Casebook.*

Ferguson, Margaret. 1983. *Trials of Desire: Renaissance Defenses of Poetry.* New Haven, CT: Yale University Press.

Fernández Márquez, Pablo. 1967. *Los personajes de* La Celestina. Mexico City: Finisterre.

Fineman, Joel. 1986. *Shakespeare's Perjured Eye: The Invention of Poetic Subjectivity in the Sonnets.* Berkeley and Los Angeles: University of California Press.

Finucci, Valeria, and Schwartz, Regina. 1994. *Desire in the Renaissance: Psychoanalysis and Literature.* Princeton, NJ: Princeton University Press.

Fisher, Sheila, and Janet E. Halley. 1989. 'The Lady Vanishes: The Problem of Women's Absence in Late Medieval and Renaissance Texts.' In *Seeking the Woman in Late Medieval and Renaissance Writing: Essays in Feminist Contextual Criticism,* ed. Sheila Fisher and Janet E. Halley, 2–17. Knoxville: University of Tennessee Press.

Fontes, Manuel da Costa. 1984. 'Celestina's *Hilado* and Related Symbols.' *Celestinesca* 8, no. 1:3–13.

– 1985. 'Celestina's *Hilado* and Related Symbols. A Supplement.' *Celestinesca* 9, no. 1:33–8.

– 1992. 'Fernando de Rojas, Cervantes, and Two Portuguese Folk Tales.' In *Hispanic Medieval Studies in Honor of Samuel G. Armistead,* ed. E. Michael Gerli and Harvey L. Sharrer, 85–96. Madison, WI: HSMS.

Fothergill-Payne, Louise. 1989. *Seneca and Celestina.* Cambridge: Cambridge University Press.

Fothergill-Payne, Louise. 1993. '*Celestina* as a Funny Book: A Bakhtinian Reading.' *Celestinesca* 17, no. 2:29–51.

Foucault, Michel. 1978. *The Order of Things: An Archaeology of the Human Sciences.* New York: Pantheon.

Fox-Davies, Arthur Charles. 1969. *A Complete Guide to Heraldry.* 1909. Revised and annotated by J.P. Brooke-Little. London: Nelson.

Fraker, Charles F. 1993. 'The Four Humors in *Celestina*.' In *Fernando de Rojas and* Celestina *Approaching the Fifth Centenary*, ed. Ivy A. Corfis and Joseph Snow, 129–54. Madison, WI: HSMS.

Fraker, Charles F. 1966. 'The Importance of Pleberio's Soliloquy.' *Romanische Forschungen* 78:515–29.

Frantz, David. 1989. *Festum Voluptatis: A Study of Renaissance Erotica.* Columbus: Ohio State University Press.

Freedman, Barbara. 1991. *Staging the Gaze: Postmodernism, Psychoanalysis, and Shakespearean Comedy.* Ithaca, NY: Cornell University Press.

Freud, Sigmund. 1948. 'A Neurosis of Demoniacal Possession in the Seventeenth Century.' (1923). Collected Papers, vol. 4. Ed. Ernest Jones. Authorized trans. Under the supervision of Joan Riviere. London: The Hogarth Press/The Institute of Psycho-Analysis.

– 1953–74. *The Standard Edition of the Complete Psychological Works of Sigmund Freud.* Trans. James Strachey et al. 24 vols. London: Hogarth Press.

– 1953–74. *Three Essays on the Theory of Sexuality.* In *Standard Edition of the Complete Works of Sigmund Freud*, vol. 7, 123–245. London: Hogarth.

– 1955. 'Totem and Taboo and Other Works.' In *The Standard Edition of the Complete Psychological Works of Sigmund Freud.* vol. 13 (1913–14), trans. James Strachey in collaboration with Anna Freud. London: The Hogarth Press/The Institute of Psycho-Analysis.

– 1960. *Jokes and Their Relation to the Unconscious.* Ed. and trans. J. Strachey. New York: Norton.

– 1961. *Beyond the Pleasure Principle.* Trans. James Strachey. New York: W.W. Norton and Co.

– 1965. *The Interpretation of Dreams.* Trans. and ed. James Strachey. New York: Avon Books.

Friedman. Mira. 1989. 'The Falcon and the Hunt: Symbolic Love Imagery in Medieval and Renaissance Art.' In *The Poetics of Love in the Middle Ages: Texts and Contexts*, ed. Moshe Lazar and Norris J. Lacy, 157–83. Fairfax, VA: George Mason University Press.

Galán Sánchez, Angel, and María Teresa López Beltrán. 1984. 'El *status* teórico de las prostitutas del reino de Granada en la primera mitad del siglo XVI (Las Ordenanzas de 1538).' In *Las mujeres en las ciudades medievales. Actas de las III Jornadas de Investigación Interdisciplinaria*, ed. Cristina Segura Graiño, 161–9. Madrid: Seminario de Estudios de la Mujer, Universidad Autónoma de Madrid.

Garber, Marjorie. 1987. *Shakespeare's Ghost Writers: Literature as Uncanny Causality.* New York: Metheun.

García Cárcel, Ricardo. 1976. *Orígenes de la Inquisición Española. El Tribunal de Valencia, 1478–1530.* Barcelona: Ediciones Península.

Gardner, John. 1977. *The Life and Times of Chaucer*. New York: Knopf.

Gariano, Carmelo. 1975. 'El erotismo grotesco en *La Celestina*.' *Vórtice* 1, no. 3:2–16.

Gaunt, Simon. 1990. 'Marginal Men, Marcabru and Orthodoxy: The Early Troubadours and Adultery.' *Medium Aevum* 59, no. 1:55–72.

– 1995. *Gender and Genre in Medieval French Literature*. Cambridge: Cambridge University Press.

– 2001. 'A Matryr to Love: Sacrificial Desire in the Poetry of Bernart de Ventadorn.' *Journal of Medieval and Early Modern Studies* 31, no. 3: 477–506.

Gaunt, Simon, and Sarah Kay. 1999. *The Troubadours: An Introduction*. Cambridge: Cambridge University Press.

Gaylord, Mary Malcolm. 1991. 'Fair of the World, Fair of the World: The Commerce of Language in *La Celestina*.' *Revista de Estudios Hispánicos* 25:1–28.

Gerli, E. Michael. 1976. *Alfonso Martínez de Toledo*. Boston: G.K. Hall.

– 1994. *Poesía de cancionero: historia y texto*. Madrid: Akal.

– 1995. 'Complicitous Laughter: Hilarity and Seduction in *Celestina*.' *Hispanic Review* 63:19–38.

– 2000. 'Leriano and Lacan: The Mythological and Psychoanalytical Underpinnings of Leriano's Last Drink.' *La Corónica* 29, no. 1 (Fall):113–28.

Gilman, Stephen. 1972. The Spain of *Fernando de Rojas: The Intellectual and Social Landscape of* La Celestina. Princeton, NJ: Princeton University Press.

– 1974. *El arte de* La Celestina. Madrid: Editorial Taurus.

Gilson Étienne. 1940. *The Mystical Theology of Saint Bernard*. Trans. A.H.C. Downes. London: Sheed and Ward.

Ginzburg, Carlo. 1989. *Clues, Myths, and the Historical Method*. Trans. John and Anne C. Tedeschi. Baltimore: Johns Hopkins University Press.

Ginzburg, Carlo. 1986. *The Worms and the Cheese: The Cosmos of a Sixteenth-century Miller*. Trans. John and Anne Tedeschi. New York: Peguin.

Girard, René. 1965. *Deceit, Desire, and the Novel*. Trans. Yvonne Freccero. Baltimore: Johns Hopkins University Press.

Goldin, Frederick. 1967. *The Mirror of Narcissus in the Courtly Love Lyric*. Ithaca, NY: Cornell University Press.

González Echevarría, Roberto. 1993. *Celestina's Brood: Continuities of the Baroque in Spanish and Latin American Literatures*. Durham, NC: Duke University Press.

Gossy, Mary S. 1989. *The Untold Story. Women and Theory in Golden Age Texts*. Ann Arbor: University of Michigan Press.

Gottfried von Strassburg. 1930. *Tristan und Isold*. Ed. Friedrich Ranke. Berlin: Weidmannsche.

Goux, Jean-Joseph. 1990. *Symbolic Economies: After Marx and Freud*. Trans. Jennifer Curtiss Gage. Ithaca, NY: Cornell University Press.

Green, Otis H. 1968. *Spain and the Western Tradition*. Madison, WI: University of
Wisconsin Press.

Green, Otis H. 1965. 'Did the World Create Pleberio?' *Romanische Forschungen*
77:108–10.

Greenblatt, Stephen. 1986. 'Psychoanalysis and Renaissance Culture.' In
Literary Theory/Renaissance Texts, ed. Patricia Parker and David Quint.
Baltimore: Johns Hopkins University Press.

Greene, Roland. 2005. 'The Protocolonial Baroque of *La Celestina*.' In
Postcolonial Approaches to the European Middle Ages: Translating Cultures, ed.
Ananya Jahanara Kabir and Deanne Williams, 227–49. New York and
London: Cambridge University Press.

Grieve, Patricia E. 1990. 'Mothers and Daughters in Fifteenth-century Spanish
Sentimental Romances: Implications for *Celestina*.' *Bulletin of Hispanic Studies*
67:345–55.

Gumbrecht, Hans-Ulrich. 2004. *On the Production of Presence: What Meaning
Cannot Convey*. Palo Alto, CA: Stanford University Press.

Gurevich, A.J. 1985. *Categories of Medieval Culture*. Trans. G.L Campbell. London:
Routledge and Kegan Paul.

Hale, D.G. 1971. *The Body Politic: A Political Metaphor in Renaissance English
Literature*. The Hague: Mouton.

Hall Martin, June. 1972. *Love's Fools: Aucassin, Troilus, Calisto and the Parody of the
Courtly Lover*. London: Tamesis.

Hamilton, Michelle. 2007. *Representing Others in Medieval Iberian Literature*. New
York: Palgrave.

Haren, M. 1985. *Medieval Thought: The Western Intellectual Tradition from Antiquity
to the Thirteenth Century*. London: Macmillan.

Hathaway, Robert L. 1993. 'Concerning Melibea's Breasts.' *Celestinesca*
17:17–32.

Hartunian, Diane. 1992. La Celestina: *A Feminist Reading of the* Carpe Diem
Theme. Potomac, MD: Scripta Humanistica.

Hatto, Arthur T. 1957. 'Der minnen Vederspil Isot.' *Euphorion* 57:302–30.

Haywood, Louise M. 2001. 'Models for Mourning and Magic Words in *Celestina*.'
Bulletin of Hispanic Studies 78:81–8.

Herrero, Javier. 1984. 'Celestina's Craft: The Devil in the Skein.' *Bulletin of
Hispanic Studies* 61:343–51.

– 1986. 'The Stubborn Text: Clisto's Toothache and Melibea's Girdle.' In
Literature Among Discourses: The Golden Age, ed. Wlad Godzich and Nicholas
Spadaccini, 132–47. Minneapolis: University of Minnesota Press.

Heugas, Pierre. 1973. La Célestine *et sa descendance directe*. Bordeaux: Institut
d'études ibériques et ibéro-américaines de l'Université de Bordeaux.

Hollander, Anne. 1975. *Seeing Through Clothes.* Berkeley and Los Angeles: University of California Press.

Hook, David. 2001. 'Celestina's *frayles devotos.*' *Bulletin of Hispanic Studies* 88:89–102.

Huchet, Jean-Charles. 1982. 'La Dame et le troubadour: Fin'amor et mystique chez Bernard de Ventadorn.' *Littérature* 47, no. 1:12–30.

– 1987. *L'amour discourtois:'Fin'amors' chez les premiers troubadours.* Toulouse: Privat.

Irigaray, Luce. 1985. *This Sex Which Is Not One.* Trans. Catherine Porter with C. Burke. Ithaca, NY: Cornell University Press.

James, E.O. 1958. *Myth and Ritual in the Ancient Near East.* London: Thames and Hudson.

Jameson, Fredric. 1981. *The Political Unconscious: Narrative as a Socially Symbolic Act.* Ithaca, NY: Cornell, University Press.

Jardine, Lisa. 1983. *Still Harping on Daughters.* Sussex and New York: Barnes and Noble.

Johnson, Mark Albert. 2007. 'Bearded Women in Early Modern England.' *Studies in English Literature 1500–1900* 47, no. 1:1–28.

Johnson, Carroll. B. 1983. *Madness and Lust: A Psychoanalytical Approach to Don Quixote.* Berkeley and Los Angeles: University of California Press.

Jones, Ernest. 1955. *The Life and Work of Sigmund Freud.* 3 vols. New York: Basic Books.

Joubert, Laurent. 1980. *Treatise on Laughter.* Trans. and ann. Gregory David de Rocher. Tuscaloosa, AL: University of Alabama Press.

Juan Manuel. 1981. *Libro de la caza.* Ed. José Manuel Blecua. *Obras completas.* Vol. 1, 515–96. Madrid: Gredos.

Kantorowicz, Ernst. 1957. *The King's Two Bodies: A Study in Medieval Political Theology.* Princeton, NJ: Princeton University Press.

Kay, Sarah. 1990. *Subjectivity in Troubadour Poetry.* Cambridge: Cambridge University Press.

Kernberg, Otto F. 1986. *Object-Relations Theory and Clinical Psychoanalysis.* New York: Jacob Aronson.

Kristeller, Paul Oskar. 1964. *The Philosophy of Marsilio Ficino.* Trans. Virginia Conant. Gloucester, MA: Peter Smith.

Kristeva, Julia. 1985. *Au commencement était l'amour: psychanalyse et foi.* Paris: Hachette.

Kristeva, Julia. 1991. *Strangers to Ourselves.* Trans. Leon S. Roudiez. New York: Columbia University Press.

Kuhn, Annette. 1982. *Women's Pictures: Feminism and Cinema.* London: Routledge amd Keegan Paul.

Kurzweil, Edith. 1977. La Celestina *y su contorno social: Actas del I Congreso Internacional sobre* La Celestina. Under the direction of Manuel Criado de Val. Barcelona: Hispam, Borrás Ediciones.

– 1980. *The Age of Structuralism: Lévi-Strauss to Foucault.* New York: Columbia University Press.

Lacan, Jacques. 1968. *The Language of the Self: The Function of Language in Psychoanalysis.* Trans., notes, and commentary by Anthony Wilden. Baltimore: Johns Hopkins University Press.

– 1977. *Écrits: A Selection.* Trans. Alan Sheridan. New York: W.W. Norton.

– 1981. *The Four Fundamental Concepts of Psychoanalysis.* Trans. Alan Sheridan. New York: Norton.

– 1982. *Feminine Sexuality: Jacques Lacan and the* école freudienne. Edited by Juliet Mitchell and Jacqueline Rose. London: Macmillan.

– 1988. *The Seminar of Jacques Lacan.* Ed. Jacques-Alain Miller. New York: W.W. Norton.

– 1992. *The Ethics of Psychoanalysis* (Seminar 1959–1960). Trans. and notes by Dennis Porter. New York: Norton.

Lacarra, María Eugenia. 1990. *Cómo leer La Celestina.* Madrid: Ediciones Júcar.

– 1993. 'La evolución de la prostitución en la Castilla del siglo XV y la mancebía de Salamanca en tiempos de Fernando de Rojas.' In *Fernando de Rojas and Celestina: Approaching the Fifth Century,* ed. Ivy A. Corfis and Joseph T. Snow, 33–78. Madison, WI: HSMS.

Lawrance, Jeremy N.H. 1993a. 'On the Title *Tragicomedia de Calisto y Melibea.*' In *Letters and Society in Fifteenth-Century Spain: Studies Presented to P.E. Russell on His Eightieth Birthday,* ed. Alan Deyermond and Jeremy Lawrance, 79–92. Llangrannog: Dolphin.

– 1993b. 'The *Tragicomedia de Calisto y Melibea* and Its "Moralitie".' *Celestinesca* 17, no. 2:85–110.

Lazar, Moshe. 1964. *Amour courtois et fin'amors dans la littérature du XIIe siècle.* Paris: Librairrie Klincksieck.

Lecertua, Jean-Paul. 1978. 'Le jardin de Melibée: Métaphores sexuelles et connotations symboliques dans quelques épisodes de *La Celestina.*' *Travaux et Mémoires de l'Université de Limoges* 2:105–38.

Lefebvre, Henri. 1991. *The Production of Space.* Trans. Donald Nicholson-Smith. Oxford: Blackwell.

Le Gentil, Pierre. 1949–52. *La Poésie Lyrique Espagnole et Portugaise á la fin du Moyen Âge.* Rennes: Plihon.

Le Goff, Jacques. 1989. 'Head or Heart: The Political Use of Body Metaphors in the Middle Ages.' In *Fragments for a History of the Human Body,* ed. Michel Feher et al., vol. 3. New York: Urzone.

Lewis, C.S. 1959. *The Allegory of Love.* Oxford: Oxford University Press.

Lida de Malkiel, María Rosa. 1970. *La originalidad artística de La Celestina.* 2nd ed. Buenos Aires: EUDEBA.

Literary Theory/Renaissance Texts. 1986. Edited by Patricia Parker and David Quint. Baltimore: Johns Hopkins University Press.

Lotman, Juri. 1977. *The Structure of the Artistic Text.* Trans. Ronald Vroon. Ann Arbor: Department of Slavic Languages and Literatures, University of Michigan.

Lovejoy, Arthur. 1960. *The Great Chain of Being.* New York: Harper Torch Books.

Lutwack, Leonard. 1984. *The Role of Place in Literature.* Syracuse, NY: Syracuse University Press.

Lyotard, Jean-François. 1993. *Libidinal Economy.* Trans. Ian Hamilton Grant. Bloomington: Indiana University Press.

MacKay, Angus. 1987. 'Ritual and Propaganda in Fifteenth-century Castile.' In *Society, Economy and Religion in Late Medieval Castile,* 3–43. London: Variorum Reprints.

– 1989. 'Courtly Love and Lust in Loja.' In *The Age of the Catholic Monarchs, 1474–1516: Literary Studies in Memory of Keith Whinnom,* ed. Alan Deyermond and Ian Macpherson, 83–94. Liverpool: Liverpool University Press.

Maravall, José Antonio. 1968. *El mundo social de* La Celestina. 2nd ed. Madrid: Gredos.

Márquez Villanueva, Francisco. 1993. *Orígenes y sociología del tema celestinesco.* Barcelona: Anthropos.

– 1994. '"Nascer e morir como bestias" (Criptojudaísmo y Criptoaverroísmo).' In *Los judaizantes en Europa y la literatura castellana del Siglo de Oro,* ed. Fernando Díaz Esteban, 273–93. Madrid: Letrúmero.

Marx, Karl. 1976. *Capital.* Trans. Ben Fowkes. Harmondsworth: Penguin.

McCulloch, Florence. 1962. *Medieval Latin and French Bestiaries.* Studies in the Romance Languages and Literatures 33. Chapel Hill: University of North Carolina.

McPheeters, D.W. 1954. 'The Element of Fatality in the *Tragicomedia de Calisto y Melibea.*' *Symposium* 8:331–5.

The Meaning of Courtly Love. 1973. Ed. Francis X. Newman. Albany: State University of New York Press.

Medieval Mysteries, Moralities, and Interludes. 1962. Ed. Vincent F. Hopper and Gerald B. Lahey. Great Neck, New York: Barrons.

Memorias de don Enrique IV de Castilla. Colección diplomática compuesta y ordenada por la Real Academia de la Historia. 1835–1913. Madrid: Fortanet.

Mérida Jiménez, Rafael M. 2000. 'Teorías presentes, amores medievales. En torno al estudio del homoerotismo en las culturas del Medioevo occidental.' *Revista de Poética Medieval* 4:51–98.

Metz, Christian. 1975. 'The Imaginary Signifier.' Trans. Ben Brewster. *Screen* 16:58–72.

Moi, Toril. 1986. 'Desire in Language: Andreas Capellanus and the Controversy of Courtly Love.' In *Medieval Literature: Criticism, Ideology, and History*, ed. David Aers, 11–33. Sussex, UK: Harvester Press.

– 1989. 'Patriarchal Knowledge and the Drive for Knowledge.' *New Directions in Psychoanalysis and Feminism*, ed. Teresa Brennan, 189–205. New York and London: Routledge.

Morón Arroyo, Ciriaco. 1984. *Sentido y forma de la* Celestina. 2nd ed. Madrid: Cátedra.

– 1994. Celestina *and Castilian Humanism at the End of the Fifteenth Century*. Center for Medieval and Early Renaissance Studies, Occasional Papers, no. 3. Binghamton, NY: Medieval and Renaissance Texts and Studies.

Mulvey, Laura. 1989. 'Visual Pleasure and Narrative Cinema.' In *Visual and Other Pleasures*, 14–26. Bloomington: Indiana University Press.

Nancy, Jean-Luc. 1993. *The Birth to Presence*. Palo Alto, CA: Stanford University Press.

Nelson, John Charles. 1958. *Renaissance Theory of Love: The Context of Giordano Bruno's* Eroici furori. New York: Columbia University Press.

Newman, Francis X. 1973. See *The Meaning of Courtly Love*.

Opitz, Claudia. 1994. 'Life in the Late Middle Ages.' In *A History of Women: Silences of the Middle Ages*, ed Christiane Klapisch-Zuber, 267–317. Cambridge, MA: Belknap Press of Harvard University.

Ovid. 1977. *Heroides* and *Amores*. Trans. G. Showerman. Rev. G.P. Goold. 2nd rev. ed. Cambridge, MA: Harvard University Press.

Pagden, Anthony. 1993. *European Encounters with the New World: From Renaissance to Romanticism*. New Haven, CT: Yale University Press.

Panofsky, Erwin. 1969. *Problems in Titian: Mostly Iconographic*. New York: New York University Press.

Parker, Patricia. See *Literary Theory/Renaissance Texts*.

Patterson, Lee. 1991. 'The Wife of Bath and the Triumph of the Subject.' In *Chaucer and the Subject of History*, 280–321. Madison: University of Wisconsin Press.

Pattison, David G. 2001. 'Deaths and Laments in *Celestina*.' *Bulletin of Spanish Studies* 78, no. 1:139–43.

Perniola, Mario. 1989. 'Between Clothing and Nudity.' In *Fragments for a History of the Human Body*, ed. Michael Feher et al., vol. 2, 237–65. New York: Zone Publishers.

Perry, Mary Elizabeth. 1990. *Gender and Disorder in Early Modern Seville*. Princeton, NJ: Princeton University Press.

Pine, Martin L. 1986. *Pietro Pomponazzi: Radical Philosopher of the Renaissance*. Padua, Italy: Antenore.

Pinedo, Ramiro. 1930. *El simbolismo en la escultura medieval española*, Madrid: Espasa-Calpe.

Pitkin, Hanna F. 1984. *Fortune Is a Woman*. Berkeley and Los Angeles: University of California Press.

Quint, David. See *Literary Theory/Renaissance Texts*.

Rasmussen, Ann Marie. 1997. *Mothers and Daughters in Medieval German Literature*. Syracuse, NY: Syracuse University Press.

Redondo, Augustin, ed. 1990. *Le Corps dans la Société Espagnole des XVIᵉ et XVIIᵉ Siècles*. Paris: Publications de la Sorbonne.

Rico, Francisco. 1986. *El pequeño mundo del hombre*. Rev. and corr. ed. Madrid: Alianza.

Ricoeur, Paul. 1976. *Interpretation Theory: Discourse and the Surplus of Meaning*. Fort Worth: Texas Christian University Press.

– 1992. *Oneself as Another*. Trans. Kathleen Blamey. Chicago: University of Chicago Press.

Riquer, Martín de. 1957. 'Fernando de Rojas y el primer acto de *La Celestina*.' *Revista de Filología Española* 41:373–95.

Rivera, Isidro J. 1995. 'Visual Structures and Verbal Representation in the *Comedia de Calisto y Melibea* (Burgos, 1499?).' *Celestinesca* 19:3–30.

Roffé, Mercedes. 1996. *La cuestión de género en* Grisel y Mirabella *de Juan de Flores*. Newark, DE: Juan de la Cuesta.

Rogers, Edith. 1974 'The Hunt in the Romancero and Other Traditional Ballads.' *Hispanic Review* 42:143–3.

Rojas, Fernando de. 1987. *Celestina*. Trans. James Mabbe (1631). Ed. Dorothy Sherman Severin. Warminster, UK: Aris and Phillips.

– 1989. *La Celestina*. Ed. Dorothy Severin. Madrid: Cátedra.

– 1991. *Comedia o tragicomedia de Calisto y Melibea*. Ed. Peter E. Russell. Madrid: Castalia.

– 2000. *La Celestina*. Ed. F.J. Lobera et al. Barcelona: Editorial Crítica.

Rossiaud, Jacques. 1988. *Medieval Prostitution*. Trans. Lydia G. Cochrane. Oxford: Basil Blackwell.

Rougemont, Denis de. 1956. *Love in the Western World*. Trans. Montgomery Belgion. New York: Pantheon.

Rouhi, Leyla. 1999. *Mediation and Love: A Study of the Medieval Go-between in Key Romance and Near-Eastern Texts*. Leiden, Boston, Cologne: Brill.

Rubin, Gayle. 1975. 'The Traffic in Women: Notes on the "Political Economy" of Sex.' In *Toward an Anthropology of Women*, ed. Rayna R. Reiter, 157–210. New York and London: Monthly Review Press.

Ruggerio, Michael J. 1966. *The Evolution of the Go-between in Spanish Literature through the Sixteenth Century*. Berkeley and Los Angeles: University of California Press.

Russell, Peter E. 1978a. *Temas de* La Celestina *y otros estudios.* Barcelona: Ariel.

– 1978b. 'La magia como tema integral de *La tragicomedia de Calisto y Melibea.*' In *Studia Philologica: Homenaje a Dámaso Alonso.* Madrid: Gredos, 1963. Expanded in his *Temas de* La Celestina *y otros estudios del* Cid *al* Quijote. 243–76. Barcelona: Ariel. 3:337–54.

– 1989. 'Why Did Celestina Move House?' In *The Age of the Catholic Monarchs, 1474–1516: Literary Studies in Memory of Keith Whinnom,* ed. Alan Deyermond and Ian MacPherson, 155–61. Liverpool: Liverpool University Press.

– 1991. See Rojas. *Comedia o tragicomedia de Calisto y Melibea.*

Salinas, Pedro. 1962. *Jorge Manrique, o tradicion y originalidad.* 3rd ed. Buenos Aires: Editorial Sudamericana.

Samoná, Carmelo. 1972. 'La Celestina.' In *La Letteratura Spagnola dal Cid ai Rei Cattolici,* 215–49; 232–43. Florence: Sansoni-Accademia.

Sanmartín Bastida, Rebeca. 2005. 'Sobre el teatro de la muerte en *La Celestina:* El cuerpo *hecho pedazos* y la ambigüedad macabra.' *eHumanista* 5:113–25.

Sanz Hermida, Jacobo. 1994. '"Una vieja barbuda que se dice Celestina": Notas acerca de la primera caracterización de Celestina.' *Celestinesca* 18, no. 1:17–33.

Sbarbi, José María. 1943. *Gran diccionario de refranes de la lengua española.* Ed. Manuel J. García. Buenos Aires: Joaquín Gil.

Schevill, Rudolph. 1913. *Ovid and the Renascence in Spain.* Berkeley: University of California Press.

Schwartz, Regina M., ed. 2004. *Transcendence: Philosophy, Literature, and Theology Approach the Beyond.* New York: Routledge.

Scott, Joan Wallach. 1996. *Only Paradoxes to Offer: French Feminists and the Rights of Man.* Cambridge, MA: Harvard University Press.

Sears, Theresa Ann. 1992. 'Love and the Lure of Chaos: Difference and Disorder in *Celestina.*' *Romanic Review* 83:94–106.

Severin, Dorothy Sherman. 1995. *Witchcraft in* Celestina. PMHRS, 1. London: Queen Mary and Westfield College.

– 1978–9. 'Humour in *La Celestina.*' *Romance Philology* 32:274–91.

– 1970. *Memory in* La Celestina. London: Tamesis.

– 1989. *Tragicomedy and Novelistic Discourse in* Celestina. Cambridge and New York: Cambridge University Press.

Severin, Dorothy S., and Joseph T. Snow. 1988. 'La casa de Pleberio en Salamanca.' *Celestinesca* 12, no. 1:55–8.

Shipley, George. 1973–4. '*Non erat hic locus;* the Disconcerted Reader in Melibea's Garden.' *Romance Philology* 27:286–303.

– 1985. 'Authority and Experience in *La Celestina.*' *Bulletin of Hispanic Studies* 62:95–111.

Sluhovsky, Moshe. 2006. 'Discernment of Difference, the Introspective Subject, and the Birth of Modernity.' *Journal of Medieval and Early Modern Studies* 36:169–99.

Sicroff, Albert. 1965. 'Clandestine Judaism in the Hieronymite Monastery of Nuestra Señora de Guadalupe.' In *Studies in Honor of M.J. Bernardete*, ed. Izaak Abram Langnas and Barton Sholod, 89–125. New York: Las Américas.

Silva, Feliciano de. 1988. *Segunda Celestina*. Ed. de Consolación Baranda. Madrid: Cátedra.

Snow, Joseph. 1986. 'Celestina's Claudina.' In *Hispanic Studies in Honor of Alan D. Deyermond: A North American Tribute*, ed. John S. Miletich, 257–77. Madison, WI: Hispanic Seminary of Medieval Studies.

– 1989. '¿Con qué pagaré esto? The Life and Death of Pármeno.' In *The Age of the Catholic Monarchs, 1474–1516: Literary Studies in Memory of Keith Whinnom*, ed. Alan Deyermond and Ian Macpherson, 185–92. Liverpool: Liverpool University Press.

– 1997. 'Hacia una historia de la recepción de *Celestina*: 1499–1822.' *Celestinesca* 21, nos. 1–2:115–72.

Solalinde, Antonio G. 1958. *Cien romances escogidos*. Madrid: Espasa-Calpe.

Solterer, Helen. 1995. *The Master and Minerva*. Berkeley and Los Angeles: University of California Press.

Spearing, A.C. 1993. *The Medieval Poet as Voyeur: Looking and Listening in Medieval Love-Narratives*. Cambridge: Cambridge University Press.

Stallybrass, Peter, and Allon White. 1986. *The Politics and Poetics of Transgression*. London: Methuen.

Steele, Valerie. 1996. *Fetish*. New York: Oxford University Press.

Stone, Marilyn. 1990. *Marriage and Friendship in Medieval Spain*. New York: Peter Lang.

Summit, Jennifer, and David Wallace, eds. 2007. *Rethinking Periodization. Journal of Medieval and Early Modern Studies* 37, no. 3.

Sutherland, Madeline. 2003. 'Mimetic Desire, Violence and Sacrifice in the *Celestina*.' *Hispania* 86, no. 2:181–90.

Swietlicki, Catherine. 1985. 'Rojas' View of Women: A Reanalysis of *La Celestina*.' *Hispanofila* 29, no. 1: 1–13.

Szittya, Penn R. 1986. *The Antifraternal Tradition*. Princeton, NJ: Princeton University Press.

Thiébaux, Marcelle. 1974. *The Stag of Love: The Chase in Medieval Literature*. Ithaca, NY, and London: Cornell University Press.

Thompson, B. Bussell, and J.K. Walsh. 1988. 'The Mercedarian's Shoes (Perambulations on the Fourth *tratado* of *Lazarillo de Tormes*).' *Modern Language Notes* 103:440–8.

Traub, Valerie. 1992. *Desire and Anxiety: Circulations of Sexuality in Shakespearean Drama*. New York: Routledge.

Tuan, Yi-Fu. 1982. *Segmented Worlds and Self: Group Life and Individual Consciousness*. Minneapolis: University of Minnesota Press.

– 1974. *Topophilia: A Study of Environmental Perception, Attitudes, and Values*. Englewood Cliffs, NJ: Prentice-Hall.

Valbuena, Olga Lucía. 1994. 'Sorceresses, Love Magic, and the Inquisition of Linguistic Sorcery in Celestina.' *Publications of the Modern Language Association* 109, no. 2:207–24.

Valdés, Juan de. 1969. *Diálogo de la lengua*. Ed. José F. Monetsinos. Madrid: Espasa-Calpe.

Vasvári, Louise. 1992. 'Why Is Doña Endrina a Widow?: Traditional Culture and Textuality in the *Libro de buen amor*.' In *Upon My Husband's Death: Widows in the Literature and Histories of Medieval Europe*, ed. Louise Mirrer, 259–87. Ann Arbor: University of Michigan Press.

Vendôme, Matthew of. 1980. *The Art of Versification*. Trans. Aubrey E. Gaylon. Ames: Iowa State University Press.

Von der Walde Moheno, Lillian. 2000. '*Grisel y Mirabella*, de Juan de Flores: fuente desapercibida en la obra de Fernando de Rojas.' In *Actas del XIII Congreso de la Asociación Internacional de Hispanistas I. Medieval, Siglos de Oro*, ed. Florencio Sevilla and Carlos Alvar, 249–55. Madrid: Asociación Internacional de Hispanistas–Castalia–Fundación Duques de Soria, Madrid.

– 2007. 'El cuerpo de Celestina: Un estudio sobre fisonomía y personalidad.' *e-Humanista* 9:129–42.

Wack, Mary F. 1990. *Lovesickness in the Middle Ages*. Philadelphia: University of Pennsylvania Press.

Wallace, David. See Summit and Wallace, eds., *Rethinking Periodization*.

Wardropper, Bruce W. 1964. 'Pleberio's Lament for Melibea and the Medieval Elegiac Tradition.' *Modern Language Notes* 79:140–52.

Weber, Alison. 1997. '*Celestina* and the Discourses of Servitude.' In *Negotiating Past and Present: Studies in Spanish Literature for Javier Herrero*, ed. David T. Gies, 127–44. Charlottesville, VA: Rockwood Press.

Weinberg, Bernard F. 1971. 'Aspects of Symbolism in *La Celestina*.' *Modern Language Notes* 86:136–53.

Weiss, Julian. 1991. 'Alvaro de Luna, Juan de Mena, and the Power of Courtly Love.' *Modern Language Notes* 106:241–56.

– 2002. '¿*Qué demandamos de las mugeres?* Forming the Debate about Women in Late Medieval and Early Modern Spain.' In *Gender in Debate from the Early Middle Ages to the Renaissance*, ed. Thelma S. Fenster and Clare A. Lees, 237–74. New York: Palgrave.

Weissberger, Barbara. 1996. 'El "voyeurismo" en el teatro de Diego Sánchez de Badajoz.' *Criticón* 66–7:195–215.

West, Geoffrey. 1979. 'The Unseemliness of Calisto's Toothache.' *Celestinesca* 3, no. 1:3–10.

Whinnom, Keith. 1994. 'Towards the Interpretation and Appreciation of the *Canciones* of the *Cancionero general* of 1511 (1970).' In *Medieval and Renaissance Spanish Literature: Selected Essays by Keith Whinnom*, ed. Alan Deyermond, W.F. Hunter, and Joseph T. Snow, 114–32. Exeter, UK: University of Exeter Press.

– 1980. 'The Problem of the Best Seller in Spanish Golden Age Literature.' *Bulletin of Hispanic Studies* 57:189–98.

– 1983. *La poesía amatoria de la época de los Reyes Católicos.* Durham Modern Languages Series: Hispanic Monographs, 2. Durham, UK: University of Durham.

White, Hayden. 'The Forms of Wildness: Archaeology of an Idea.' In *Tropics of Discourse*, 150–82. Baltimore: Johns Hopkins University Press, 1986.

Zizek, Slavoj. 1989. *The Sublime Object of Ideology.* London: Verso.

– 1992. *Looking Awry: An Introduction to Jacques Lacan through Popular Culture.* Cambridge, MA: MIT Press.

– 1994a. 'Courtly Love, or, Woman as Thing.' In *The Metastases of Enjoyment*, 89–112. London: Verso.

– 1994b. *The Metastates of Enjoyment: Six Essays on Woman and Causality.* London: Verso.

Index